THE
PRINCESS ROYAL

By the same author

KING OF FOOLS

THE
PRINCESS ROYAL

John Parker

HAMISH HAMILTON · LONDON

HAMISH HAMILTON LTD

Published by the Penguin Group
27 Wrights Lane, London W8 5TZ, England
Viking Penguin Inc, 40 West 23rd Street, New York, New York 10010, U.S.A.
Penguin Books Australia Ltd, Ringwood, Victoria, Australia
Penguin Books Canada Ltd, 2801 John Street, Markham, Ontario, Canada L3R 1B4
Penguin Books (N.Z.) Ltd, 182–190 Wairau Road, Auckland 10, New Zealand

Penguin Books Ltd, Registered Offices: Harmondsworth, Middlesex, England

First published in Great Britain 1989 by
Hamish Hamilton Ltd

Copyright © 1989 by John Parker

1 3 5 7 9 10 8 6 4 2

British Library Cataloguing in Publication Data

Parker, John, *1938*–
The Princess Royal
1. Great Britain. Anne, Princess, daughter
of Elizabeth II. Queen of Great Britain
I. Title
941.085′092′4

ISBN 0–241–12721–1

Typeset and Printed in Great Britain by
Butler and Tanner Ltd
Frome and London

Contents

v

List of illustrations

The author and the publishers are very grateful to Syndication International and award-winning Royal photographer Kent Gavin of the *Daily Mirror* for the use of pictures.

Author's acknowledgements

Many people have assisted me in the preparation of this book, through interviews and guidance. In particular, I would like to thank the former Prime Minister, the Right Hon. Edward Heath, MBE, MP, for his intriguing recollections of both sporting and political associations during the last twenty years. My thanks also to: author and politician Jeffrey Archer for his comments on Princess Anne; Mr Donald Trelford, editor of the *Observer*, for his observations and for permission to use extracts from the Kenneth Harris interview with Princess Anne; Mrs Marje Proops, of the *Daily Mirror*, for her recollections and comments; Mr Magnus Linklater, editor of the *Scotsman*, for his outspoken view on Fleet Street's relationship with the Royal family; Mr David Montgomery, editor of *Today* and former editor of the *News of the World*, for his observations on the same theme; Mr Brian MacArthur, executive editor, *Sunday Times;* Mr Joe Haines, former press secretary to Prime Minister Harold Wilson, and now *Mirror* Group political editor; Mr Victor Knight, political journalist who until his recent retirement spent much of his working life in the House of Commons; Mr Hugo Vickers, biographer of Cecil Beaton, for permission to include extracts relating to the Royal photographer's encounters with Princess Anne; Mr James Whitaker, *Daily Mirror* Royal correspondent, and Mr Tony Frost, assistant editor of the *Sunday Mirror*, for their recollections of Royal tours with Princess Anne; Mr Brian McConnell for his first-hand account of the kidnap attempt on Princess Anne in which he was shot; Miss Jean Rook, of the *Daily Express*, whose witty and piercing commentaries through the years were a valuable source of reference; Mr Dennis Pitts, for his research assistance. And Edda Tasiemka of the exceptional Hans Tasiemka Archive in London, which once again provided me with invaluable research material.

AUTHOR'S ACKNOWLEDGEMENTS

My thanks also to many others whose requests for anonymity
I have respected.

J.P.
Northamptonshire
November 1988

Prologue

We have come a long way from the image of Royalty inherited and rejected by King Edward VIII, restored with loving and romantic care by the Court of King George VI, and nurtured with deep concern during the long reign of Queen Elizabeth II which has seen many fundamental changes. The process has brought with it a dangerous trivialization of the Monarchy, the one institution that binds, by George Orwell's invisible chain, a politically divided nation.

Although this book is principally to chronicle the life and times of the Princess Royal, it is impossible to separate her from the rest of her family. Her influence and importance within this immensely high-profile little group is vast, and she can only become even more stalwart in future years. If, as many believe, the Monarchy faces critical times in the run up to the twenty-first century and beyond, then the reliable figurehead of the Princess Royal will be one member of the family, at least, to continue to carry on the tradition.

For years, I have been writing about the Royal family, preparing headlines, sizing up endless photographs to present their various activities to their adoring public. If they now suffer from over-exposure, I must confess my own guilt as party to that. As a reporter, I was an "accredited" person at many Royal events and later, as an editor, I planned countless front pages adorned with one or other of them.

During the time I was researching this book, I was invited with my wife and daughter to one of the traditional summer garden parties in the grounds of Buckingham Palace. There we saw, at a distance of just a few paces and at times face to face, the stars of the British Royal family in their element, surrounded by respectful, admiring crowds politely jostling each other to get a closer view. Members of the Royal family came out on to the great steps leading from the Palace down

1

to the lawns, after the assembled company of public servers, assorted do-gooders, industrialists, diplomats, military people, and local presidents of townswomen's guilds had consumed their carefully manicured cucumber sandwiches and drunk tea from crested crockery under the lines of marquees especially erected for the Queen's treat for those from all walks of life recommended to the Office of the Lord Chamberlain for this simple reward. Flunkeys stood to attention and the band played *God Save the Queen.* Her Majesty led the way, followed a few paces behind by Prince Philip, and then the Queen Mother, aided down the steps to the lawn by Prince Charles, the Princess of Wales, the Princess Royal, and the Duke and Duchess of Gloucester. Garden party marshals, well versed in organization, indicated that the crowds should form themselves into lines, to make corridors of straining, eager faces, through which the Royal family strolled, stopping occasionally to chat. They then went into a special enclosure reserved for special people where the Queen and her family took tea and chatted some more.

This is Monarchy at work. It is a minuscule example of their very public existence which puts each and every member of the Royal family within close public scrutiny for most of their working lives. Another sea of faces, another line of outstretched hands, another stifled yawn.

In the past three decades, this British group of remarkable individuals (or, as some would have it, entirely unremarkable individuals), who have no direct power or authority over a nation, have become throughout the world a fetish, a phenomenon which is impossible either totally to explain or to ignore. Since the reign of Queen Victoria, who hid herself away after the death of her beloved Prince Albert, the Monarchy's relationship with its public has come full circle. Then, republican groups emerged and the Queen's infrequent public appearances were occasionally jeered. Today, it is familiarity that has bred contempt. The Monarchy has mass appeal, but, for the first time in centuries, there is also a measure of indifference.

After Queen Victoria's death, the Royal family courted their public's acclaim and favour. They were presented in many ways which endeared them to the people through two World Wars, numerous crises in government and the gradual dissolution of the great British Empire. But latterly, in keeping with the technological and psychological advances of the twentieth century, the Monarchy has become an endangered species. Bared of dignity through the all-seeing eye of the camera lens, the Royal family is losing its very life-blood through the exploitation of its own popular image.

The way in which some members of the Royal family have been reduced to the level of sarcastic banter was well demonstrated when Princess Anne stared icily at the editor of *Paris Match* and inquired with a coolness that showed not a tinge of humour: "Am I divorced yet?" It was a remark that succinctly summed up her feelings towards the media. Her twenty years in the public eye have been punctuated by controversy. At times, it has been self-inspired, but what makes Anne and other members of her family bitter is the stream of gossipy stories and innuendo that leads into vindictive inquisitions into their personal lives. These are the results of popularity and public appetite.

King Farouk once said: "Eventually there will only be five kings left in the world: Diamonds, Hearts, Spades, Clubs and England." In that, he was right, for many of those Monarchs who reign outside the United Kingdom have been reduced to pale shadows of a past age – pleasant people of no great importance. Many believe that the only reason the British Monarchy has survived with such strength thus far is due to the nation's love for the Queen herself. How else, they argue, could the World's Greatest Family remain so revered through the avalanche of truths, half-truths and outright lies that have been written about them in the last few years?

That the Royal family has become the daily diet of newspapers is partly due to the behaviour of some of its members. If the Queen was originally unamused by Malcolm Muggeridge's description of her family as "Royal Soap Opera", at times in the recent past she might have been inclined to agree that the actions of some of them could be leading in that direction.

But the Queen herself has presided over the modernizing of Royalty as she faces the pressures of changing attitudes and public needs. She has set a new tone which has brought her closer to the people. At the same time, members of her family have found themselves more vulnerable to open comment from which they had been protected in the past.

Of course, the Royal family are concerned about their ratings. The right kind of publicity is desired and sought. The

Queen and Prince Philip have retained dignity in their private lives, but disclosure about others in the "Soap Opera Family" knows no bounds, from the size of the Duchess of York's hip measurements to whom Captain Mark Phillips dined with while on a visit to Canada. For the past two decades, Princess Anne has borne the brunt of press prominence and has only been relieved recently by her two sisters-in-law, the Princess of Wales and the Duchess of York. Anne's has been a running battle with reporters and photographers and that, as they say, is an ongoing situation that still has its moments.

And, as the publicity and media machine reached absurd levels, the Princess Royal has given back almost as good as she got. Mr Edward Heath, the former British Prime Minister, recalled for me such a moment: "On one of her visits abroad, she faced a journalist who asked 'What criticism do you have of the way the government here is handling the crisis?' Quickly but firmly the princess replied: 'I am not here to criticize. I am here to help.' That is an example of her self-composed, charming directness." Similarly, Jeffrey Archer, the author and politician who is himself no stranger to public controversy, told me: "I quite believe that had the Princess Royal been born the Queen's first child, there might well have have been a constitutional crisis because of her strength and forthrightness. I say that without any diminution of Prince Charles, but the Princess has become what I would term one of our leading non-political figures, one of the world's outstanding leaders who shows amazing persistence and courage from the belief that she will not be thwarted simply because she is a woman. She has devoted herself to public service in a way which resembles early Victorian Royalty and, as I travel the country, it is always clear to me that she is one of the most popular of our Royals. With regard to her attitude towards the media, and the tabloid press, I would say that like most people in public life today, she has come to terms with the fact that her good deeds seldom get the space they deserve; certainly this is true of the popular press."

I know from my own experience that she was certainly very unpopular among journalists in her early days in public life. I know also that disdain for her has been replaced by respect, but one veteran reporter of Royal events told me: "You can admire her, but that doesn't mean you have to like her." She remains aloof, slightly snobbish and a trifle arrogant.

Since her earliest days of public engagements, there has always been a hostile relationship between her and the press but, as I recall, it moved into a rather more bitter phase during the period when everyone, including Anne herself, denied that her engagement to Mark Phillips was in the offing, right up to the day it was confirmed. The skirmishes became more strident with Anne berating her ever-attendant press corps with venom and not infrequent expletives made up of a variety of four letters.

But then, who could blame her? She had walked into a situation that was outside her control. A new age of newspaper circulation battles and television technology, the like of which had never been seen in Britain, began just as the young princess was being launched into her demanding public duties. The world's eyes were on her: she was the first young Royal star of the television age. The media attention she would receive had not been equalled since the Abdication and scandal of the weak and wilful Edward VIII's adulterous affair with Wallis Simpson which had left a permanent scar on Anne's family. Edward and Mrs Simpson constituted Part One of Muggeridge's "Royal Soap". Anne's grandfather, King George VI, and her grandmother, Queen Elizabeth, restored the Monarchy to its former place of prestige and respect through their very ordinariness. The turning point in Royal relationships with the press was the Abdication itself. The King had flown, long live the King. George VI came reluctantly to the throne, dragging with him a Royal family who had sunk in the esteem of its public to a particularly low ebb, at a time when the nation sought confidence from its leaders as the worrying prospect of another war edged closer. Edward VIII's rejection of the Throne had cast doubts over the Royal family's "divine right" to rule, and the public was suddenly painfully aware that Monarchs can be only too human and frail. The new King was a handsome man but an unknown quantity, desperately shy and, initially, agonizingly tense in his impeded speech. Many expressed concern. Kingsley Martin, editor of the *New Statesman*, for instance, wrote "... if we drop the trappings of Monarchy in the gutter, Germany has taught us that some guttersnipe will pick them up."

The art of corporate public relations was in its infancy in Britain, but already well used under Goebbels' insidious propaganda machine in unifying the Third Reich behind its rabid leader. The King's courtiers were anxious to project their new man, although such modern thinking is unlikely to have been actually voiced in the red-velvet corridors of Buckingham Palace. The emphasis was on his homely family, a warm and reassuring image, so that the memories of the Abdication could be expunged. Photographs of the family would be an important element. Staid, stuffy pictures, stiffly posed, unsmiling groups, were banished. Enter the sophisticated Cecil Beaton with his lush Fragonard backcloths and mastery of the quietly lit soft-focus portrait. Beaton was a surprising choice. He had come into prominence with his pictures of Wallis Simpson, a close friend, and yet he was selected as the official photographer of the 1937 Coronation (and also, incidentally, by the Duchess of Windsor for her wedding) and was to dominate the Royal photographic scene for decades. Marcus Adams and Studio Lisa played their part in this Royal photographic renaissance; but it was Beaton who transformed the public image of the Royal Family and gave Royalty a human, albeit regal face. With all the embellishments and chiffon garniture (Norman Hartnell was co-operating with the photographer-Royal), many of those pictures were ideal for newspapers, stark in black and white. The wartime photographs of the King and Queen in the East End, as the German bombs fell, had an enormous effect on public morale; so, too, did the picture of the elder princess in her ATS uniform wielding a spanner like thousands of other women. With the war over, and Britain in the grip of austerity, Beaton's photography returned the Royal family to a lush arcadia and established him once more as the floppy-hatted Gainsborough of the twentieth century.

Shortly before Princess Elizabeth married Prince Philip, in 1947, the King wrote: "Our family, the four of us [The King, Queen, and Princesses Elizabeth and Margaret], the 'Royal Family' must remain together with additions of course at suitable moments. I have watched you grow up all these years with pride under the skilful direction of Mummy who, as you know, is the most wonderful person in the world in my eyes." King George was not long for this world when he wrote those words and Princess Anne and her brother Prince Charles would be born into a Monarchy that was about to undergo radical change.

The Queen Mother, who had been the power behind the Throne since the Abdication, would remain in the background, though with strong influence. The Queen, when she assumed her father's mantle, would seek the advice of her mother daily. But there would be other influences, particularly from Prince Philip who was outspoken, unconventional, radical and impatient with protocol, in all of which he was to be followed in thought and deed by his daughter. There was new thinking at the Palace which would mould the young Princess Anne.

The Coronation of Queen Elizabeth was the celebration of an almost hysterical public and support for the Monarchy. Past misdemeanours were forgiven and even Princess Margaret would be given more sympathy than criticism over her desire to marry a divorced man which had brought back temporarily memories of that awful era of Wallis Simpson.

King George had rejected the suggestion that his daughter's wedding to Prince Philip in Westminster Abbey should be televised and, when the question arose again over the Coronation, even Winston Churchill agreed with the majority view in the Cabinet that film crews would be an intrusion and impose upon the young Queen a burden which she might not welcome; it was agreed that permission for a live broadcast could be withheld, and that viewers would be shown only recorded highlights. Lord Mountbatten, ever the showman, was, however, strongly in favour of live television, and eventually the Queen herself agreed that the burden upon her was something that she should and could endure for the sake of her subjects. The BBC, the only television channel at the time, was profoundly respectful and sycophantic in its commentary and observations. But the age of the mass microscope had begun. Three hundred million people would watch the Coronation; the edited film would be played to fascinated cinema audiences for months to come. Homely "just the four of us" had become mass-market at home and abroad. Could the Queen have imagined that thirty-four years later her children and their various spouses would be seen on television cavorting in a most unroyal way to a chorus of criticism in *It's A Knockout*!?

The Queen's own actions of allowing the public and the press to get closer came at an embarrassing time as the drama surrounding her sister, Princess Margaret, who seemed determined to marry Group Captain Peter Townsend, unfolded. For weeks, the affair was mulled over at the breakfast table until Prime Minister Anthony Eden, a divorcé himself, had the official task of instructing the princess that she could not marry the Group Captain and remain a working member of the Royal family. Her alternatives were to follow her uncle into exile with the man she loved, or to end it there and then. *The Times* was the first to congratulate Princess Margaret on deciding to finish the romance: the peoples of the Commonwealth would feel gratitude to her for taking the selfless, Royal way which was expected of her.

Princess Margaret would never let anyone forget her sacrifice, least of all the Queen. The effects of these events on the Monarchy itself would soon become apparent. Politicians, the Church, the Establishment, the press and even minor courtiers tried to use the Princess Margaret affair for their own ends. The mystique had been punctured, revealing once again the frailty and vulnerability of the Royal family and exposing it in two-inch headlines throughout the world.

The Times insisted that the Royal House of Windsor ought to remain aloof, untouched by the vulgarity of popular press. At the other end of the spectrum, the *Daily Mirror*, then at the height of its popular appeal and mass circulation with a daily sale exceeding five million, insisted in a prominent leader article that the nation was demanding a new openness from the Monarchy through which the Royals should mix with commoners and protocol be swept aside.

Somewhere between those two extremes, the Queen and her husband would try to guide their family. But an inch becomes a yard, and a yard becomes a mile. Before long, the press and television would be forcing their own pace to the extent that the publishers and proprietors of national newspapers would no longer dictate to their editors what was acceptable and what should be kept back. This had been an open sore, anyway, ever since the press barons had plotted to keep the Wallis Simpson story under wraps in the 1930s. The newspaper-buying public wanted Royal stories. Commercially, disclosure was the thing to do. Nothing sells popular newspapers like good gossip.

The "scandal" of Princess Margaret started the ball rolling and the press was now for ever on the look-out for more Royal revelations. The fact that Prince Philip had managed to turn his official opening of the 1956 Olympic Games into a 40,000-mile world tour, which he described as his personal contribution to the Commonwealth ideal, didn't go down too well either. Perhaps more experienced courtiers should have warned him that the slightest indiscretion would be taken out of all proportion; perhaps they did. The Continental and American press soon began to turn the rumours into stories; suddenly half Europe was saying the Queen and Prince Philip had marriage problems. Why else would he be away from her for five months? His assistant secretary, Mike Parker, was named as Philip's companion in bachelor life in Australia. Then a great shudder hit London (where the press had hitherto largely ignored the story) as Mrs Parker sued for divorce over her husband's alleged adultery. The American and European newspapers took it further and headlines appeared abroad stating "Queen and Duke in a marriage split".

Prince Philip learned a lesson that year. At the same time, the Queen was drawn into the Suez crisis. The young Queen, with limited experience in the affairs of State, was consulted by her Prime Minister, Anthony Eden, at their bi-weekly meetings. Eden led the country into a bungled military intervention and humiliation in the eyes of even Britain's closest allies. What became clear as Eden's plot for an Anglo-French occupation of the Canal area emerged was that the taint of defeat and duplicity would be attached to the Queen herself for which the Palace would be awarded vitriolic press attacks.

After that, a period of calm was needed and the Queen would be seen in her best light – a warm and homely picture of her and her growing family. There were some dissenters, of course, and when Malcolm Muggeridge wrote a fairly ordinary piece for an American newspaper on the British Monarchy, his remarks were taken out of context and used in a stinging attack on the Queen by Lord Beaverbrook, in which she was described as dowdy, frumpish and banal. There was a similar furore when John Grigg (Lord Altrincham) described, in an intellectual magazine, the Queen's manner of speech as that of a "priggish schoolgirl". The effect was remarkable: the popular press rounded on Grigg and Muggeridge, but delighted in reprinting every single one of the offending words. There was a further result, also. The Queen took voice production lessons and her delivery changed dramatically for the better in a matter of months.

The spotlight then moved for the moment towards the growing-up of the Queen's children and the attendance of Prince Charles at an "ordinary" preparatory school. Her press secretary was ordered to complain, on her behalf, to the Press Council and cautioned Fleet Street editors that the education of Prince Charles could not continue to be disrupted. A new focus for attention was at hand, however, and it would be from the newspapers' own ranks that a new Royal star was gleaned. Anthony Armstrong-Jones, a social photographer of increasing but unspectacular note, had arrived in Palace circles when commissioned to take photographs of Prince Charles and Princess Anne. Surprisingly, his entry into the Princess Margaret social set had remained a matter of little concern and only those closest to them recognized a more lasting attachment between the Princess and the commoner when she began to join him at his tiny apartment overlooking the Thames, which would eventually become noted by tourist guides on boats sailing up and down the river as the hideaway where the Royal romance flourished in secret. Of his arrival, Cecil Beaton said: "I don't think his pictures are that interesting but his publicity value is terrific." In later years, Beaton's view of Snowdon's work would become very much more complimentary. The *Daily Mirror* welcomed the new blood to the House of Windsor: a young man of the people whom they insisted upon calling plain Tony Jones, and whose arrival was also applauded by the Duchess of Windsor who commented from her Paris palace: "At least I'm keeping up with the Joneses."

As the wedding neared, it was noted Princess Margaret's Civil List income would rise to £15,000 upon her marriage when the average wage was but a tenth of that. The £56,000 to be spent on refurbishing a Royal apartment for the couple brought a greater broadside and the news that their floating honeymoon aboard the Royal Yacht *Britannia* would cost £10,000 a day brought the whole financial turmoil to an unpleasant head. Worse, Mr Jones had to change his best man after it was "exclusively revealed" that his first choice had a criminal conviction for a homosexual offence. So it went on. The boundaries of public disclosure about the Royals were being pushed ever further outward, and rightly say the guardians of a free press. They could no longer expect secrecy or even good taste.

Events of the sixties prodded such coverage still further and it was against this background and the increasingly insatiable public appetite for Royal "news" that the Queen's two eldest children, Prince Charles and Princess Anne, were launched to become the Royal megastars. How much further can the press coverage of the Royal family go? Donald Trelford, editor of the *Observer*, is one of a number of national newspaper editors I have spoken to who firmly believe that the outer limits have long since been reached and that certain elements of the media should restrain their inventiveness. Discussing the Princess Royal in particular, he told me in August, 1988: "I do feel that she has been unfairly treated. In her serious public work she has not been given adequate recognition until very recently. I also believe that some of the gossip published about her private life has been an unacceptable intrusion that papers would not have dared to publish about someone able to answer back with a libel action."

Much of the material published in Europe is so incredible that it does not bear repeating. For example, three years after Princess Anne's launch into public life, *France-Dimanche* analysed its press cuttings on the British Royal family over the previous fourteen years. It discovered that during this time, the Queen was preparing to abdicate on sixty-three occasions, was divorcing Prince Philip in seventy-three stories, had fallen out with Lord Snowdon in one hundred and fifteen cuttings, was not speaking to Princess Grace of Monaco on seventeen separate occasions, and was pregnant ninety-two times. Now it was Princess Anne's turn, and she would become the main attraction until the arrival of Lady Diana Spencer and Sarah Ferguson.

The press had played its part in reducing the Royal family to utter triviality, much of it not even true. But the Queen and some other members of her family have retained dignity and the standard of hard work, and it is this role that Princess Anne has latterly assumed. Throughout the 1980s, she has been a solo performer on her own public stage. She has travelled hundreds of thousands of miles around the world and into some of its more remote and unwelcoming parts, often with only a detective and a lady-in-waiting for company. She has journeyed into areas where the Save the Children Fund, of which she had been head since 1970, has discovered the most appalling poverty and suffering. Nor has she shown any lack of courage in tackling other major issues, such as AIDS, or in her prison visits as Patron of the Butler Trust. There must have been many occasions when she has contemplated life without the prefix of "Princess" or "Royal". But just as her aunt, Princess Margaret, was told years before, she has a duty to do what is expected of her. In April 1989 Princess Anne, now the Princess

Royal, completed twenty years of that very public duty. She herself admits that her life during that time has been a see-saw of magnificent highs and frustrating low points. One of the things of which she is justly proud is the firm establishment of the Save the Children Fund, which in 1970 had an annual income of two-and-a-half million pounds and which by the end of this decade will be exceeding fifty million pounds a year.

But twenty years is just a beginning; ahead lie many more years of public service from which she is bound to emerge as a most significant member of her family, a key anchor-figure whose influence will be as important as that of the future King Charles himself, and whose experience, in the years I now chronicle, will be a vital mainstay in the survival of the British Monarchy.

ONE

Like Father, Like Daughter

By the time she had reached her twenty-first birthday, Princess Anne had created an image confusing to the public, and had generated a hostility from the press pack. She had been tagged with every conceivable adjective by those who took her apart and stripped her bare, metaphorically speaking, to analyse every single aspect from clothes to candour, from language to lingerie.

Her strong Hanoverian inheritance was giving a new shape to her face. The prettiness of earlier years was giving way to a sterner facial form and the sharp Greek-based temperament of her father, the Duke of Edinburgh, was apparent in her public displays of mood and temper. Like him, she was impatient, spoke her mind, and didn't suffer fools gladly. By the time she had come of age, she had been described as beautiful, yet ugly; truculent, yet modest; bubbly, yet boring; hot-tempered, yet patient; snobbish, yet caring. Anne was all these things and more: a person so complex that the real and underlying character had yet to emerge and, like a good wine, would take years to mature.

As an infant, there had been little to indicate that she would be anything other than a pretty and charming princess who would eventually take her place as a high-ranking British Royal who, for the rest of her life, would be on public view. She was born into a country still scarred by the War, physically and emotionally; a nation in the grip of a depressing poverty. Ration books and identity cards (hers was Number MAPM3/96) were still very much the order and good cheer was in short supply. However, it was the beginning of a hopeful new era: there were energy and expectation in the air. Clement Attlee had become Prime Minister the year Anne was born and his Labour Government promised better days for everyone. Britain and the Monarchy were ready for happier times. Anne's own family had come through a traumatic time in the preceeding years. Russian, German and other European relatives had been decimated and divided by Revolution and two World Wars. Her grandfather, King George VI, exhausted and ill after the ordeal of Edward VIII's abdication, had been tireless in his morale-building efforts during the War years. He was now drained, and would not be on this earth to witness his darling granddaughter's second birthday.

Yes, the nation and the family were ready for good news to help relieve the vivid memories of the past decade – and a Royal birth was taken up immediately as a cheering diversion in an austere climate. By the end of the evening of August 14 1950, crowds were already gathering in the Mall, outside Clarence House where the birth would take place at 11.50 the following morning. The Duke of Edinburgh had been waiting all morning in an adjoining room and was delighted to be told he had a daughter. He telephoned members of the family and Queen Elizabeth arrived almost immediately and mouthed to the cheering crowds: "It's a girl", which would please everyone since the first child of Princess Elizabeth and the Duke of Edinburgh had, of course, been a boy, Charles, delivered two years earlier. As with so many Royal events, then as now, the build-up to Anne's birth had been almost hysterical, even though pending Royal confinements were more secretive. Princess Elizabeth retired from public engagements in the latter months of her pregnancy which, however, only served to heighten interest of both press and public.

The baby princess's arrival on this earth was marked in a way that would have embarrassed her in later life. There was a forty-one gun salute from the King's Troop, the Royal Horse Artillery in Hyde Park, and a twenty-one gun salute fired by the First Regiment of the Honourable Artillery Company at the Tower of London. Bells pealed for an hour at Westminster Abbey and half an hour at St Paul's. Coldstream Guardsmen on duty at the time of the Royal birth were awarded one shilling and six pence each and the King ordered the Royal Navy to splice the mainbrace. The Home Secretary, Chuter Ede, was told by telephone of the birth, the Government having agreed at the King's request to dispense with the seventeenth-century tradition of having a Minister present at the birth of a child in line to the Throne, the rule having been strictly observed until it was lifted for the birth of Prince Charles.

Parliament was in recess and Ede was therefore unable to perform the further tradition of being the first to announce the birth to the House of Commons and the nation. The recess also robbed anti-Monarchists among MPs of the chance to persist with their vitriolic attacks on the Royal family (whose cost to the nation and value to the public were then, and probably always will be, challenged). However, there was sufficient comment in the newspapers in the coming days to make up for any lack of rhetoric from the House. Those against the sheer wealth and privilege of the British Monarchy had been given plenty of ammunition in recent years with the wasteful and at times obscene display of opulence by the former King and his bejewelled bride, the Duke and Duchess of Windsor, whose photographs at night-clubs and parties and aboard luxurious liners continued to adorn the front pages of newspapers the world over. Nor did the new Monarchy escape without its critics. King George, recovering from illness, was on holiday in Scotland, shooting grouse. His daughter, Princess Elizabeth, was receiving an annual income of £50,000 a year from the Civil List and her husband, the Duke of Edinburgh, was, on the day of their daughter's birth, promoted in his naval role to Lieutenant-Commander of HMS *Magpie*.

In that age of make do and mend, here was a child born with a golden spoon who, the critical observers insisted, would want for nothing, would never know hunger, or cold, or debt, or homelessness, all of which plights faced a good percentage of the British populace at that time.

Here began the challenge for a princess, as yet unimpressionable, but whose later life would take on the role of dedication to the underprivileged.

But, as Britain went into a new decade, the highly vocal critics of Royalty pointed out that the average weekly wage was a mere £8 and the State family allowance for the second child was five shillings, while the cost just of announcing the baby princess's birth would have kept the average family in food for a year.

Messengers were sent from Clarence House with letters to each Ambassador at the Court of St James and every Governor General was informed by telegraph. The great British public was undeterred and, despite the shortages, baby clothes and toys began to arrive by the sackload. There were hand-knitted garments of every description and colour from every part of the globe. A complete wardrobe of baby clothes was presented by the children of Swindon, Wiltshire, and from Ontario, Canada, came five dolls, nine inches high, representing various members of the Royal family. There were hundreds of toys ranging from dolls to train sets, a bale of cotton from Texas and two blankets from Australia with Princess Elizabeth's Coat of Arms embroidered upon them. Few of the presents were retained. Most were passed through the various family- and poverty-agencies to the needy. There were other minor accolades and tributes that fuelled the voices of dissent: Princess Anne was made the one millionth member of the Automobile Association, and Locomotive 46202 in service on the Euston line became the Princess Anne.

The nursery on the top floor of Clarence House needed little adjustment to accommodate the new addition to the family. The nanny, Mrs Helen Lightbody, who had previously worked for the Duke and Duchess of Gloucester at Barnwell Manor in Northamptonshire, had been brought in at the birth of Prince Charles, along with nursery assistant, Mabel Anderson, the daughter of a Liverpool policeman, who got her job simply by placing an advertisement offering her services in a magazine to which the Palace replied. Naturally, as press interest continued, everything from nursery routine to the pale blue decoration of the walls was written about and devoured; and when Anne's names were revealed, a new round of adulation began. She was to be called Anne Elizabeth Alice Louise: the first after her mother's best friend Lady Anne Nevill; the second and third after her maternal and paternal grandmothers respectively; the fourth a tribute to Uncle Dickie, Lord Louis Mountbatten.

The Duke of Edinburgh did not sign the official National Registration Form until nine days after the birth and even then he made a quite deliberate error, omitting from the form his wife's family name of Windsor. At the time, Mountbatten had been pressing the King to allow Princess Elizabeth to take his own family name which had been adopted by his nephew Prince Philip and would have followed under the normal rules of the marriage contract. Had Mountbatten succeeded in this, the family name of the British Monarchy would thus have changed from Windsor to Mountbatten upon the accession of Princess Elizabeth to the Throne. The King and his daughter, however, refused to change her name and she retained her own family name of Windsor. It was only after continued pressure that, some ten years later, she agreed to alter her family name to Mountbatten-Windsor which would eventually be shown on Princess Anne's marriage certificate.

The baby princess was, unsurprisingly, like any ordinary child. Cecil Beaton, who took the photographs at the christening, noted that she was quite a small baby, with a definite nose for one so young, large sleepy green eyes and a particularly pretty mouth. Beaton recalled: "Babies are difficult to photograph at the best of times: and this was one of the worst times, because she just wanted to sleep. I wasn't allowed to take a jack to keep her eyes open; so we made bird noises, rattled keys, clapped our hands, jumped up and down, and the more idiotic the performance, the more bored she became. Only a drop of glycerine on the tongue seemed to do the trick." With the help of Beaton's pictures, Anne made her entrance in style. This was her first appearance on the front pages. Beaton's photographs went round the world. One with Prince Charles kissing his new sister was particularly popular. The homely foursome of Royalty was among the warmest family portraits ever published. (Beaton wasn't as keen on photographing Anne in future years. According to his biographer, Hugo Vickers, when he met her at the age of ten, he "loathed her on sight".)

When Anne was four months old, her mother began increasingly to become more deeply involved in affairs of State and official engagements. When Charles had been born, Princess Elizabeth had been given a year free of all commitments; this time, as her father was visibly deteriorating, both she and Prince Philip were required to take a greater role in the running of the Monarchy. Anne was barely a year old when Princess Elizabeth and Prince Philip began an arduous tour of Canada and America and, upon their return, plans were immediately put in hand for their Commonwealth tour due to begin in February of 1952. Modern psychiatrists would speculate that the absence of parents during the formative years of a child could have a lasting effect in the evolvement of the child's character, but Princess Elizabeth then, as in future years, did her best to remain a mother as well as an important national and international figure.

Nanny Lightbody's nursery routine was geared to the movements of Princess Elizabeth and Prince Philip so that they could be with their children as often as possible. The day began at seven each morning, when the children would be bathed and fed. At nine they would be taken to their parents' bedroom for half an hour and, whenever engagements allowed, their mother would be in and out of the nursery. Whenever Princess Elizabeth was not at home, their grandparents, King George VI and Queen Elizabeth, would make a point of having the children with them.

Greater demands upon the young parents were on the immediate horizon. The Commonwealth tour, which was to have been a lengthy one, visiting East Africa, Australia, New Zealand, Kenya and Ceylon, was to begin on February 1, 1952. The previous day, the King was seen on the newsreels standing in the bitter cold at Heathrow Airport waving goodbye to his daughter and son-in-law. He returned to Sandringham and there on February 5, he came in from a hare shoot and went straight up to the nursery where Charles and Anne were having their supper. He knelt with them and prayed, then tucked them up in bed and said goodnight. In the early hours of the following morning, King George died peacefully in his sleep and, at that moment, Princess Elizabeth became Queen Elizabeth II. Anne moved to second in line to the Throne. The infant princess was, of course, unaware of the drastic changes that confronted her family but the immediate effect was an upheaval in domestic life itself.

The new Queen would be required to leave the comparative comfort of Clarence House and take up residence in Buckingham Palace, which successive Monarchs have hated for its museum-like appearance and endless corridors. Initially, it had been suggested that she might retain Clarence House as the family home and use the Palace for official duties, but Winston Churchill, now Prime Minister again after the election of a Conservative Government, would not hear of it. Queen Victoria and the four successive kings had lived in this great yet gloomy house; Royal tradition could not be interrupted.

From the outset, however, the Queen was clearly intent on spending as much time as possible with her young family. It would have to become a matter of planning and definite routine if she were to achieve her aim without affecting the massive responsibilities and huge programme of affairs of State that lay before her. She asked her Prime Minister to delay his weekly audience by one hour so that she did not miss the children's bathtime. By the nature of her own strictly administered life, in which her duties and engagements were planned months in advance, she was able to see more of her children than was the case in the homes of some members of the aristocracy. Also the Queen Mother, who remembered the routine she was forced to establish to see her daughters when they were young, saw her grandchildren as often as possible. With her help, they were taught hide-and-seek and other games played in every home where there are children. She was as keen as the Queen for them to have a pony almost as soon as they could walk and Anne, the Queen Mother herself recalled, showed considerably more enthusiasm at that age for riding than Charles. When their first pony was brought to the Royal mews, Anne was barely three. She was a natural on horseback; she wanted to canter when others wanted to trot, and gallop when others were cantering.

One of Princess Anne's own earliest recollections is that of her mother's Coronation in June 1953. She was thought to be too young to attend and even her brother, then five, could not be kept attentive throughout the ceremony and had to be led from Westminster Abbey before the end. Anne, in later interviews, remembered at the time a feeling of being left out of something good and of being quite angry that Charles should be taken but not herself. The independent spirit that would dominate her character was already beginning to show. The Queen Mother had already noticed a considerable difference in the developing characters of the two Royal children. Charles was watchful and protective towards his younger sister. He was also inclined to be somewhat shy and anxious, traits which he had inherited from his mother. Princess Anne, on the other hand, had acquired her father's confidence and determination to the point that, even as a toddler and looking every inch a beautiful girl child with golden ringlets and big blue eyes, she showed an inclination towards being a tomboy. Her need to be pushy and occasionally rebellious was perhaps a natural reaction to always having to take second place to her brother, the future King. She was too young to understand the implications and when Queen Mary, her great-grandmother, used to insist on a curtsy from Anne purely as a mark of respect for a former Queen, Anne would not always conform. Prince Philip himself has suggested that the attention paid to Charles, as heir to the Throne, led to Anne feeling rather neglected as a child and consequently the brother-sister relationship between the two of them was at times quite abrasive, particularly as Anne's temper flourished. Similarities have also been drawn between the two princesses, Elizabeth and Margaret, and the relationship between Charles and Anne. Elizabeth, as a child, apparently felt embarrassed that the sentries on duty at Buckingham Palace were under orders to present arms with the usual ceremonial clatter whenever one of the children walked past; Margaret, on the other hand, was quite taken with the ritual. Two decades later, Charles would avoid bringing the guards to attention; Anne, like her Aunt Margaret, would walk back and forth just to bring the frustrated guards into action, like real-life toy soldiers.

Nanny Lightbody brought a note of strictness to the young princess. But she remained little Miss Mischief. Artist Ulrica Forbes, who was commissioned by the Queen Mother to draw a portrait of Anne, recalled her experiences. She arrived at the Palace and after a long journey through corridors and up flights of stairs she was shown to a door where a footman waited outside. He opened it and there stood Princess Anne "a little figure of sheer loveliness . . . she solemnly regarded me with her big blue eyes". Ulrica handed her a posy of flowers which she smelled, her eyes lighting up. There was a hint of mischievousness, but not a trace of being spoilt. The artist noted: "You don't get spoiled children with Palace discipline which is rigorous compared with that of middle-class families whose children I have drawn." When she wanted Anne to pose lying on a settee, she wouldn't, because Nanny did not permit children to put their shoes on furniture. On another occasion, a footman brought elevenses of tea and biscuits. Ulrica's biscuit was one decorated with raspberries, Anne's was rather dull. "I must have a biscuit like yours," the princess exclaimed. "Anne, eat your own biscuit," the nurse curtly ordered. The eager look on the child's face vanished and tears began to flow.

On her next sitting, Ulrica arrived at the Palace to find both Charles and Anne waiting for her, clearly plotting something. Suddenly Anne produced a great hairy spider which she pushed into the artist's sleeve. Ulrica shrieked and tried to shake it out, while Charles and Anne danced around in delight. The spider turned out to be a toy brought back from abroad by Prince Philip.

Even at that age – she was six when Ulrica completed her sittings – Anne's life was controlled to a certain degree by an appointments book, in which were listed her lessons, study times, out-of-palace visits and so on. There was, in the background, formality and protocol, which different children, unaccustomed to such rigid atmosphere, might have found inhibiting. Princess Anne, for example, had very little free time; but Ulrica Forbes said that she always managed to have fun.

This potential was increased with the arrival at the Palace during school hours of two girls of similar age. When Charles was sent to boarding-school at Cheam, the Queen decided that Anne should have two more children with her in "class". Caroline Hamilton, granddaughter of the Dean of Windsor, and Susan Babington-Smith, granddaughter of a former equerry to King George V, her companions for the next seven years, formed a threesome, who would be among the most pampered pupils in Britain. They were taught alongside the princess under the watchful eye of governess Catherine Peebles, who had taught the Duchess of Kent's two children, Princess Alexandra and Prince Michael. She formed a curriculum that was as close as possible to normal schooling, and Anne's interest in geography and travel was highlighted when she was able to plot the course of her parents' various travels around the world. Susan, who was known in class as Sukie, recalled many years later just how much theirs was *unlike* a normal education. What impressed her most was the number of trips: the best seats at Wimbledon tennis, ice-skating at Richmond. They took it for granted that other children got the same treatment as they did. There were also weekly music lessons. Additional children were brought in to form a small class for ballroom and ballet dancing. The school year was strictly adhered to and, because the autumn term began while the Royal family were still on their summer holidays at Balmoral, it would normally be necessary to send Miss Peebles and the two girls to Scotland for the first four weeks of the term. And while press and public attention focused heavily on Charles's school days, Anne remained largely out of the limelight except for public functions with the rest of her family. So it would remain until she was twelve, when she was moved to an outside school. At that point, the two girls who had formed such a close bond with Anne during those years would depart the Palace schooling system and would have little contact with Anne again.

There were other regular companions at the Palace for the young princess. Princess Margaret herself revived the Buckingham Palace Brownie Pack, especially for Anne, with girls from Holy Trinity, Brompton, and daughters of the Royal Household joining in. It was to be Anne's first real association with "ordinary" people. The Brownies included children of a taxi driver, an electrician and a hotel boiler engineer whose daughters, Sally and Carol Lewis, were among the first members of the Pack. Carol was a sixer and expected to be patrol leader, but Anne herself was voted leader. Their mother Ann, a typist, said at the time: "We got the shock of our lives when the letter came from Buckingham Palace. But it's a good thing to do, both for my kids and the princess. And it will make her more democratic." The children were collected by car every week, until they left the Guides. Like Anne's school chums, they would have little future contact with her. And a new phase in her life was beginning.

The birth of Prince Andrew in 1960 had moved her down a notch in the line of succession to the Throne and, perhaps for the first time, she could discover how a normal family occasion, like the arrival of a brother, could be projected around the world as a major event. She was old enough now to witness and appreciate the press and public interest in the activities of her parents. The announcement of the Queen's pregnancy, her confinement and the eventual birth of Andrew commanded immeasurable column inches of newsprint and television time. The awareness that she was A Princess was beginning to dawn.

This was obvious in her poise, even posing, at public events to which she accompanied her parents. She was getting "a bit above herself", according to one courtier, and this was borne out by Cecil Beaton's experience when it was arranged that he should photograph the Queen's latest addition, along with Anne and Charles, at the Nash rooms. The children arrived first with Nanny. Hugo Vickers tells us that Beaton had set up his equipment and announced: "Oh well, I suppose we had better start photographing right away if that would be all right," to which Anne replied: "Well, I don't think it will be." Eventually the Queen and Prince Philip arrived and Beaton tried to make the most of what was a fairly formal and conventional family group. "I felt as if I were being chased in a nightmare," Beaton wrote in his diary, "when one's legs sink into the mire. The family stood to attention ... I said something to make them smile, and clicked. The baby, thank god, behaved itself and didn't cry or spew." He found Prince Philip awkward and organizing, making suggestions about where Beaton should stand or where he should position his camera. Then Anne started playing up. Beaton had taken her to a window. "The wretched girl shrugged her shoulders and pulled a face," he wrote. "I said, 'You hate it, I know. But hate it by the window, hate it looking this way, hate it looking that way, hate it in profile. Now detest it looking straight at the camera.'"

Anne's appearance was becoming important, and fashion writers were beginning to take note of what she was wearing at the age of eleven. The Queen was criticized in *Woman's Mirror* in 1961 for what was described as obvious economy in the Royal nursery where the rule was that hems, sleeves and turn-ups should be let down as the children grew. It was a practice which by necessity had to be adopted in most households. Was it really necessary for a family in such public view? Anne often appeared in clothes made from her mother's dresses and tended to be old-fashioned for a modern miss. Fashion commentator Susan Curtis-Bennett wrote: "What a pity the Queen's advisers don't take a walk round some of our stores to see just what is available for children of this age."

Princess Anne herself showed little interest in clothes. Already, her fondness for casual wear was beginning to show, and that went naturally with her increasingly passionate love of riding at which she had become the Royal family's most proficient exponent. She had long been a member of the local Pony Club and had advanced instruction over her own course set up at Windsor. She was also keen on sailing, encouraged by her father, and was already learning to drive on the private roads of the various Royal estates.

Anne was also showing occasional impatience and a certain dislike at being "gawped at" and photographed constantly. She wanted to be like her contemporaries. Newspapers recorded with some surprise that she had been allowed to join a Girl Guides' camp, in which she slept under canvas with other "normal middle-class girls, daughters of businessmen, policemen and palace servants". The Royal tradition of keeping princesses on a pedestal was being swept away. But the wealth and privilege of Royalty could not be ignored and it could never be true that Anne was being brought up just like any other child of her age. When she showed interest in tennis, for example, Dan Maskell was engaged to coach her; when she showed an aptitude for show-jumping, she received the best extra tuition.

The Queen and Prince Philip were concerned lest Anne should grow up in isolation from her own generation. Charles was now at Gordonstoun, and in September 1963, she was enrolled as a pupil at Benenden School in Kent where she joined three hundred children from the ranks of the upper-middle classes.

The school was carefully chosen. It was close enough to London for access to her parents, yet suitably situated to avoid siege by reporters and cameramen who had dogged Prince Charles at Cheam. It was also close to the home of the Queen's friend, Lady Anne Nevill, with whom Anne could stay at weekends when the Queen and Prince Philip were away.

She arrived at Benenden with her mother. The entire three hundred and forty staff and pupils were waiting to greet her, standing in groups under oak trees outside the main entrance. The princess wore the regulation blue suit and carried her school hat with the orange band of her house. On the school terrace overlooking the two hundred acres of parkland, house-mistresses were presented to the Queen and Princess Anne and then the headmistress, Miss Elizabeth Clarke, showed them the dormitory she was to share with two other girls. Everyone would try their best to welcome her as just another new girl. But there was no getting away from the fact that she *was* a princess; a Very Important Person, who would be watched day and night, and who would be treated differently from any other girl, however much the tutors and fellow schoolgirls insisted that she would not, or however much they tried not to. The Queen made a rather poignant comment as she left her only daughter in the care of Benenden. "The girls all look so alike in their uniforms I don't know whether I shall be able to pick her out when I come next." That, basically, was why Anne was there, to be like other girls and so proceed, it was hoped, unnoticed through her school career. But was this possible?

For Anne herself, the experience must have been something of a culture shock, coming as she did from the formality and calm of the corridors of Buckingham Palace where staff talked in whispers and "home" was too large for two or three noisy children to be even noticed. The bustle, chatter and general mêlée of a girls' school can take your breath away.

Pupils were told to address her simply as Anne, the mistresses called her Princess Anne. If she had any nerves, she didn't show them. One girl warned her that her dorm was haunted by a ghost called Kitty Fisher, and walked into her room one night wailing and wearing ghostly apparel. "Anne simply remarked: 'You must do better than that. You forget I have seen real ghosts at Balmoral.'" She was quickly accepted as one of the girls, but her Royal status could never really be ignored, especially with Perkins, her detective, constantly hovering in the background. In sports and in athletic activity, Anne was always ahead of the field. Swimming, tennis, skiing, rock-climbing, she tried the lot, and was generally above average. Academically, she was just about, and quite often below, average in most subjects. Her housemistress, Cynthia Gee, said Anne "never worked especially hard. She wasn't stupid, but economy of effort was her style."

But perhaps that was to be expected of a teenager discovering a blossoming world, and freedoms and friendships she had never before experienced. Nor had she to consider any special qualifications for a career. That was already mapped out for her: a life in public view, attending official engagements as a senior representative of her family and, frankly, one which she might have looked upon with some dread. In her more despairing moments, she might hate the prospect; but then she might remember that, in an earlier age, she would not even have had a school education. She would have been a princess who would have married at an early age some other member of European Royalty whom she barely knew. Even two decades before, her mother and her aunt had been confined almost throughout their youth to the extremities of Windsor, Buckingham Palace and Balmoral, beyond whose boundaries they seldom ventured until their late teens.

Whether Anne totally appreciated her good fortune at the age of thirteen or fourteen is unlikely, but she could certainly see the duties which would be expected of her looming perilously close. Public speaking, quelling nerves in front of an audience in the school play, above all a greater consideration for others, would all form a part of her education, perhaps more important than actual scholarship.

Her horse, High Jinks, was brought to the Benenden stables where she continued instruction in her true love, riding and competing. In this she was assisted by Cherry Kendall, a successful Badminton three-day eventer, who helped bring the princess on to a higher level of ability than those girls around her. It also helped to dispose of some of the puppy fat which was so apparent in photographs of Anne when she was one of the train-holders at the wedding of King Constantine of Greece and Princess Anne-Marie of Denmark in 1964. She had put on almost a stone and a half in weight and could now fit into her mother's clothes without much cutting down or alteration.

Another four years at Benenden, however, would make her ready, if not entirely willing, to undertake the duties expected of her. She was still capable of throwing a tantrum and pulling rank. But her mistresses remained undaunted and ignored such threats. In her last year at the school, she was made "housemother" which the headmistress insisted she got through merit and achievement as a pupil and not merely because she was a princess. Anne herself has also rapidly rejected any suggestion to the contrary. She had in the last couple of years become one of the school's most conspicuous and confident pupils. "Lively and vigorous" was how one of her former tutors described her. She was always neat and tidy and in her last term, having passed her driving test first go, borrowed a new Bedford van from the Palace to ferry some of her departing chums home, rather than let them face the school train.

She left in 1968 with a handful of O-levels and two A-levels, a D in History and an E in Geography. The economy of academic effort noticed by her housemistress had not changed and Anne herself saw no point in going on to university. To begin with, she wasn't really equipped mentally for further education. "Many of my friends were going to university simply because it was university," she said, "not for any real reason."

So there she was, going out into the world and away from the discretion and support of the few close friends she had made at Benenden. Was she ready for the task ahead? Hardly. As we shall see, being housemother at a girls' boarding school, or learning to live on an allowance of £2, or taking part in special studies on nursing, sociology and occupational therapy, would not be sufficient grounding for A Royal in the Real World. Her education in that was about to begin. Most of all, she would quickly discover that her developing obsession for privacy would never be fulfilled; and though she had perhaps acquired experience of compassion, she had yet to moderate her responses to those with whose views, or even presence, she might disagree. Impatience holds no virtue and sometimes it is necessary to suffer fools. As yet, Princess Anne had not taken that on board.

TWO

Harsh Realities

As the latest member of the Royal family to take on public work, Princess Anne knew she was in for a mixed reception when she stepped out of the private world she had enjoyed at Benenden into a totally public arena, where the whirring of motorized cameras would record her every move and eavesdropping ears would note her every word.

At eighteen, she was coming out at a particularly fashionable period when young people were for the first time making serious inroads into the higher echelons of fashion, showbusiness and industry. It was the age of youth, more sensible and determined now after an erratic and irresponsible few years which would be dubbed the Swinging Sixties. The Beatles and the Rolling Stones were still at the top of the pop charts, the mini-skirt was the fashion and *Monty Python's Flying Circus* was on television.

Anne came into this world with a degree of nervousness. She did not hurry to her public stage and, for the first few weeks after leaving school in the summer of 1968, she stayed close to her parents. Her eighteenth birthday was spent aboard the Royal yacht *Britannia* sailing off the Scottish coast, a holiday intended as a final staging post before she was launched into her job with the family firm. She was awarded an allowance of £6,000 a year from the Civil List; her parents bought her a Rover 2000 for her birthday; and she was given her own suite of rooms at Buckingham Palace.

She listened to the advice of relatives experienced in years of this work, and she was particularly influenced by her father who encouraged her to be herself. "The idea that you don't do anything on the off chance that you might be criticized for it would mean you'd end up like a cabbage and it's pointless; but you've got to stick up for something you believe in," he told her. There was no school of Royalty she could attend; there were no endless sessions in front of mirrors, practising and posing, though, to watch some of Anne's family on occasions, one might be forgiven for thinking they had done just that.

Anne had no illusions. She wasn't a fairy-tale princess. There was a job of work to be done, and she would do it. What she faced was a daunting career in public service; most girls of her age could not begin to contemplate it and would be racked by nerves. Anne was, too, but she put on a front of confidence which could often be misconstrued as arrogance; it was the only way she knew of overcoming "the butterflies". As public speakers and actors will confirm, such attacks of self-consciousness, nerves and the forgetting of lines can occur with alarming frequency, but no one out there in the audience will take account of this. Perfection is expected every time.

Her training was picked up as she went along, but, unlike her contemporaries in the film world, for example, there were no second chances. A mistake was a mistake. It could not be erased or cut or edited out. The Duke of Windsor, in his autobiography, recalled the instruction from his father when he was setting out on his round of world tours. "All eyes will be upon you. Remember to conduct yourself at all times with dignity and set a good example. You must be obedient and respectful and kind." And the sheer weight of public engagements horrified Queen Mary when she wrote to her son: "I feel angry at the amount of handshaking and autograph writing you seem compelled to face ... This does not sound dignified, though no doubt the people mean it well. Your speeches quite surprise us ... your Papa [King George V] made himself so miserable over speeches that it often spoilt the pleasure and interest of visiting new places." There was telling advice from Sir Frederick Ponsonby, Keeper of the Privy Purse, who told the young Duke: "There is always a risk in making yourself too accessible ... The Monarchy must always retain an element of mystery ... and remain on a pedestal."

Princess Anne's only route to excellence at her job would come through experience. And with her own rebellious streak she, like her great-uncle Edward VIII, would find difficulty at times in achieving all that was expected in terms of dignity – and humility.

Meanwhile, she turned more to her family for advice and support. She herself would always admit that she had never been a "family person". "When I was a child," she said in an interview, "and up to my teens I don't think I went along with the family bit at all, not until later than everyone else. I know its value now but I don't think I did up to my middle teens." For example, her appreciation of her grandmother developed later than, say, her brother's. Prince Charles had established a very special relationship with the Queen Mother and, as Anne went to work, she, too, would begin to rely more and more on her grandmother's help and advice, although it was her father's guidance she would seek most in those early years, and it would be from him that she took her cue on so many things. "I think that goes for most daughters," said Anne, "especially when there is one girl and three brothers ... but the greatest advantage of my life was the family I grew up in. We don't always agree. When we were children Charles and I used to fight like cat and dog but the family was always there and we are stronger for it. And the family is still there."

There would be many occasions when she would need that family support, as she began her public life in the autumn of 1968.

Fresh from school and still with some puppy fat that would soon disappear through sheer work, her aura of confidence was immediately dented by an article in a woman's fashion magazine which said: "Poor Princess Anne ... she's eighteen and nobody thinks she's a pretty girl. If I were her mother, the first thing I'd do is slim her down. The frumpy fur stoles, the middle-aged evening gowns, the overdone hair, the underdone hair, the sloppy grooming. It's about time Anne was allowed to bloom on her own." Another writer branded her frumpy, dumpy and grumpy. It was hardly a welcoming start to public endeavour and Anne could well be excused for running home and burying her head in her pillow. But that, she would find, was mild compared to some of the criticism she would have to face.

In the autumn of that year, Anne went temporarily back to school. Her French was passable but not fluent. She used to practise as a child by talking in French to one of the palace footmen who was French-speaking. But her final results at Benenden had not been good enough to see her through a conversation and she decided to take a crash course. She booked in for six weeks at the Berlitz language school in Oxford Street, London, for a fee of £525. French was still the language of diplomacy; and, as she began her world travels, the six weeks' hard work alone in that classroom over the bustle of busy shoppers would prove invaluable.

The ability to communicate, she would find, was another aspect of her work that was vital. She would be confronted with many people who were more nervous of her presence than she of theirs and often she, like a dancer, would have to lead by asking questions of her hosts and thus get the conversation moving. In this, a second language would be a necessity.

In the autumn of 1968, the Queen gave a reception for British athletes returning from the Olympic games in Mexico. The equestrian team, in which Anne was obviously very interested, had taken a gold and in that team, though only a reserve, was Lt. Mark Phillips whom she sought out again after a chance meeting at a dinner earlier in the year.

He had made a lasting impression on her. They didn't meet again for some weeks and, in the New Year, Princess Anne was to begin her career in earnest. Some diversion was just as well: when the annual Civil List came up for discussion with the Budget, Mr Willie Hamilton, the most vocal of MPs who were critical of the Monarchy, challenged yet another Royal "sponging" off the taxpayer.

In March 1969, Anne went solo for the first time.

She administered the age-old custom of presenting leeks to the Welsh Guards on St David's Day. She had taken the advice of the fashion writers and slimmed down considerably and came dressed in bright colours and a stylish cap. The newspapers couldn't resist a little dig. One suggested her knobbly knees were hardly suited to high hemlines. However, she was bright and cheerful; and confident. In the *Sunday Telegraph*, Victoria Reilly wrote: "Suddenly it is all happening to Princess Anne. The Queen's daughter has blossomed into a young woman with a fashion flair that is assuring her front-page coverage wherever she goes. This time last year, she was still a schoolgirl; now she is a much-in-demand public figure. What a transformation!"

In May, she launched her first ship, an Esso tanker; toured the Rover plant at Solihull; opened the Young Farmers' Club Centre in Kenilworth; and visited the National Equestrian Centre at Stoneleigh Abbey. The following week she accompanied the Queen and Prince Philip on a State visit to Austria. Victoria Reilly again: "The Austrians were clearly charmed by her, if a little alarmed at the shortness of her skirts. As for the princess, she was utterly determined not to waste a second; the daffodil yellow coat and matching bowler were discarded in favour of full riding gear and a try-out session on one of the famous Lipizaner horses at the Spanish riding school whose head was amazed at her skill. I found the princess remarkably poised and not in the least unnerved by questions."

The launching of Anne would be completed later that month when she made her first public speech, which she wrote herself to launch the Festival of London Stores. Twenty-six stores were taking part and Anne worked out she had already been a customer at twenty-five of them. It was an amusing, unassuming first public utterance that bears a second look: "I think I can claim to have supported almost all the stores represented here at some time or other. The other one that has escaped my needs is Aquascutum but no doubt this can be rectified. Harrods have had a long association with my family which I am successfully continuing every Christmastide, not forgetting a few other odds and ends at other times of the year. The same applies to Burberry's although I am ashamed to admit that I dislike macs so intensely that my present Burberry is going to last me a good many years. I was tempted into Fenwicks by way of being stuck in Bond Street traffic jams on my way back from my language course; Selfridges supplied me with what an outraged woman described as a Zebra coat and 'How could I be so cruel'; but I have never seen a blue and white zebra. I have bought articles in Peter Robinson but I do not think they are the sort of things you discuss here. Simpsons provided me with my reefer jacket which easily bears the title of my most worn garment, much to the irritation of a good many people."

The last remark was a reference to criticism of her casual dress in her off-duty moments. These were the times of privacy. She seemed to believe that she could draw a curtain across her life at the point at which she became non-public and assume, like a child covering its face with its hands, that no one could see her. Privacy was one of the reasons she immersed herself totally in riding. It was an area of her life, she would say, that she considered Private with a capital P. Though her competitive riding was done in public, and treated by the media as if she was at a public function, Anne herself did not see it that way. It was during these events, which she considered her private domain, that she would become angry at press intervention.

In some respects, too, she would make a definite effort to

appear a "casual" person who liked things that ordinary people enjoyed. She caused something of a sensation, for instance, when she went twice to see the avant-garde musical *Hair* in London's West End with her regular escort at that time, Sandy Harpur, her first "true love" whom many thought she would marry. On the second occasion, she and other members of the audience accepted an invitation from the cast to join them on stage for one of the numbers. Her clothes brought a few raised eyebrows. She was wearing a trouser suit.

She was also casual enough once to walk into Marks and Spencers to exchange a sweater which was too tight. She asked to be measured at the counter by the nervous assistant. She walked out with a thirty-six-inch sweater, two inches larger than the one she had originally bought.

However friendly and approachable she *liked* to appear, there was an element of a naturally-split personality that even Anne herself seemed to have difficulty in coping with. When one of her friends made reference to "her mother", Anne testily responded: "I take it you refer to Her Majesty the Queen." It was a difficult period for her to come through. She wanted obviously to be in the company of lively friends of her own age, who felt they could relax and not be formal with her. At the same time, she refused to lower her defences to the point where her family and the Monarchy could be taken lightly. Once she went to the Royal College of Art, which she had heard had good parties. But she found few people would dance with her and spent most of the evening accompanied on the dance-floor by her detective. One young man, who plucked up the courage to ask her to dance and was clearly overawed at holding a princess in his arms, was quickly advised by Her Royal Highness: "I'm not a piece of china, you know." It was in search of friends who would not be scared of her position that she gravitated further into the world of the horse – her "private" world.

The pomp and pageantry of the Investiture of her brother as Prince of Wales at Caernarfon Castle in July brought the princess back into the total formality of her public life. It was a moving ceremony for her entire family and one which, she admitted some years later, gave her a feeling of strange isolation. As the only girl in a family of four, she stood alone. The ceremony would also indicate once more that she would always remain in the shadow of her brother, who would one day be king. She had yet to discover that her work for the Save the Children Fund would be the route out of that shadow, into a limelight that would be her very own. On that summer's day in Wales, she did indeed feel isolated. She said in an interview: "I have always accepted being second in everything from quite an early age ... you start off life at the back of the line; you don't think anybody's paying much attention to you, then much later you find out public attention is on you too. It comes as a nasty shock because you were behaving as an ordinary human being and you felt you were doing the right thing and you now realise people are looking at you in a special kind of way and often critically."

People looking at her in that special kind of way would intensify during that first year of her "going public". Apart from the Investiture, she attended the FA Cup final, her first experience of a football match. She drove a nine-ton double decker bus at the Road Transport Industry's training centre; joined her parents on a semi-official visit to Norway in August; and in October went to Paderborn, to the 14th/20th King's Hussars of which she had been made Colonel-in-Chief. She soon endeared herself to the entire British Army by putting on a uniform, driving a fifty-two-ton tank and firing a machine gun.

Her engagements were coming thick and fast and she barely had time to prepare for a major tour in the spring, when she would join the Queen and Prince Philip in Fiji, Tonga, New Zealand and Australia. Her return to England saw her embark on a new round of luncheons, dinners, visits, trips to various parts of the country and another Channel crossing back to Paderborn and then on to lay the foundation stone of the Florence Nightingale Hospital at Dusseldorf-Kaiserwerth. She hardly had time to catch her breath before the family was packing again, for a ten-day tour of Canada and the United States, which would end with Prince Charles and Princess Anne making a three-day visit to Washington as guests of President Nixon.

Her diary was crammed: in one six-day period she carried out seventeen engagements at home. Was she doing too much? That was certainly one of the reasons put forward to explain why the American trip was labelled a total fiasco. For several days, the American press, while applauding the Queen and Prince Philip, turned on Princess Anne in the most vitriolic attack ever mounted against a member of the British Royal

34

family. Even the Duke of Windsor had not suffered quite such a personal onslaught. The *Washington Daily News* described her as "snobbish, pouting, spoiled, bored, sullen and disdainful". Another newspaper wrote: "Why not limit Anne to opening rhododendron shows in Kent before unleashing her again on foreigners?" One writer complained that the princess looked plainly exhausted while her parents and her elder brother, with greater stamina and experience, still had genuine smiles on their faces and buoyancy in their bones.

Anne's particularly moody arrival in Washington in that July of 1970 followed an arduous tour of Canada. She was apparently hoping for some relaxation when she arrived at the White House – to go riding, see the shops, visit a discotheque – none of which were permitted by the American security advisers. Charles and Anne were kept within constant view of the armed protectors, and, as usual, under the minute-by-minute scrutiny of the press. She complained: "There are twenty million reporters on my heels." Anne had lost interest in Washington and the Americans, and failed to conceal her desire to be out of it. By the time she returned to London, the British press were full of headlines like "ANNE'S ANTICS" and "SPOILED BRAT".

Royal biographers Graham and Heather Fisher suggested the fault lay with Buckingham Palace for working their new star too hard. They wrote: "The worlds of pop and entertainment are littered with the nervous breakdowns of young girls who have tried to do too much, too soon, for whom the strains and pressures have been too great. Is Princess Anne in danger of running the same risk in her equally demanding role? Is she, like many a young pop singer, movie starlet or model, living a life with which she is emotionally unable to cope?"

True, all those pressures experienced by the young and famous were there. But it wasn't tiredness that made Anne appear such a reluctant participant of the Royal game. Her Hanoverian features, particularly around the jaw, could set into an unsmiling look of disdain, very much like Queen Victoria. Anne, in the end, had actually to concentrate on her expressions, otherwise she could absent-mindedly look angry. Also, the plain fact of the matter was that she was bored; and, like her father, she has difficulty even now in hiding her true feelings or saying things she doesn't mean. When she had no heart for a project, she was unable to conceal her lack of interest; when she was keen, she gave one hundred per cent and was extremely articulate and modest about her involvement.

This trait showed through during the winter of 1970, when she was on her travels once again, this time – and for the first time – in connection with the Save the Children Fund. She had just become the new President of the Fund and in November nervously presided over its annual meeting. She followed in the footsteps of her great-aunt Lady Mountbatten who was President from 1949 until her death in 1960. In her maiden speech, Anne expressed a hope for more support from young people ... "a reservoir of youthful talent that remains to be tapped". Her interest had been captured. "She's mad keen on children and her enthusiasm permeates down the line," said one official. And a young volunteer girl said: "She's very easy to speak to and has really thought out the problems we're trying to tackle." And so Anne was instrumental in getting BBC television's *Blue Peter* team to join her on safari in Kenya, in the hope of attracting more interest from the young. There were some very personal moments as presenter Valerie Singleton and the crew filmed over the princess's shoulder and then put her in front of the cameras for a relaxed and frank interview. In the forty-minute film she was seen riding, photographing wildlife, swimming in the Indian ocean and visiting the Save the Children Fund centre in Nairobi. It was her first extended appearance on television, and the public's big chance to see her in action. What they saw was deep concentration, sensible probing questions, and relaxation in an intimate style rarely, if ever, seen of a member of the Royal family.

She emerged sharp-eyed and spirited and with clear values. As a person, she obviously *chose* to appear slightly reserved. When Val Singleton was talking to her about fashion, the latest craze, wearing hotpants, came up. "There is a limit to what you can do and that's it," said Anne. "People complain that one is not with it but honestly, there are certain things I will not do." She was cool and poised and displayed the same gift for laconic observation as her father. She was also clearly uncomfortable that a greater part of the film was about her, rather than the Nairobi centre for destitute boys or the African village where the Fund was trying to resettle children. Nevertheless, when the TV film and the subsequent BBC book on the expedition went out, there was substantial criticism that the Fund took second place to showing the princess in a new light.

She had, moreover, allowed herself to be manipulated by the producers. When she was photographed with Val Singleton in the midst of a huge sea of black faces of boys watching a football match, the two women sat in those seats only for the few moments during which the cameras shot the scene. They clapped and cheered to the producers' orders and then moved away to a position among the Fund officials, well away from the children. A scene where she walked to Treetops, the hotel in the bush where her mother became Queen, was obediently re-enacted by the princess. Her appearance in a swimming costume was exclusively for the television cameras. The Fund was her motive, and the BBC took advantage of the fact.

At the end of the week, she was supposed to give an hour of her time to press photographers who were there in force but had been given sparse pickings because the television cameras took the lion's share. Suddenly, Anne's mood changed. She became sulky and frowning. Her face set and she found the hour almost unendurable.

Sometimes, she said in the film, the awful feeling came over her "Why do I do this?" And there were always plenty of critics waiting in the wings to insist that no one was forcing her to do anything. It has undoubtedly been the thought of every member of the Royal family at some time or other to wish herself or himself out of public life and into a "normal" existence. That was the desire so often expressed by Edward VIII but, fortunately for those who believe in the Monarchy, he has so far been the only member of the Windsor family this century to walk out on his heritage and his Royal duty in favour of personal gratification.

Princess Anne's way of coping has been to pursue her alternative career as a horsewoman. In this, her private world, she can disappear. Being atop a horse is also her greatest natural talent. She is also an excellent yachtswoman. As she approached her twenty-first birthday she was beginning to realize that one of the main advantages of her life was that she had the means, outside her public duties, to follow her own pleasures. When she left Benenden, she turned to the sport of eventing. Unlike show jumping, it was something she could do on a fairly casual basis because it could fit in with her other work. It was only "casual" in terms of the time she could allot to it. In every other sense, she approached it with commitment and seriousness. Speed was the thrill, just as it was for her when driving her new Scimitar sports car, bought for her by her parents as a joint Christmas and birthday present to replace the staid Rover. She chose horses which were lively, even rejected by others as being none-too-safe. She selected Mrs Alison Oliver, one of the nation's greatest instructors, as her trainer and acquired three first-class horses, Doublet, Purple Star and Royal Ocean. She got up at first light to spend three hours in the saddle, learning and practising, before taking a shower and changing into formal clothes for a full day of official engagements.

No one quite realized how hard she was working at it: by 1971 she had become a thoroughly proficient three-day eventer with her sights set on the Olympics.

Her increasingly successful appearances at various horse trials were made all the more difficult by the press pack at her heels. She said: "When I'm approaching a water jump with dozens of photographers waiting for me to fall in, and hundreds of spectators wondering what's going to happen next, the horse is the only one who doesn't know I'm a Royal." Her new horse, Doublet, gave the photographers plenty of opportunities of catching the princess on the deck. She admitted he was never an easy ride – "the quickest stopper I ever rode" – and, when she began to disappear over his head with alarming frequency, Mrs Oliver was asked: "Why is she riding that dangerous horse when she keeps falling off?" Anne persevered and gradually moved up the scale to the point where top riders who had once viewed her with scepticism were now competing against her.

Her most significant achievement came at Badminton Horse Trials of 1971 where hopefuls for the 1972 Olympics in Munich were showing their best over what was the hardest and longest course to be staged there. She was among the cream of British and European riders. After day one, the dressage, she was leading the field with Mark Phillips in second place. On the second day, the steeplechase and cross-country, she showed what her trainer later described as "innocent courage" over a course made treacherous by overnight rain, and finished up fourth. By now, the country's television viewers were beginning to take notice and join her family in its applause, as the tension rose towards the end of the three punishing days. It was a triumph for her to finish fifth out of forty-seven, which won her a place in the European championships at Burghley in September.

The winner of Badminton that year was Mark Phillips on Great Ovation whose congratulatory kiss of Princess Anne went unnoticed by the cameramen.

Public duties had by no means slackened off during Anne's rise to stardom in eventing. In May, she was back in Canada for a ten-day tour and, on her return, travelled the length and breadth of Britain in a gruelling succession of engagements during which she collapsed with agonising stomach pains. She was admitted to the King Edward VII hospital where it was discovered she had an ovarian cyst. Visitors came by to comfort her and to commiserate on her ill-fortune on now being unable to compete at Burghley in six weeks' time. "Who says so?" said Anne. She was already up and walking around the ward in spite of doctors' advice to stay in bed and it was clear she had no intention of missing the big event. During the summer, she joined her parents at the family holiday at Balmoral and set herself a rigorous fitness programme which included some tiring hill walking. She took time out to relax for her twenty-first birthday party on board the Royal yacht and a week later she was back in the saddle for Eridge Horse Trials to warm up for Burghley.

In the meantime she had to contend with a variety of press coverage to "celebrate" her official coming-of-age. If her relationship with Fleet Street had so far been sustained by the occasional skirmish, it would now turn into a running battle. The *Daily Mirror* said she was a princess in search of a role and was emerging as the odd-Royal out, a young woman with an inquiring mind and obvious intelligence who had not quite found her feet; while other members of her generation were forging new freedoms, there was little apparent difference between Anne's life and that of her great-aunt, the late Princess Royal, and she gave every appearance of boredom and impatience. The *Sun* took the opportunity of trying to get her married off and suggested various men in her life who might take her down the aisle. They included Prince William of Gloucester who was killed the following year in an air crash, Crown Prince Gustaf of Sweden, Mountbatten's grandson Norton Knatchbull, and the twin princes Rupert and Albert, cousins on her father's side. Mark Phillips was not mentioned as a possible candidate.

One observer described Anne as "determined to differentiate between her own and her brother's identity. Charles is charming, intelligent, obviously anxious to please while Anne remains resolutely unimpressed and deliberately downbeat." There were other assessments, too. Those who claimed to know her told a variety of anecdotes. Some said she was good fun. Example: When Prince Charles tied a firework to the ignition of the Queen's Landrover at Balmoral, the princess thought it "a great hoot". At the Royal Highland Show in Edinburgh she saw her first black pudding and asked: "What can you do with these? Hang them in the sitting room," a remark which led to a consignment of black puddings arriving for her at Holyrood House the next day. She was said to be informal. "My kid brother rings her up out of the blue and cadges a free ride to polo," said a one-time escort. "He gets over to Buck House on his bike, she slings it in the back of her car and off they go." Another time, coming in from riding, she dismounted and helped a motorist push a car that had broken down. But she had a sense of position. A young man introduced to her at a dance said: "Your face is familiar. Where have I seen you before?" She replied: "I don't think that's very funny." She didn't smoke or drink. When taken out to dinner, she drank coke and she could dance at a ball until five and be up at seven. In conversation she was amusing and sarcastic rather than witty. She told funny stories herself and was not a prudish listener to other people's. She liked imitating people, particularly politicians. She wasn't gifted at arguing but skilful at turning the conversation away from tricky topics.

Anne was tense, slightly angry with the press and very ready to disappear into her world of riding. She took her three horses to Burghley, and Alison Oliver for moral support. Together they walked the course and Alison could feel the tension and excitement coming from Anne. Other riders, though her friends, were unsure whether she had the ability and there had always been the nagging doubt that she had been given the chance to compete at Burghley as an individual, rather than a team member, simply because she was the Queen's daughter. Some foreign competitors and certain sports writers were convinced that she hadn't either the skill or the stamina to stay with such experience.

Princess Anne and Doublet went into an early lead, which was sustained throughout the first day. At the end of the dressage, she was leading the field with 41.5 penalty points only. In the English team, only Richard Meade got less than 50 penalties. On the second day, over the tough cross-country course, Doublet retained the lead, and the third day, with the Queen and Prince Philip among the spectators, opened in a tense and exciting atmosphere. Could the young, inexperienced princess pull it off? She admitted later that, as she rode Doublet for the warm-up, her stomach was in knots. As she entered the show-jumping arena, there was hardly a sound. She finished on a clear round and a wild cheer rang out. Princess Anne was the 1971 European Champion, for which she received a gold medal and a £250 cheque presented to her by the Queen. The other British riders were down the field, including Richard Meade at fifth and Mark Phillips who came sixth. For Anne, it was a moment of total joy and achievement: commentators were unanimous in the view that she would be included in the British Olympics team for Munich the following year. There were instant opponents, of course, including show-jumper Harvey Smith who publicly said: "In her own class, she is the best there is but she's nowhere near Olympic standard." Her good friend Richard Meade rushed to her defence and challenged Harvey to a duel of horsemanship at Badminton, which was never taken up.

Princess Anne became the BBC Sports Personality of the Year; Fleet Street awarded her their coveted Sportswriters Award; and the *Daily Express* named her Sportswoman of 1971. (Their Sportsman of that year was racing driver Jackie Stewart who met the princess at the various presentation ceremonies and became one of her closest friends.)

In the event, the much-discussed Olympic place would elude the princess. A week before the Badminton Trials the following April, at which prospective British team members would consolidate their positions, Doublet sprained a tendon and had to be withdrawn. She tried out Columbus, a horse owned by the Queen, as a replacement but he was too big and muscular for her to control. The Queen asked Mark Phillips if he would like to take him on, and here was the first hint of a Royal friendship in the offing, although it wasn't immediately picked up by the press. At the Olympic Games later in the year, Princess Anne was there to cheer the British team to a gold medal and, according to several of the tabloids, she "made no secret of her admiration when Richard Meade won the individual gold".

The *Daily Mirror* reported that the event was charged with a "special kind of emotion" for the princess whose name had "often been linked romantically with Meade". When Meade finished his ride she "rushed to the paddock to congratulate him ... and she was flushed with excitement". All this was but a few months away from the engagement of Mark Phillips and Princess Anne and she was playing a cat-and-mouse game with the press. There had been rumours of a romance with a famous rider, but they had picked the wrong man. They would soon realize that, of course, and then the fun would really start. But now Princess Anne and her arch enemies were shaping up for a battle from which relations between the Palace and the press would never recover.

Apart from the intense interest in her love life, there were two or three other incidents which would put her on the front pages before the year was out. First, she was stopped on a motorway for exceeding the seventy miles per hour limit in her Scimitar which obviously brought a substantial press reaction. The Tory MP, Sir Gerald Nabarro, who had appeared in court on a motoring charge in which he claimed he wasn't driving, began to use a joke typical of the time. "Between you and me," he would say, "it wasn't my secretary driving, it was Princess Anne." The same sort of humour was applied by the *Evening Standard* cartoonist, Jak, after the princess had been involved in angry scenes while out fox-hunting. Jak showed a Palace footman announcing her arrest on a mugging charge.

All this encouraged the *Sunday Telegraph* to run a note of caution under the headline "Princess and Public": "Her style is essentially a continuation of Prince Philip's. She has two kind and devoted parents but not for nothing is she called a father's child. Her whole way of attack, the concentration on physical achievement, her riding and driving skills, her directions and use of phrase, is stamped with the accumulated memories of him ... swearing or sweating in the muck on the polo field ... beseeching a *Daily Express* man to get stuffed ... all this has helped shape her individuality. Yet if PR is the Royal family's primary job, millions will look to Princess Anne for leadership by example which Royalty is expected to supply."

Princess Anne must have been exuding nervous energy on a par with Battersea power station. She was by no means as confident as she appeared to be, and the more daunting functions would cause her loss of appetite and lack of sleep for days beforehand. Further, it had to be exceptional courage and determination that could turn a princess into a European riding champion at such an early age and against such competition; failure would have brought with it equally exceptional risk of personal stress.

At this particularly touchy time, the press and the Palace exchanged complaints over coverage of Princess Anne's presence at Burghley. There were rights and wrongs on both sides, but as usual photographers had been somewhat over-zealous. There was one incident when two cameramen spotted Anne wearing brightly coloured slacks and a red, white and blue sweater, her hair down and looking stunning. One of them called out: "Sorry ma'am, but if we can get a picture of you now we'll be off. We don't want to be pests." Anne replied coldly: "You are pests by the very nature of the cameras in your hands."

Here was the princess, barely twenty-two years old, with perhaps another fifty years ahead of her in the public eye, taking on the very people who would be in front of her every footstep throughout those years. The modern media would soon be pressing even more exhausting demands on the Royal family. And, as we shall see, it would get worse. It would open issues which this author believes can only be resolved by head-to-head agreements between Palace and newspaper proprietors.

Edward Heath told the author: "We appeared together with other sportsmen and women at a luncheon given at the Mansion House by the Lord Mayor of London in honour of sporting successes. It was, I suppose, an unusual occasion for us both, to be guests as sportsmen in our own right. She, a princess, feted for her triumph as a rider in the European Individual three-day event. I, as Prime Minister, was invited as captain of the British Ocean Racing Team which, including my own boat *Morning Cloud*, had that summer successfully regained the Admiral's Cup at Cowes. I was impressed by Princess Anne's modesty, as well as her confidence. The journalists at that time had concentrated, not on her skill as a rider but on her ill-disguised dislike of intrusive photographers interfering with her riding. I understood her feelings completely. In *Morning Cloud* on the start line we were subject not only to the attentions of all our rivals – some fifty odd boats – attempting to push us over the line and in some way get us disqualified, and also the distraction of innumerable photographers and reporters in fast outboards rushing around us, to say nothing of their helicopters circling overhead, regardless of the effect they had by blowing our sails inside out. But on the course, Princess Anne's sportsmanship was unquestioned, as was that of the British Ocean Racing Team."

THREE

Betrothal Denied

The build-up to the engagement of Princess Anne and Mark Phillips was marked by the most intense press speculation ever witnessed for a Royal story. Anne herself was partly to blame. She was insistent on keeping her friendship with the young Army officer secret as long as possible and their friends went to extraordinary lengths to assist them. There would be "coincidental" but carefully arranged meetings at dinner parties to which they were both invited; there would be out-of-the-way arrangements for dining out; and they would see each other regularly at Alison Oliver's stables where the Queen's horse, Columbus, which Mark had taken over, was kept.

The press finally dismissed Richard Meade as a "red herring" because he was too old at thirty-three; he had also, incidentally, been dismissed by the Queen and Prince Philip for the same reason and their feelings had been made known to Anne. Sandy Harpur had always been the other main contender for Anne's hand, but he had since gone off and married a model, from whom he was subsequently divorced. The Palace 'in' crowd thought he might have become her spouse, but those who knew him well had already noticed the strain he suffered when escorting Princess Anne, although they would suggest later that Anne had taken up with Mark on the rebound from Harpur.

The penny eventually dropped when Anne was discovered out fox-hunting with Mark in November 1972. She was a guest at his family home in Great Somerford, Wiltshire. His mother, Anne Phillips, recalled that they had only six weeks of calm from the point when Anne first visited Wiltshire until all hell broke loose. The villagers had kept it secret. So had the couple's friends who had been watching them grow ever closer for months. "Once the media latched on, they didn't get a moment's peace," said Mrs Phillips.

And the more the newspapers insisted that a Royal engagement was on the cards, the more Anne and Mark were equally insistent with their denials. Mark himself recalled: "The press would be surprised how often we went out to dinner and they hadn't cottoned on. In the spring [immediately prior to the official announcement of their engagement] and the last winter one was almost driven mad because one was given so very little private life. Everywhere we went, and some of the places we didn't go, we read about it in the papers. There was one Sunday when three papers said we had been to three different places." The princess added: "One of the things they got frightfully over-excited about was that he had been invited down to Sandringham for the weekend. We have people at Sandringham and we have had them for years. I have had my friends down on numerous occasions but because the papers got a bee in their bonnet they suddenly decided he was the only person staying there."

Did they regard dodging the press as a sort of game? "We didn't think it was funny," said the princess. "We were forced to do it as we were getting absolutely no privacy whatsoever. At that particular point of time one's friends were getting badly treated as well." Mark said: "Reading in the press every day that you were about to get engaged and about to get married is enough to make one think that that is the last thing one is going to do because one has been told to do so every day by the press. At that time we were very friendly but I had no intention of getting married. I was a confirmed bachelor."

The princess: "He kept telling me he was a confirmed bachelor and I thought at least one knows where one stands. I mean I wasn't thinking about it. One of the myths of my career is that people have written over the years that the only thing I wanted to do when I left school was get married. It has been one of the bugbears of my life. It couldn't have been further from the truth."

Princess Anne obviously felt outraged by constant intrusion into her private life, but the press would counter with the explanation that they were merely fulfilling public demand for stories and photographs.

The press pack followed her on a visit to Ethiopia which included a mule trek in the Simien Mountains. What Fleet Street would remember most about this episode was that Princess Anne and Mark Phillips continued to deny her forthcoming engagement until almost to the day when it was announced. After that, there was a gradual but definite deterioration in the relationship between the Palace and the press to the point where most newspapers rang the Palace press office for a comment on a particular story purely as a matter of course, knowing full well that, whereas previously they had got an "unofficial steer" as to the accuracy of a story, all they could now expect was a bland response which usually amounted to no comment at all. What began as an irritation would in the next ten to fifteen years develop into a crisis of confidence between the two sides, particularly regarding the Palace's view of certain newspapers.

Princess Anne and Mark Phillips had their own explanation of why they kept up the denials. Lieutenant Phillips, as he then was, said in a public interview after their engagement: "People don't believe us when we say that in March [1973] we had no intention of getting engaged. In fact, it is absolutely true and it was only after Badminton [horse trials held in April] when the pressures of competing were less and we weren't so busy and had time to look and think about the future that it seemed like a good idea." The princess agreed: "It is very difficult, I know, because people say 'How naïve can you get, saying that you weren't going to get married.' But that is a well-known disease that the last people who know are the people who are actually involved themselves. The boring part is that they say 'Oh you must have been fibbing' because it seemed to them a very obvious conclusion. Well, I am sorry, it didn't seem very obvious to us at the time. I know it sounds silly and it is probably difficult to understand but that is often the case. Not only that, but of course we are the ones who have to make the decisions and therefore one is not going to take them as lightly as the newspapers."

But there were other reasons why the press were getting on Anne's and Mark's nerves. During the latter part of 1972 and early 1973, they had both been involved in important eventing competitions at which Anne lost her patience with the photographers on a number of occasions. She said: "I accept the press when on an official engagement as part of the scenery. But at horse trials, the 'me' that does official duties couldn't possibly ride a horse. It is a different sort of me. I have to concentrate on what I am doing. If I appear to lose my patience, I would appear to lose my patience with anyone who got in the way ... when they think I am being bolshie ... all I am trying to do is concentrate." She gave as an example a cross-country course with a jump out of the woods into a lane. There was a fence in front of her which was just one stride away; the horse required his full attention because there was no room for error. Six cameramen all went "*click*" together – and the horse just stopped. He had lost his concentration and was unable to make the leap. "Even when you have got off the horse they tend to follow you around when you are not actually doing anything, and I think you can't get away from them at all ... you never have time to relax and relaxation is very important for competitors," she said.

So the engagement was finally announced on May 29, 1973, and even *The Times* was moved to record that "months of speculation ended last night ..." *The Times* also noted in its second sentence that (in spite of the denials) the couple had actually become engaged at Easter. Mark had flown over at the Bank Holiday weekend from his regiment in Germany to ask Prince Philip formally for his daughter's hand. He had been "petrified" at the thought of performing that duty but was put totally at ease by the prospective father-in-law, who was not, however, entirely overjoyed by his daughter's choice of husband, whom he considered rather dull and capable of talk only about horses and the Army. There were several reasons for not announcing the engagement right then, one of which was to sort out Mark's career. It could hardly be feasible that the husband of the Queen's daughter who had a busy schedule of official duties to perform could be expected to live in Army quarters in Germany, or Northern Ireland, or wherever the Regiment was posted. The Army was naturally told secretly that the couple would have to be suitably accommodated. Lieutenant Phillips, who was then twenty-four, was serving with The Queen's Dragoon Guards and the Regiment, it became known, was on stand-by to be moved from its present base in Germany to Northern Ireland. In fact, it had already been established that Lieutenant Phillips would not be going into the danger zone. He had already accepted a new posting to the Royal Military Academy at Sandhurst as an Acting Captain Instructor. His commanding officer, Lieutenant Colonel Maurice Johnston, who had been one of the first to know of the engagement since a serving officer must ask his permission to marry, said: "It's certainly been a well kept secret. Now the whole regiment can share the joy and pride I have felt all these weeks."

Mark's current salary in the Army was £2,300 a year. Upon her marriage, Princess Anne would receive £35,000 allowance from the Civil List, a rise of some £20,000 a year on the amount she received while single. Mark himself would not receive a penny from the List and his income would be derived purely from his Army pay, but there was immediate speculation on what honours, titles and other attributes the young officer might be afforded by the Crown. Mr Anthony Armstrong-Jones had accepted the title of Lord Snowdon upon his marriage to the Queen's sister, Princess Margaret, and it seemed natural to observers of Royal tradition and protocol that Mark would accept something similar, if only to ensure that their children would also receive titles in keeping with offspring of a princess who was, after all, still fourth in line to the Throne. Princess Anne said there had never been a discussion on the question of marrying an untitled man when she announced her intention to the Queen and Prince Philip. "I don't think there was ever any question, as far as the family was concerned, that one should ever marry anybody in particular. It isn't a duty because I'm not a boy. That side of it doesn't apply to me. One's parents might have possibly said 'we don't like him' or 'we do like him'. But I think they trusted one enough."

Mark Phillips had had a fairly uneventful background which was typical of many fellow officers. He was sent away to Stouts Hill prep school as a boy and then moved on to Marlborough College where he gained just five O-levels and one A-level, followed by Sandhurst. Much would be made of the fact that his A-level was not sufficient to get him directly into Sandhurst as an officer. He joined up as a private soldier, signing on as potential officer material. He stayed in the ranks only six months and could never therefore claim to have experienced a worm's eye view of life. He had few major interests other than horses. He didn't read a lot and seldom, if ever, went to the theatre or the cinema ... "One is generally so exhausted after eventing, that one tends to get one's head down and sleep." He was good-looking, dressed neatly but dowdily, and seemed agreeable. He was a keen sportsman but was outstanding on horseback. He had his first pony when he was eighteen months old; his mother was once Master of the local hunt; and he could

49

ride before he could walk properly. He had come fourth in a highly competitive field at Burghley when he was eighteen, was fourth at Badminton twice and won Badminton outright in 1972, with his future wife among the riders he beat. He was in the British Olympics contingent in Mexico at twenty, in 1968, and it was as part of the equestrian team that he first met the princess. As the Queen Mother remarked, had their particulars been run through a computer dating service, it is likely they would have matched each other's requirements. Although seemingly reserved, Mark was, like Anne, strong willed and at times quite stubborn.

It was his own proviso that he would remain the master in his own household. Both of them were aware of the problems that might confront them: perhaps like a film star, the wife's career would totally overshadow that of the husband. This was one of the reasons why Mark Phillips, with Anne's unqualified support, was insistent at that time on not taking a title. Whether it would be as a soldier, a professional horseman or a farmer, he wanted to retain charge over his own destiny. He could not begin to contemplate the role only of the princess's consort and the father of her children, which is what many expected he would retire from the Army to become. When asked whether he would join the princess on her official engagements, even then he said he would as far as possible, but added a note of caution that it would always depend on his own career commitments.

Mark was also by nature a shy person in unfamiliar surroundings. He had been given an insight of what it was like in the glare of the public spotlight during his riding activities and during the speculation over his association with the princess. He had been surprised at the extent that this had altered his view of life; and those experienced at publicity might well have forecast that he would attempt to avoid being an up-front person. He was also not a good public speaker; his voice was not strong and he was once described by Colonel Frank Weldon, director of Badminton, as having a rather "unfortunate manner". It was Anne who rounded on a girl reporter who had been sent out to watch them on horseback in a Berkshire field. It was Anne who did the talking at the Buckingham Palace garden party which followed their engagement.

So, from the outset, it seemed unlikely that he would join to the full what his future wife had already described as a "funny sort of existence". Anne did her best in the months before the wedding to prepare him for the kind of public and press attention that she knew they could expect. A Royal engagement and wedding would be treated in true fairy-tale tradition with total exposure and complete overkill. It was already evident that the Monarchy's image was increasingly popular and accessible. Opponents would say that, in this age of modernizing the Monarchy, largely as a result of the Queen's own policy of how her children should be brought up, it could never be expected that any Royals would be treated in the way Anne craved, like "ordinary" people. Even when Anne and Mark went to discos and other "ordinary" places, there was a definite boundary between them and the rest. Quite simply, they weren't ordinary: they were good "copy".

This "popularizing" of the Royal family was hastened by the circulation battle among the newspapers. Rupert Murdoch had acquired the *News of the World* and the *Sun*. The latter he got almost as a gift from the *Mirror* Group. Murdoch couldn't believe his luck in getting hold of a title to launch his downmarket popular daily, and by the early 1970s it was clear to everyone at the *Mirror* that the sale of the old *Sun* to Murdoch had provided the opening for what would become the *Mirror*'s greatest rival and competitor.

The *Sun* had increased its sales figures at an incredible rate, in spite of *Mirror* boss Hugh Cudlipp's assessment that "the *Mirror* has nothing to worry about there." Soon the *Sun* would be challenging the *Mirror* for the title of best-selling daily newspaper in Britain. At the same time, Murdoch wanted to see the *News of the World* retain its lead in the Sunday market and crucify the opposition, the *People* and the *Sunday Mirror*. It was one of the most competitive periods in newspaper history and when news editors, picture editors and even editors themselves are locked in battles like this, standards are eroded and the men out doorstepping famous faces and Royalty tend to become more strident and venturesome in the quest for material.

Princess Anne and Mark Phillips walked straight into it. For the rest of 1973, they were surrounded by cameramen, followed, spied upon, jostled for pictures, shouted at for a hoped-for responsive comment, particularly of the expletive kind. They were the superstars of the age: young, attractive and in love, and Royalty too. The adrenalin of the daily newsgatherers

51

surged. And if the couple felt they had been unfairly admonished by the press for denying their forthcoming engagement, this would rate as a minor ticking off compared to the kind of criticism about to be unleashed upon them. Everything from the cost of the wedding to their choice of home would come under scrutiny both from columnists and some left-wing MPs who said it was all shaping up to become a highly expensive and obscene circus. "I fear ," said Mr Willie Hamilton, "there's a spate of bilge on the way."

The weekend after the engagement became public, the prospective bridegroom got his first solo encounter with the press when he returned to his regiment in Germany. The Army had laid on a press conference. Mark was lined up for photographers from the Sunday papers beside a Chieftain tank. Printed sheets containing his curriculum vitae were handed out to the hundred journalists who had gathered from around the world. He was shown off as a man highly suited to become the husband of the Queen's only daughter. What also showed was that he was a wholly unexceptional person, such as could be found anywhere in the middle-class, shire families of Britain.

Yet it would be argued that every Royal mate should be vetted, because in the end they could affect the outlook and influence the thinking of key members of the Royal family. Princess Anne's choice would not have any national significance. But it is the behaviour and outlook of members of the Royal family that help form the public's regard for the Monarchy itself. There had been grave public concern over Princess Margaret's wish to marry a divorced man. Her eventual choice of husband, a commoner, Mr Anthony Armstrong-Jones, and the Princess Alexandra's similar move in marrying Mr Angus Ogilvy, were considered to be a radical updating of the Royal family's attitude. No longer would a princess like Anne be expected to scour the ever-dwindling ranks of European Royal families for a suitable prince. Her work and her needs were here, in Great Britain. And while Mark Phillips could hardly be classed a man of the people, he was closer to their ranks than Royalty had previously elected, and his family, too, were viewed as pleasant and down-to-earth.

Mark was popular with his friends, and a charming if somewhat limited young man. He was dissected and analysed. And then it was the turn of his parents who would be discovered, by the dozens who knocked on their front door, rather nervous and word-shy. His father, Peter William Garside Phillips, MC, had returned from the War, having gone straight into the Army from school, to have nationalization put paid to his ambitions in the family business, which was mining. He went to agricultural college and then farmed in Gloucestershire for nine years. "I was under-capitalized and made some mistakes which were difficult to rectify," he admitted honestly to those who asked. "And when they put a motorway through the best part of my farm, that was the end of that." He joined Walls in 1957 as an area manager and rose to become purchasing director. Mrs Phillips, sought out by the "women's interest" reporters, faced interminable questioning about the wedding which, through protocol, she could not answer. They came over as a homely couple – "a goose and a chicken wandered by the front door, a whippet and two labradors romped in and out of the house" – who were somewhat bemused by the prospect of a princess in the house. Neither parent had Royal ancestry, although Mrs Phillips was the daughter of Brigadier John Tiarks of the banking family who was aide-de-camp to King George VI. The details were recorded, down to the minutiae.

The press corps followed Anne a couple of months later to Russia, for the three-day European eventing championships at Kiev where she rode the Queen's horse, Goodwill. After falling badly at a notorious fence which claimed thirty-five other victims, she shouted to waiting photographers: "I hope you got your money's worth."

There would be further flurries of press activity when it was revealed that Captain Phillips and his bride were house-hunting around Sandhurst where he was taking up his appointment as an instructor. They settled on Oak Grove House, which had traditionally been occupied by the academy's Director of Studies. It was a home normally offered only to the rank of Colonel in the Army's strict grading system. Captain Phillips would have to pay the same rent as a Colonel, which was £8 a week for a five-bedroomed Georgian house, standing in half an acre with its own drive, and protected from prying eyes by a shield of mature trees. The house needed a lot of redecoration, largely to Princess Anne's choice, all of which would be noted by the critics who were already denouncing as exorbitant the costs of the wedding and the honeymoon on board the Royal yacht *Britannia*. That autumn, Britain's industry was facing stage three of a wages freeze enforced by Mr Edward Heath's Tory Government, which was also taking on the coal miners. Inflation was rising, there was an oil crisis looming, talk of power cuts, petrol rationing, coal shortages and gloom, not to mention the constant bomb threats in London from the IRA. The country would be cheered up by a Royal wedding, but at what cost, they asked?

The couple found it all quite hurtful. The princess said in a television interview: "The answer to the [cost of the] wedding is that it is none of their business; the honeymoon on *Britannia* is quite simple. The half-truths about it are numerous but the yacht is on its way to New Zealand for the Queen and has to pass through the West Indies to get there." On the question of the house, Mark said: "There has been a lot in the press about it. If a married officer goes to Sandhurst as an instructor he is given quarters and that is normal practice." The princess added: "When someone asks 'Has the criticism distressed us?' it is distressing because it is not accurate and it puts the blame at our feet when we don't think it really has anything to do with us. There is a myth going around that there are an awful lot of empty houses in Windsor Great Park which we somehow should have been able to step into. The answer is that there isn't one and it just doesn't exist. The myth that we could have had another house and we were just being plain difficult about Sandhurst was another very irritating criticism because it was misinformed again."

The big day arrived with all the pomp and pageantry that only British Royalty can muster. It was also the world's largest ever television event: five hundred million people around the globe were watching. The programme was even beamed out behind the Iron Curtain.

Wednesday November 14, 1973, was an ice-cold day but the spectacle would bask in brilliant sunshine. As someone pointed out in the freezing temperatures of Westminster Abbey, this could be the norm in the very near future as Heath was squaring up to do battle with the nation's coal miners. Hundreds and then thousands had begun their vigil on the streets of London up to thirty hours before the ceremony, bedding down with blankets and plastic sheets as the only protection from a torrential downpour during the night. The great gothic doors of Westminster Abbey swung open to allow in the glittering

The shape of things to come:
Princess Anne (*above*) faces a
barrage of popping flashbulbs
at a Beating the Retreat
ceremony on Horse Guards
Parade in 1958. (*Right*)
Stepping out confidently with
her mother, and already
wearing the kind of clothes she
prefers. Windsor Horse Show,
May 1955.

1964: at fourteen, Anne was described as dowdy. Viewing the Acropolis (*above*) during a family visit for the wedding of Greece's King Constantine and Denmark's Princess Anne Marie.

Preparing for her launch into public life (*below left*). Early in 1969: attending charity show at the London Palladium.

The spring of 1969: she had done something about her wardrobe and her weight. She looked stylish in (*right*) a new above-the-knee coat bought especially for the occasion when she launched her first ship, the *Esso Northumbria* oil tanker. A crowd of 10,000 turned up to see her perform the ceremony on Tyneside.

Going solo: Princess Anne's first public engagement on her own. She had to stand in biting wind while Army wives in the background sat with blankets round their chilled knees. The occasion was the traditional presentation of leeks to the Welsh Guards at Pirbright in Surrey in March 1969.

Sandy Harpur became her regular escort during 1969. This picture of them at a polo match at Cowdray Park, Sussex, naturally found its way into the news pages, but the speculated romance was short-lived.

Next to riding, Anne's favourite pastime was messing about in boats. This casual moment (*right*) was captured during Cowes Week in 1970.

She became president of the Save the Children Fund in 1970. The first of the overseas visits which have become a hallmark of her career (*below*) included Nairobi in February 1971.

East Africa, 1971: Anne joined BBC's *Blue Peter* presenter, Valerie Singleton, in a sea of faces watching a football match. The tour was being filmed for her first major television appearance which was tinged with controversy.

Back in Britain, Anne continued her passion for eventing. Here she was captured in a cheerful mood of mimicry, yet seconds later she was dismissing the photographers as "pests".

The wedding. After weeks of
speculation and denials, the
engagement was announced
in May 1973 which gave the
media six months to prepare
for the most public Royal
wedding to date. Presents
flooded in from around the
world and, because of their
love of riding, there were
enough horsey accessories to
equip a cavalry.

A night to remember on March 20, 1974: Princess Anne steps out of her Palace limousine (*top*) to attend the showing of a film for another of her favourite charities, Riding for the Disabled. Later, as she left the engagement with Mark and her lady-in-waiting, a lone gunman attempted to kidnap her and hold her for ransom. He ambushed her car as it was driving down the Mall, and in the space of ten minutes shot and wounded her bodyguard, her chauffeur, a policeman and a journalist.

Five days after her escape, Anne visited the wounded heroes in hospital: journalist Brian McConnell (*left*) and Inspector James Beaton (*below*).

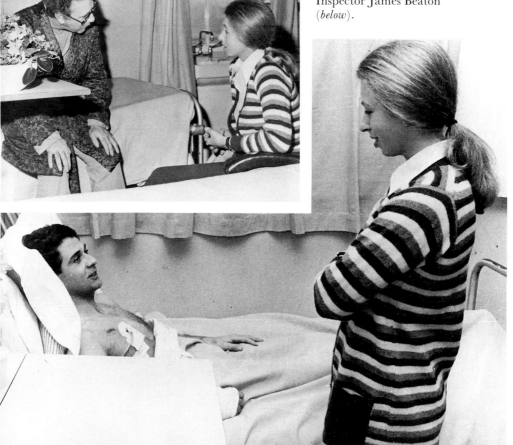

Anne and Mark had a single-minded target, which was to perform in the 1976 Montreal Olympics. Dressage (*right*) on Goodwill in Kiev in 1973 and cross-country (*left*) on the Queen's horse, Candlewick, in Dorset in 1976. She fell in both events, was mobbed by photographers eager for the sensation, but bravely went on riding and won her place in the British team.

parade of wedding guests: dukes and duchesses with rustling brocades and sparkling with jewels released from the family vaults; peers in crimson velvet tipped with ermine; military men in gold braid, like scrambled egg on their dark uniforms; and the Archbishop of Canterbury in his gold mitre and ivory robes. Royalty included Princess Grace of Monaco and King Constantine of Greece, rubbing shoulders with the commoners, Army comrades of the groom, the odd stable boy and Mrs Fred Smith, the Phillips's family charlady. At the stroke of 11.17, the nine Royal coaches began arriving at the ancient Abbey steps, accompanied by the plumed and breastplated cavalry, and deafening trumpets blasted out to announce the arrival of the Queen. Any ordinary bride might have been extinguished by such ostentation. Anne outshone them all in her superbly woven wedding gown of rich ivory silk sprinkled with pearls and with a magnificent train. A diamond tiara held her headdress and stunning gossamer veil as she walked the aisle to stand beside her groom, in his striking scarlet tunic and tight blue trousers, black boots shining like a mirror, and silver spurs.

Any acrimony between Anne and the press was, for the moment, put aside and there was but a touch of acidity as the heavyweights of Fleet Street were trotted out. Jean Rook, whose own biting and occasionally bitchy remarks must have been among those which Anne and Mark found "distressing", wrote: "Did the bride's mother cry? Was that why TV cameras were ordered to switch away from the Queen's face at that moment her only daughter said I Will. The Royal jaw was clenched as hard as her tightly gripped handbag. They couldn't squeeze a word of the opening hymn past the obvious lumps in her throat. But she didn't cry . . . Out peal the trumpets. Up goes the mink on the back of our hats and the blood rushes and tingles – thank God – down to our very frozen feet. How did the bride really look to me who was a diamond's throw away from her? Ice-beautiful. Chaste. Tudor. Flower-faced. Every bit as good as Norman Parkinson's pictures. Maybe he didn't re-touch those 'medieval portraits' after all . . . and just as they reached the great scar of poppies that covered the Unknown Soldier's tomb, they turned to each other and smiled . . . they looked hugely, wide-mouthed and toothily happy. Because at last they had jumped the fence."

The author's colleague, Donald Zec at the *Mirror*, homed in on the fact that the princess had agreed to "obey" which, he suggested, was the most loaded four-letter word of the year. Catching the mood of the moment, he wrote: "And when Mark declared 'With this ring, I thee wed, with my body I thee worship, with all my wordly goods I thee endow' it was clearly no time to think of Anne's £35,000 a year stipend, or the eight-pounds a week mansion. Here in the sturdy masonry of centuries Anne has got her man and five hundred million viewers are permitted to share in the phenomenon of a slightly hard-up Britain laughing all the way to the Abbey."

Afterwards, it was back to the Palace for a wedding breakfast with family and close friends, and of course the traditional balcony scene. As they left the Abbey for the journey past the thousands who had braved the bitter cold for hours on end for a few minutes' glimpse of the pageant, Anne guided her new husband in the art of public relations. As they reached the west door she said: "Get ready to acknowledge the crowds on the way back," and later, on the balcony, she told him: "Come on, wave."

In the following day's newspapers, you could win the hat (or a copy of it, more truthfully) that Anne wore to go away. Readers were given minute details on what was in her trousseau, right down to her lingerie and night attire which had been exclusively revealed to a newspaper by one of the shop girls who had been sworn to secrecy. Attempts at copying the wedding dress, which one store boasted would be on sale within an hour of the wedding at £12, had to be abandoned because of the intricate work of the Susan Small design.

Just before the wedding, Anne and Mark gave a joint television interview which was screened on both BBC and ITV, as well as around the world. It was Mark's first television appearance and he had been given special coaching by Army instructors in the art; but it was a difficult task for him, nerve-racking and uncomfortable. Princess Anne gave her usual immaculate performance, and against her Mark seemed unsure, hesitant and stammered often. It was an embarrassment for them both, and one which would be parodied by many a television mimic for their constant use of the third person, referring all the time to themselves as "one".

One thousand five hundred wedding presents went on public display in the State apartments of St James's Palace. And as Mr and Mrs Mark Phillips embarked upon life's path together, they would be equipped with a most prodigious collection of most useful items, including two dozen backgammon sets, three *Oxford Dictionary of Quotations*, fifty-nine assorted silver horses and statuettes of soldiers and enough horse brasses and prints completely to cover the walls of their first sitting-room. The Queen Mother gave Anne a magnificent diamond and aqua-marine tiara. The Queen gave a diamond brooch, two pairs of diamond earrings, two gold and enamel bell-pushes and a gold dress pocket watch; the Duke of Edinburgh a 1765 Chippendale desk. The Prince of Wales gift-wrapped two leather gun cases and a diamond brooch. Then there were more practical "household presents" such as an ice-bucket of considerable value from Prince and Princess Georg of Hanover, eight dozen coathangers from Princess Margaretha, a colour TV from the Society of Film and Television Arts, a refrigerator, deep freeze and vacuum cleaner from an electrical manufacturer.

President Nixon and the people of the United States gave four glass and gold candlesticks and a crystal bowl supported by four golden eagles. The Soviet people sent a lacquered box with a highly attractive portrait of Princess Anne and Captain Phillips on the lid; President Pompidou of France donated a table cloth and napkins. The huge mass of horsey presents would equip a cavalry; and there were enough trays and table mats showing hunting scenes, various, to kit out the Savoy Grill.

The press, of course, followed the couple on honeymoon and there were rumours that they might go ashore on the island of Mustique where Princess Margaret was moving into her house. A dozen or more chartered light aircraft carrying reporters and photographers landed on the tiny airstrip, only to be politely turned away by the Hon Colin Tennant. In fact, Anne and Mark never went to the island and hardly set foot off the yacht for the entire honeymoon, much to the disgust of the press hordes who were following like a Dunkirk flotilla. On board the *Britannia*, it was a case of Just the Two of Us – except for the twenty-one officers and two hundred and fifty-six crew who were under instructions to make sure the couple were not disturbed and that their every need was catered for.

After two weeks of relative seclusion, Princess Anne and Captain Phillips began their first dual engagements. Buckingham Palace had arranged an exhausting round of engagements which took them to Ecuador, Colombia, Antigua, Jamaica and Montserrat. Mark was apparently overwhelmed:

seas of faces, a thousand handshakes, guards of honour to inspect, a dozen speeches, endless polite conversation and dinners and receptions galore. Anne took the full force of the engagements, with Mark close by her side or hovering somewhere in the background. He was rarely called upon to speak publicly, and rightly realized that his wife was the star of the show. Meantime, he watched and learned as the seasoned campaigner of countless similar official duties sallied forth with confidence and a smile. She would give him plenty of useful advice, and one of the first tips he learned was that members of the Royal family eat very little at public functions and drink even less. Princess Anne usually drinks Coca-Cola, or the occasional glass of wine. Mark Phillips himself was on an almost permanent diet to keep his weight down for eventing, though he admitted to drinking champagne until it was coming out of his ears on his stag night. Light meals, scrambled eggs and the like, were the order of the day and, apart from dinner parties, the domestic staff who had been taken on at Oak Grove House, in Sandhurst, would not find their culinary role particularly challenging.

So now it was back to England, and to their first taste of home life. But what was in store? Would Mark be forever the man at his wife's side? There were clues already. First, he had already discounted the probability that he would accompany his wife everywhere she went. For the first year or so, he would certainly travel on the major trips abroad but it was by no means a foregone conclusion that he would be there every time she cut a tape or launched a new ship. Secondly, though their marriage was being likened in some quarters to *The Taming of the Shrew*, it was not really like that. Anne was probably attracted to him in the first place because he was strong willed enough to disregard her autocratic and at times wilful manner; and yes, he could tame her temper. He had stated quite categorically on television, and in front of millions, that at home he would be the boss. He knew that there would be times when Anne would have to rule the roost, have the supremacy, and when it would be barely credible for him to expect Anne to serve and obey. On the other hand, Anne herself was sensible enough to realize that both must have well-defined areas of their lives and, on occasions, he must lead.

He already had thoughts about being a farmer, and she would dearly have loved to have joined him in raising and training horses and riding competitively. But those were just day-dreams. She was a Royal; she had responsibilities; her duties had to be attended to. The girl who had been something of a tearaway, though that term was used to describe everyone in the 1960s and early 1970s, had had her fling and her marriage to Mark Phillips, over which she had not been entirely quick to decide, meant that she had now in her own mind decided to adopt the life and style the Queen wanted; in fact the Queen's own style rather than the more casual and rebellious approach of her aunt, Princess Margaret.

Her marriage had brought Royalty closer to the British middle classes. The British public of the time, downtrodden by the economic plagues of freeze and squeeze, could identify with Mark and Anne.

FOUR

The Kidnap Attempt

The joy and splendour of the wedding was already a fading memory as the newly-weds returned to a damp and cold Britain, beleaguered by political and industrial strife that in the end would demolish Mr Heath's Government as he battled with trade deficits, a feeble pound and a winter fuel crisis.

Anne and Mark joined the rest of the Royal family for the warmth of their traditional Christmas holiday, which was cut short by the plans for the Queen and the Duke of Edinburgh, accompanied by Anne and Mark, to make a major overseas tour, taking in New Zealand, Norfolk Island, New Hebrides, the British Solomon Islands, Papua New Guinea and Australia. The tour would mark a new dimension in the Queen's increasingly off-the-pedestal tendency of being seen at close quarters, in her now famous walk-abouts. Her security advisers were already warning the Royal family about its apparent disregard of danger from terrorist attacks to which the Queen always responded: "We will not live in bullet-proof cages." There were other fears on the horizon, too. Intelligence reports suggested that the IRA was mounting a campaign of bombing in Britain that would surface in 1974 with a sickening and horrific orgy of violence and, early in that year, Scotland Yard Special Branch and senior officers of the Royal Protection Squad had already begun a review of security arrangements around members of the Royal family. But even as that was going on, Princess Anne would be the target of an attack which came from a totally unexpected and unforeseen source.

They had been married barely five months. After the overseas tour, they moved into their first home together at Sandhurst. What Princess Anne didn't know then was that her every move was being watched and recorded. Among the first duties they undertook together was the special showing of a film *Riding Towards Freedom* produced by the Riding for the

Disabled Association of which Princess Anne was patron. The day was March 20, 1974, and one which they will remember for the rest of their lives. The events of that evening have seldom been told in complete detail, and it is worth once again recalling just what happened, if only as a tribute to the courage of Princess Anne and her husband and the four people who, within the space of ten minutes, would be lying shot beside the Royal car.

Just after 7.30 pm they left Sudbury House in Newgate Street in the City of London where the film had been shown, and settled into the ageing, maroon Austin Princess limousine that was to take them back to Buckingham Palace. Princess Anne and Captain Phillips got into the back with Miss Rowena Brassey, Anne's lady-in-waiting, who sat on the folding seat immediately behind the partition. In the front was the princess's bodyguard, Inspector James Beaton, sitting alongside the chauffeur, Alexander Callender.

The car moved off through Ludgate Circus, up Fleet Street, over Trafalgar Square and into the Mall. No one had noticed that a white Ford Escort which had been parked in Newgate Street slid out behind them as they made their way along what would normally have been a ten-minute drive to the Palace. At the wheel of the Escort was a strange, gaunt young man who had been brooding for three years over a most audacious crime he was about to attempt. His plan was to kidnap Princess Anne and to hold her to ransom for £3,000,000. And, like the assassin who had tried to kill General de Gaulle in Frederick Forsyth's novel *The Day of the Jackal*, he had meticulously planned his attack and his false identity.

It was an ambitious plan. If challenged prior to the kidnap, his driving licence would identify him as John Williams, of Christchurch Road, Crouch End, North London, one of the three aliases he had established for himself using accom-modation addresses to hide his true name. He had sold his own Austin 1100 and hired the Escort in the name of Williams; he had removed all the labels from his clothes; he had burnt his passport issued in his real name of Ian Ball, aged twenty-six and born in Uxbridge, Middlesex. He also destroyed his pilot's licence for which he had qualified at Biggin Hill, Kent. It was an attempt to obliterate his past, totally, in a bizarre attempt to cover up his identity which could only be established by his fingerprints, already on police files after his career as a petty

61

crook. For two years before this night, he had been out of work. He had been arrested three times for receiving stolen property and obtaining goods by deception. He had left his parents' home and taken cheap lodgings; he ate little, lived the life of a loner and his only expense was the cost of his flying lessons. Throughout his life, he had been virtually friendless, such a nonentity that no one at his school could even remember him. Alone and haunted, he began to dream and plan, and, gradually, in his sick mind he devised a major crime that would get him world headlines.

In December, while Anne and Mark were still abroad, Ball had travelled to Spain where he had obtained a firearms permit, and at a gunshop in the Plaza de Espana in Madrid, he equipped himself with four weapons: two Astra revolvers, a five-round .38 and an eleven-round .22 which he brought back to England. He scoured the area around Sandhurst where, he had read, the princess would be living. His aim was to rent a house as close to her as possible and it was, in a strange way, a credit to his cunning that he was able to take a smart detached house, number 17 Silverdale, a quiet cul-de-sac in Fleet, Hampshire, just a few miles from Oak Grove House. The street was known locally as Brigadier's Row, because there were so many Army officers living there. It was from this house that Ball began the final planning of his mission and it was to this house that he planned to bring Princess Anne after the kidnap. He had paid a large cash deposit to the estate agents handling the rental, and given a month's rent of £27 in advance. He called himself Jason Van Der Sluis, whose name he had usurped from a letter he stole from the members' rack of a London club and who had an account at Barclays Bank in Covent Garden. When the agents applied to the bank for references, there would be a glowing report. Two other references taken up by the agents were directed to accommodation addresses and answered in equally glowing terms by Ball himself. He moved into the house in March, and stocked it with all the items he would need for the princess: new bedding, towels, food and even a toothbrush. He would choose his moment carefully, stalking her for days to track her movements as far as he could. His aim was to snatch her in the quiet of the Surrey countryside, and never had he contemplated his attack being launched in the centre of London.

His last act before the kidnap attempt was to rent a typewriter for £1.50 from a shop in Camberley, Surrey, where he aroused the suspicions of a shop assistant when he admitted he only wanted the machine for one day, to type out two letters. One would be a ransom note, the other a letter to a firm of solicitors whom he wanted to act as the "middlemen" in negotiations. He continued to shadow Princess Anne in the final days and his actions in the white Escort almost led to his earlier arrest. A Staff Sergeant in the Army Catering Corps, who regularly went past the rear gates of the Royal Military Academy through which Princess Anne often took a short cut, noticed the car parked in the same spot on a number of occasions. He memorized the number, SVL 282L; often the windows were misted over, indicating that the driver had been sitting there for some time. Between March 17 and March 20, he had seen the car there on eleven different occasions. Furthermore, that Wednesday morning the white Escort was spotted by Detective Chief Inspector John Horton, who was investigating a local burglary. He stopped his car and went over to Ball, who was sitting in the Escort. He questioned him about his movements, searched the car and checked his driving licence which appeared to be in order, but was in fact the forged document in the name of John Williams. There was no reason for Horton to be suspicious; he accepted Ball's explanations and drove away, leaving Ball himself shaking with nerves.

At this point, he panicked himself into action. In that morning's *Daily Telegraph*, he had read that Princess Anne and Mark Phillips were due to attend the film show that evening; he had also established by telephoning the press office at Buckingham Palace that the couple were due to leave for Germany on March 25. By now, Ball's mental state was indecisive and tense. Inside the Escort, he hid the two revolvers along with fifty-eight rounds of ammunition, three pairs of white cotton gloves which he would wear to avoid leaving fingerprints, and four pairs of police regulation handcuffs, two of which had been linked together to form leg shackles. In his jacket pocket, he put the typed ransom note, addressed to the Queen. He had written: *Your daughter has been kidnapped, the following are conditions to be fulfilled for her release. A ransom of £3,000,000 is to be paid in £5 notes. They are to be used, unmarked, not sprayed with any chemical substance and not consecutively numbered. The money is to be packed in 30-inch unlocked suitcases, clearly marked on the outside. The following*

63

documents are to be prepared: A free pardon to cover the kidnapping and anything connected with it, ie possession of firearms, or the murder of any police officers. A free pardon for any crimes committed, from parking offences to murder. As the money is to be taken abroad, I shall be asking for a free pardon to run indefinitely for being in contravention of the Exchange Control Act. Documents are to be prepared for a civil action to be taken against the police if they disclose my true identity, with damages of not less than £1,000,000. A civil action to be taken against you or your consorts if you reveal my true identity. No excuses will be accepted for failing to compile these documents. If they cannot be drawn up under existing laws, the law must be changed. Ball also insisted that he should be given a plane to take him from Heathrow to Switzerland, that the documents and the ransom should be brought to him there, that the Queen should be brought to him and that he would ask her questions and that she would have to provide him with a specimen of her signature. When he had flown out of the country, and he was assured of immunity from the Swiss police, the princess would be released to fly home.

He put the letter in his inside pocket and drove to London. He began tailing the Palace car, with the easily identifiable registration NGN 1. From Newgate Street, Fleet Street, Trafalgar Square and into the Mall. As Buckingham Palace loomed up ahead of him, he made his move. He accelerated the nippy Escort alongside the Austin Princess and swerved in front of it, forcing the Royal car to an instant halt.

The Royal chauffeur, Alex Callender, had to brake hard to avoid a crash and, in an instant, he and the princess's bodyguard, James Beaton, saw Ball leap out of the driving seat. Beaton was already halfway out of his passenger door when Ball reached the rear door brandishing a gun, the .22. He ordered Callender to switch off the engine and then he pulled open the rear door and shouted at Princess Anne: "Come with me, I only want you for two days." Beaton had by now reached the offside of the car; Ball fired twice, hitting him in the shoulder with one bullet and grazing his arm with the other. The policeman fired back: it was only when he went to use his gun that he realized he was badly injured and, because of the wound, he missed. He tried to fire again, but his Walther PP revolver jammed and he instinctively drew back, to take cover behind the Austin as he struggled to free the Walther mechanism. Callender in the meantime got out of the driving seat and

64

lunged towards Ball, grabbing him by the arm. "I'll shoot you," shouted Ball, but the brave chauffeur would not let go and the attacker fired, point blank at his chest. During the seconds when Ball's attention was diverted to Callender, Beaton had made his way round to the nearside of the car, where Rowena Brassey was crouching, having opened the door and crawled out. Ball had got hold of Princess Anne by the arm: "Please get out of the car," he instructed. Mark Phillips had her other arm, and would not let her go; he tugged and tugged until he managed to get his wife back into the seat, and tried to slam the door shut. The blue velvet dress she was wearing, the one which she had bought for her honeymoon, was torn and the sleeve ripped out. Then Ball saw Beaton, still holding his gun: "Drop it, or I'll shoot her," he shouted, gesturing towards Anne. Beaton did as he was instructed; the gun was useless anyway. It was that moment that Princess Anne would remember so vividly in later recollections. "It was very unreal," she said. "I was amazed that things were still going on outside as usual, cars and taxis passing as though nothing was happening. I didn't have time to be frightened. I just got angry with him." Princess Anne tried to distract her kidnapper's attention with calm words and questions; what did he want, why was he trying to take her? Ball replied, "Because I'll get a couple of million."

Inspector Beaton, meantime, had edged himself into the car next to Mark Phillips and was trying to put himself between Princess Anne and the gunman to shield her with his body. Mark Phillips managed to close the door as Beaton got to the other side, and he saw Ball raise his gun and shout, "Open it, or I'll shoot." The officer raised his arm instinctively and a bullet from the second gun Ball was now holding smashed the car window and lodged in the palm of his hand. Beaton, though now wounded from three shots, whispered to Mark Phillips to release the car door gently; at a given moment he intended to kick it open, with the hope of hitting Ball, dislodging his weapons and throwing him off balance. The door swung back, missed Ball completely. Ball shot Beaton again, the bullet entering his stomach, through the intestines and pelvis and lodging in his back. The inspector fell, clutching his wound, and crawled to the pavement where he lay unable to move.

Outside the car, people in the Mall were at last beginning to take notice. The shooting had happened in a matter of

minutes and now traffic was beginning to build up behind the
Royal limousine. My friend and colleague Brian McConnell,
one of Fleet Street's best-known journalists, was in a taxi which
had left Fleet Street bound for Belgravia, and had overtaken
the Royal car on the nearside. It was thirty yards past it when
he heard shots. He called to the taxi driver to stop and ran
back. Seeing, over the bonnet of the Royal car, a man with a
gun, he kept to the nearside of the vehicle and emerged from
the rear to confront the gunman. He walked up to him and
said, simply, "Look here, old man, these are friends of mine.
Give me the gun." Ball waved him back. "Keep out of this,"
he said. McConnell pressed forward, "Don't be silly, old man."
Two paces more and Ball fired another shot. It gouged a path
through the journalist's chest as he turned to his right. "A
reflexive action," he said later, "but although the bullet cut a
line across the front of my body it missed all the clockwork."
He retired behind the car and slumped down by a tree, another
man out of the action.

McConnell, in his account of the drama to the author, said
that in fact he didn't know the Royal family at all. He met
Princess Anne for the first time when she visited him in hospital
five days later. But he explained, "Facing a gunman is like
interviewing a hostile person. You must gain the upper hand.
You must talk first, say something off-putting, placatory, outrageous if you like, and throw him off-guard. If you know your
boss is about to fire you, when you walk into his office, you
begin the conversation. Ask him if he had egg for breakfast or
whether he knew he had spaghetti on his tie. Who knows, you
might put him off his stroke and not get the sack. It was the
same in the Mall. All I tried to do was to take his mind off the
trigger while I got closer to him. Bravery is a word someone
invents after an event. In the time it takes to ask yourself
whether you should intervene it is all over, another shot fired,
someone hurt, perhaps someone dead. Everybody involved
behaved by duty or by instinct or by both. The princess is right
to wonder how everything could go on as normal nearby, but
seven people did get involved and it could have been seventeen
or seventy. From all the evidence I could gather afterwards,
she and Captain Phillips emerged the bravest. They were at
the business end of his guns, yet they reacted with astonishing
cool, tried to bargain with Ball, kept him talking, told him to
go away and forget the whole kidnapping idea. People always

seem astonished that members of the Royal family, protected, accused of living in an ivory tower, are as quick-thinking and as brave as others. They are, and more so." With McConnell shot, Ball returned to the job at hand and tried to open the door again to get Princess Anne out. Across the road, one hundred yards away, Police Constable Michael Hills, who was on duty at St James's Palace, could see some sort of commotion and began walking towards the Royal car; as he got closer he recognized the Austin and started running; closer still he saw a man leaning inside through the rear door. There were people, presumably passers-by, milling aimlessly about, but all at a safe distance. He heard someone shout: "Get away, you bloody fool, he's got a gun." PC Hills ignored the warning; he walked straight up to Ball, and grasped his arm. "What's going on?" he asked, with a degree of naivety. Ian Ball turned and fired another shot from the .22 at such close range that the bullet drove through the officer's pocket book and lodged an inch from his liver. Hills fell to the ground and crawled to the side of the Austin and out of Ball's line of fire. He pulled his radio from its clip and spoke softly to his base Cannon Row: "Alpha Delta from 739. I have been shot. Am 30 yards east of 61 Traffic [which is the police call sign for the Mall]. Royal car involved. Man with gun. Urgent assistance required."

The message was flashed to Scotland Yard and to every police car in the vicinity; soon the police reinforcements were dashing towards the scene. Meanwhile, the minutes were ticking away. Chauffeur Glanmore Martin, who was driving a Jaguar, had gone a little way down the Mall and was watching from his rearview mirror. He had the forethought to reverse his car in front of the Escort, thus blocking Ball's only route of escape. Now he courageously got out of his driving seat and edged close to the gunman. Ball stuck his gun in Martin's side and growled, "Clear off." Martin saw Hills, half conscious and weak from loss of blood, trying to make Beaton's gun fire. The young officer was half on his feet and trying to take aim. Martin saw he was about to collapse and grabbed him, and dragged him to the pavement clear of Ball's firing line. By the side of the car, they were joined by Samantha Scott, a blonde ballet teacher who had also been forced to take avoiding action when Ball's car swerved in front of the Royal Austin. Amazingly, she hadn't realized how serious was the situation until she saw Rowena Brassey crouched down beside the car, calling to her,

"Get down! There's a maniac shooting at us!"

Yet another passer-by came at Ball. Ronald Russell, six-foot-tall manager of an office cleaning business, had realized from well behind that something serious was happening ahead. He drove his own car up on to the kerb and ploughed on towards NGN 1. He then dashed across to the Royal car where Ball was trying to pull the door open; Russell punched him on the side of the head. Ball turned, fired, but missed and the bullet shattered the windscreen of a taxi. Russell dashed round the side of the car where the two policemen and the journalist were lying, bleeding; he saw chauffeur Callender in a similar state lying across the front seats of the car. Ball fired two more shots from the offside and Russell saw that Ball had now succeeded in opening the rear door and once again had Princess Anne in his grasp; Mark Phillips was holding her from the other side. Ball, now extremely agitated, said: "Come on, Anne, you know you've got to come." The princess, still outwardly cool, replied: "Why don't you go away? What good is this going to do?"

Ball stood for a moment, glaring at her as if trying to decide his next move. She took the chance and twisted her arm free of his grasp, almost at the same time as Ronald Russell began punching her attacker once again. With one huge blow, Russell almost stunned him. By now, the Mall was alive with people; wailing police cars were arriving by the second. Ian Ball took one last look at Princess Anne and ran off into St James's Park pursued by an unarmed detective, Peter Edmonds, who brought him down with a flying rugby tackle and arrested him.

The whole incident, with four people lying wounded, but the princess and Mark Phillips shocked but unharmed still in the back of the car, had taken less than ten minutes.

For those involved it had been like an eternity. Sammy Scott just couldn't believe what she had walked into. "I thought we were on *Candid Camera*," she said later. "We huddled on the ground and I could see Mark Phillips protecting Anne while the man tried to get them. I could see yellow roses [the remains of a bouquet given to Princess Anne at the film show] scattered over the floor of the car. When the gunman had gone I leaned inside and put my hand on Anne's shoulder. I said to her: 'Are you all right, love?' and she smiled sweetly and replied: 'I'm all right, thank you.'" Rowena Brassey, looking back on it some years later, said: "Really it is a wonder to me that Princess Anne and Mark Phillips were not shot. There were so many bullets flying around in such a confined space."

Police took statements from both Anne and Mark before the princess put through a telephone call to Indonesia where the Queen and Prince Philip were on a State visit. The time there was 5 am and Anne spoke first to her father, to tell him the whole story and to assure him that they were unharmed. He then woke the Queen. Prince Charles who was in San Diego as Communications Officer on board HMS *Jupiter* was also told.

Even after their ordeal, Princess Anne and Mark Phillips decided to travel back to their home at Sandhurst that evening, Anne driving herself as usual in the Scimitar and Mark in his Rover 2000. Both had a police escort.

Meanwhile, the business of the House of Commons was interrupted for the Home Secretary Mr Roy Jenkins to announce details of the kidnap attempt on Princess Anne. He faced an immediate barrage of questions over Royal security and MPs asked particularly how the movements of Princess Anne could be discovered. Mr Jenkins left Parliament to inspect the scene and, when he arrived, police were still swarming all over the area. The Royal car, with its smashed windows, and a taxi with bullet holes along the side, were still in place. Detectives had found the gunman's pistols and Sir Robert Mark, Commissioner of the Metropolitan Police, gave an on-the-spot promotion to Peter Edmonds, the man who had arrested Ball. He was made up from Temporary Detective Constable to Detective Constable.

For some time, it was feared that Ball might be either a member of the IRA or of some terrorist group that was planning attacks against prominent public figures and an instant security alert was sounded for extra vigilance. Ball had refused to identify himself and, because of his forged papers, there was no way of immediately tracing his background. When a check on his fingerprints was finally completed, Ball's true identity was discovered, and he admitted in the end that he had been working totally alone. He insisted that he had never intended to hurt Princess Anne but showed scant regard for the four people he had shot. It also seemed as if Captain Phillips was lucky to escape without injury. Ball told the police: "I didn't want him. I only wanted to take her. I thought it up a long time ago, long before the wedding. In fact the wedding made me think of giving it up. They looked such a nice couple."

When the police investigated his background further, they discovered that Ball had a history of mental disturbance. At eighteen, he apparently stopped speaking to his mother because he blamed her for his inadequate education. In the last three years he was living at home, he communicated with her by leaving notes around the house. His mother had not seen or heard of him for almost five years, until around midnight on March 20. Police called to tell her that the man who had tried to kidnap Princess Anne that evening was her son.

The following day, Ball was brought before a special court and charged with attempting to steal and carry away Her Royal Highness Princess Anne. He was also charged with two counts of attempted murder and two of wounding. On May 22, after a brief trial at which a Home Office psychiatrist gave evidence that Ball was suffering from a severe personality disorder, Lord Chief Justice Widgery ordered him to be detained indefinitely in a special hospital under the Mental Health Act. He was subsequently taken to the top security Rampton Hospital in Nottinghamshire.

Six months later, the Queen held an investiture at Buckingham Palace and a private reception afterwards for the men and women and their families who had been involved in the kidnap scare. Inspector James Beaton, who was the most seriously injured, was awarded the nation's highest honour for peace-time gallantry, the George Cross. Police Constable Michael Hills, who still had the .22 bullet lodged close to his liver, was given the George Medal. The same honour was awarded to Ronald Russell of Strood, Kent. Detective Constable Peter Edmonds, the chauffeur Alexander Callender and Brian McConnell were presented with the Queen's Gallantry Medal; and Glanmore Martin received the Queen's Commendation for Brave Conduct. Princess Anne herself was also given a medal for bravery by the Queen, the Insignia of a Dame Grand Cross of the Royal Victorian Order.

In the wide-ranging inquiry into the security surrounding members of the Royal family, there would be many questions asked. The consequences could have been far worse. Had Ball panicked, he could have shot both Anne and Mark. Had he killed the policemen and others who had tried to rescue her, he might have succeeded in snatching Anne and taking her to his hideout. Mark himself said later: "The moment help arrived, I really thought that was it. With all the blue lights flashing, it was like cornering an animal. He could see there was no escape and at that moment I really thought we would be shot. There is no question that had more than one person attempted this attack, they might well have succeeded in their aims."

In that year of 1974 the IRA bombers were becoming more daring and dangerous. There would be numerous atrocities, including a bomb explosion at the Palace of Westminster (June 17) in which eleven people were injured; a bomb at the Tower of London (July 17), killing one and injuring forty-one people including a number of children; a bomb at Heathrow Airport (July 26); two bombs at public houses in Guildford, Surrey (October 5) killing five and injuring seventy; a bomb at a Woolwich pub (November 7) killing two people; bombs in two Birmingham bars (November 7) killing twenty-one and injuring one hundred and twenty; bombs discovered at Harrods, Selfridges and outside the home of Mr Edward Heath (between December 18 and 22). It wasn't only the activities of a lone lunatic that now had to be taken into account.

The whole security network was under pressure and drastic changes in the way top people were guarded would come into effect. Electronic warning systems, bullet-proof glass in Royal cars, and a much more sophisticated system for twenty-four-hour-a-day Royal Protection Squads would be devised. It would mean that no member of the Royal family could venture out into public view without a bodyguard literally inches away. It would mean also that the guards would have to be versatile in many aspects of sport, and not just good with a gun, and this would apply particularly to those policemen attached to younger members of the Royal family; for they would have to be close at hand whether their charge was sailing, riding, on the ski slopes, or just on a friendly walk-about at some public function. On many occasions, the Royal guards would be the only other persons present and close friendships would be built between some members of the Protection Squad and their Royal employers.

But, as we know, there would be occasions when the security network would fail. In 1979, for example, the Queen's Uncle Dickie, Lord Louis Mountbatten, was murdered by the IRA, with two members of his family and a young friend, when terrorists blew up their boat off the coast of Southern Ireland.

71

In 1981, shots were fired as the Queen rode towards the Trooping of the Colour, and though the gun was loaded with blanks it illustrated once again the ease with which attacks could be made. A further tightening of the net around Royal houses would be ordered the following year after the dramatic discovery of an intruder in the Queen's bedroom: she woke to find Michael Fagan sitting at the bottom of her bed in Buckingham Palace, once thought to be the safest home in Britain. There was further trouble, too, for Princess Anne when she was constantly pestered by a man obsessed by her. He would discover her movements and regularly turn up at public engagements and attempt to speak to her. He was seen hanging around outside Buckingham Palace hoping to catch a glimpse of her; he would telephone the Palace at all hours hoping to be put through to her; and he found out the address of a lady-in-waiting, and turned up there one night wanting to talk to her about Princess Anne. Only when the police gave him a firm warning did he stop. This case was doubtlessly harmless; but in this age of terrorism world-wide, the annual cost of guarding the Queen's family is one of the most inflationary areas of public spending. It is a tribute to the Royal family that, without exception, the rule continues to be: "Let the people see us."

FIVE

Boiling Eggs

After the drama of That Night On The Mall, we in the business of producing newspapers briefly reflected the views of the majority of readers: that Princess Anne was great, and wasn't it a relief that she came through it all unscathed, and didn't she look radiant as a married woman. It was a temporary truce, but an enjoyable interlude, for there would soon again be outpourings of tittle-tattle in which Anne would be portrayed as bad-tempered, hard-to-please and the cause of constant rows in the matrimonial home.

One writer reckoned that the princess had flowered with a new prettiness. Was this due to the French make-up artist, Olivier Echaude-Maison, who prepared her for her wedding and had taught her some beauty tricks, such as wearing eyeliner and false eye-lashes?

Princess Anne's fashion sense had also improved with marriage, and she was choosing evening dresses with lower necklines and clothes that showed off her fine figure. She looked and sounded so much more attractive, her smiles had a new warmth, her face glowed with a new purpose; she was also a much nicer person. And to cap it all, there were a few choice clichés which were designed to indicate that the princess's new band of gold had given her an extra ring of confidence in that age of Women's Lib.

Soon, however, there would be stories appearing designed to show that all was not sweetness and light within the Royal household, as if by some divine intervention Anne and Mark could be expected to drive through matrimony without the occasional tiff. Two strong-willed and, let's face it, slightly spoiled young people could hardly be expected to hit it off every second of the day and night, especially when the world was peering at them through the keyhole.

One story, I remember, started off in the gossip columns and

73

was then built on for days. It began with a dinner at Claridges to launch the movie, *Murder on the Orient Express*, at which Dame Agatha Christie was a guest. The main attraction that night was not the famed authoress, but Anne and Mark. Shortly after 1 am, Mark stifled a yawn and turning to Anne announced: "Well, we had better be going. I'm on duty at seven." Anne's lady-in-waiting rose in response, but Anne waved her to be seated. "I'm enjoying myself," she said. "I see no point in leaving so early." To the astonishment of the rest of the table, Mark shrugged and said: "See you later, then," and walked off. His wife's icicled anger was broken only when Earl Mountbatten got up and asked her to dance, thus defusing the situation. Anne eventually arrived home at dawn, though according to "close friends" she was desperately sorry she hadn't gone with Mark and tried to apologize to him for days after. When this little tale became printed word, the *Daily Mail* felt able to return to the attack with a little rap over the knuckles: "Our self-willed, self-centred, ruthless golden girl hasn't changed one bit," and that certainly appeared to be the case!

The first two years of married life were centred at Sandhurst where Oak Grove had been refurbished. There were still a few critical observations about the time and money spent by the Army on the preparation of the house, and Mark's father, Peter, would admit that among the many letters he had received about his son and daughter-in-law were a number complaining: "Why should they have that house when there are so many people homeless?" to which he responded promptly "Where do you think they should live – in a council house?"

Captain Phillips was a brief walk from his job. Anne was fifty miles from her office in London; but the irritation of the travel to town several times a week was offset by the closeness of the Oliver stables at Warfield. They kept six horses there. Riding was one of the most important aspects of their early life together. When they weren't working, their time totally revolved around the determination of both to improve their eventing results and to try for a place in the British equestrian team which would go to the 1976 Olympics.

The house itself was not large in comparison with some of their upper-class contemporaries' homes. The sitting-room, fairly small and lacking in grandeur, had a couple of armchairs, a two-seater sofa, glass-topped small tables, petite china cabinet and a working desk. Fancy ornaments from their wedding gifts were everywhere, as were pictures of the wedding itself, and Mark was not the least embarrassed to say that they were able to furnish most of the house from the gifts. They had two dogs, a Dumfriesshire hound and a black labrador which were family pets and were allowed to blunder around the house without a great deal of admonishment. Because of their varying life-style and commitments, they would not become a truly Army, or Sandhurst, couple. They went to official Army do's, but Anne was not and could never be an Army wife in the real sense of the word. For a start, her honorary rank was higher than anyone at the place. Other wives whose husbands were of similar age or rank to her husband still treated her in some awe and there was a general reluctance on both sides to become too close. Apart from two or three good friends, most remained casual acquaintances whom they saw at cocktail parties or whom they entertained informally (but even "informal" meetings would always retain a degree of starchiness).

Outside her own group of friends, who were two or three girls from Benenden with whom she had maintained contact and her horsey crowd, Anne in fact had few people she could name as being "close". Some of the more enduring friendships would come from totally different worlds. Anne's relationship with the racing driver Jackie Stewart was unique and she once accepted from him an expensive gold watch as a present. Mischievous gossip-mongers would try to make more of that than ever existed; those who really knew could dismiss such suggestions as rubbish. Anne and Jackie were nothing more than very good friends; and Jackie's wife Helen was invariably with him whenever he was invited to any of the Royal households or to watch Anne and Mark at some horse competition. Equally, there were some raised eyebrows about Mark's friendship with Roman Polanski, the Hollywood film maker, whose films and relationships were, to say the least, controversial. A decade later, Prince Charles, Princess Diana and other young Royals would count a number of equally controversial showbusiness stars among their friends, but in the mid-1970s such associations were not welcomed by senior courtiers. On the other hand, Anne and Mark would be criticized equally for being too narrow-minded in their interests, which basically came down to the four-legged kind. One respected public figure was heard to complain: "All they do is talk about horses. Horses, horses. Mark, particularly. He just goes on and on." Omar Sharif also discovered that he could achieve Anne's undivided interest when he talked about his horses, but if he strayed to the subject of bridge, her attention began to wander and she said with apparent lack of interest that the card game was too difficult for her. She would also reprimand anyone who mistakenly described their passion for horses as a hobby. "Horses aren't a hobby like fishing or stamp collecting," she would say. "You stick your stamps in the book and that's that, you could then go off and do something else if you wanted. These blessed horses, you do your riding which is what you enjoy and when you get back there is still half a day's work to do just to keep the darn things on four legs. That's the biggest problem with horses; you don't have time for anything else."

At Sandhurst, she had enlisted the assistance of one of the Army instructors to teach her so that she could get a heavy goods vehicle driving licence. It was a good idea, said a friend, to indulge in other interests such as driving. That was not the reason, said Anne. She needed the licence so that when they went eventing she could drive the horse-box herself. But criticism of their single-minded interest was rejected. Anne responded: "We just want to do the things we like. Why should we go to the opera when it bores us? I don't make people come and watch me ride horses."

She was not a busy housewife. She didn't go shopping at the local supermarket, or pop down to the butcher for the Sunday joint, or vacuum the carpets, or make the beds. Domestic chores in her case would seldom extend to more than scrambling an egg.

The custom of senior military personnel retaining staff in their own quarters had long since ended, but for Anne and Mark it was necessary to hire a staff of five to run their lives at Sandhurst and to manage the princess's engagements. They included a housekeeper, Valerie Bugden, who was on loan from Buckingham Palace and who prepared their meals. Valerie is credited with the admission, when questioned about Anne's culinary talents, that "she can't even boil an egg." Valerie was in total charge of housekeeping, even down to ordering the groceries from Fortnum and Mason. When Anne occasionally had to do this chore herself, she did not prove to be entirely efficient. On one occasion she simply ordered a huge hamper containing cooked turkey and duck, Greek honey, crystallized fruit and smoked salmon. And at lunch with the rest of the Royal family at Windsor shortly afterwards, Mark was heard to moan: "Not smoked salmon again", whereupon Prince Andrew christened his sister "the smoked salmon housewife".

Perhaps Anne was more concerned with upsetting her staff than showing off her skills. She told one inquirer: "I enjoy cooking actually but I get the feeling that having got a cook, she might resent it if I pottered around the kitchen. So there are things I'm allowed to do, like scrambled eggs and omelettes, the rest I leave in her capable hands." However, it was often simply not feasible for Anne to adopt the role of loving house-wife. Housewife, in the active sense, she could not be. Some-times Buckingham Palace had booked her three or four engagements in a single day. She was all over the country and Mark often had to attend as well, though he made a point of trying to keep his Army career on an even keel. He enjoyed Army life, and was determined to make a job of it. In the long term, he was open about his ambitions to be a farmer, but while still a serving officer he would treat the Army with all seriousness, a view which was not totally shared by Princess Anne. He had repeatedly refused to attend less important functions with Anne, but by the end of the first year of their marriage, he was already having difficulty in declining some of the things the Palace staff expected of him.

In the autumn of 1974, he joined his wife on a visit to Canada for the Royal Agricultural Winter Fair at Toronto. The press across the Atlantic welcomed Princess Anne's arrival because they knew she was always good for a bit of controversy, and this occasion would be no exception. Canadian critics com-plained that the couple seemed only interested in the animals and the horsey set, and paid little regard to anything else. Anne was said to have treated the criticism as being beneath contempt; she was well used to such abuse anyway. But Mark couldn't just let it pass like water off a duck's back. He was hurt. On their return home, he suggested to Palace advisers that perhaps it would be better if he were not included on some of these trips in future, or at least could he be more selective? But another row was already in the offing. The Palace staff was planning a fortnight in Australia the following May. Mark was low-key about it. Palace secretaries were apparently horrified when he was heard to question the request to go, made by the

Queen herself. He even said he would have to check that it did not clash with any of his own arrangements. "That has already been done," he was politely told. Mark was not challenging the role he knew he had accepted when he became Princess Anne's husband; but he was determined that his own life should not be completely overtaken by her duties.

The Queen would come to accept his view. Prince Philip, with whom Mark discussed his dilemma, knew exactly what he was worried about and advised him to maintain his stance. Anne tried her best to keep any disputes within the family, but Continental journals, for example, were insistent that the marriage of the decade had already gone sour and *France-Dimanche* reported upon the "Queen's cry of agony" over the trouble her daughter was supposed to be having with the bad-tempered and stubborn Mark Phillips. The author's friend and colleague, Marje Proops, was one of the journalists Princess Anne trusted sufficiently to invite down to Oak Grove to see for herself. She would subsequently advise her readers to disregard the stories of rows and tantrums. They were both sensible enough to recognize that there would be problems adjusting to married life, particularly since their married existence would be totally different from any normal couple's. Anne said: "I think we've had problems but they're not the same kind, I'd have thought, that many couples our age have." And turning to Mark she said: "I think they're mostly your problems aren't they, like tagging along at functions and things?" Mark said: "Sometimes you can't say or do in public things you might perhaps like to say or do. Someone might pick it up and you'd soon be reading about it. One tends not to show emotion in public one sometimes feels." One of their biggest problems was not having enough time together. He'd perhaps be away on Army exercises, or she'd be out at an engagement. They met in passing, or perhaps at breakfast. A night in watching television was an absolute treat; and they desired nothing more serious than *Kojak* or *Match of the Day*. The official tours were perhaps the biggest strain. Anne, through years of experience, had developed the patter. Mark was still working on it. Her advice to him was just to ask lots of questions if the conversation flags. Mark found it all extremely tiring. It also took time to unwind. "After these tours I come back home and drive everyone mad," said Anne, "because I natter sometimes for a day or two. Then I shut up for two weeks and trying to get a word

78

out of me is like dragging blood out of a stone until I readjust."

The pressures were enormous, as Mark was just discovering. The bone-aching weariness, the anxiety to get it right, the knowledge that the slightest error would be held against him for all time. As Marje Proops discovered in her chat with them, Anne and Mark were always willing to talk about their hostile press. Anne said they took little comfort from friends saying: "Don't worry, nobody believes it." She knew full well that "it only needs a small misrepresentation and it sticks. Little stories become repeated and exaggerated and they become big stories. Quotations from a reliable source means someone invented it. We don't really mind those fantastically inventive articles they print in France or Germany. They're so hilarious no one could take them seriously. But we do mind when false stories and rumours get into the English papers. It's very frustrating not to be able to answer back [which they are prevented from doing by Royal protocol]. The best thing to do if you can do it, is to sit back and do nothing. But sometimes, when they get the facts wrong, like about money and how much this house costs and that kind of thing, you'd love to be able to say: 'Now just a minute, you've got your sums wrong.' It's so annoying. The worst was when we were in New Zealand [early 1974]. Someone said they'd seen an article in a French newspaper which said I'd had a miscarriage in a cottage hospital somewhere in New Zealand. We'd only been married four months. It was absolutely staggering – and I've had three more since then, if they are to be believed."

Mark was just as angry about his ever-increasing brushes with the newspapers. "When you're in the public eye, your life depends on public opinion. Nobody in the public eye can afford to have a continually bad press. The biggest area of conflict is when we've been riding in competitions and concentrating terribly hard and then some cameraman runs under the horse and breaks your concentration and upsets the horse. Then you're apt to get a bit waspish."

Mark can get really waspish. First, when he is on a diet. Before the start of each eventing season, he had to force himself into a rigid regime, cutting out sugar in tea, potatoes, bread and so on. And that, combined with the tiredness of heavy training sessions, with his Army duties and with his third role of being consort to his princess, means he can get tetchy. In the run up

79

to a major competition, he can, as one of his friends put it, be "damn near unapproachable". Mark himself admits to nerves. Any competition gets him like that. Anne remains calm and cool; Alison Oliver thought she was a better rider for this. She has a serenity that she passes on to the horse and consequently gives her mount more confidence. Mark, though, is overall a better competitor and has the edge on her when it comes to handling a tough horse.

It was in that year of 1974 that Princess Anne lost her favourite mount, Doublet, who had taken her to the title-winning accolades of 1971. She had entered both her leading horses, Doublet and Goodwill, for Badminton in April while her husband was on Columbus. She was lying fifth on Goodwill after the steeple-chase and cross-country but Doublet looked tired and in pain and was retired at the end of that day's event. Anne and Goodwill finally finished fourth after the show-jumping section while Captain Phillips took first place for the third time. A few weeks later, Anne was hacking Doublet in Windsor Great Park. Mrs Oliver was a few hundred yards away and saw Princess Anne come to a sudden halt and dismount. She cantered over to where Anne had stopped and discovered her white-faced. She had heard a loud crack and realized immediately that Doublet had broken his leg. There had been no clue that it might happen, nor any previous sign of weakness; but Anne knew there was nothing she could do for him. They both waited while a vet was called. Doublet in the meantime grazed unconcerned; but the vet confirmed what they both knew. Nothing could be done for him and he was put down. For Anne, it was what she described as the ghastliest experience of her life and she was shattered by it; inconsolable for several hours.

Eventing for the rest of 1974 and the early part of 1975 dulled the memory of her once-great horse. She and Mark were heavily engaged in competition riding, including three days in America for the Ledyard event in which Captain Phillips came nowhere and Anne tenth. In fact, they were both shaping up well for the extreme ambition that now lay dead ahead, to represent Britain in the 1976 Olympics in Montreal. It was an aim that Anne spoke of often and one which she and her husband considered to be their prime target for the next few months. Newspaper commentators said that she had put sporting achievement ahead of her Royal duty, which was to have children just as soon as possible. In this, so it was said, the columnists for once had the support of both the Queen and the Queen Mother. Anne herself made no secret of the fact that she did not concur at all. She had three brothers who would, she felt sure, eventually provide sufficient Royal heirs. "Yes, in time, we will have children," she said. "Right now I've got this ambition to achieve. It seems to me that having a family can wait a bit longer. I know that some people think you should have your children sooner rather than later when you are close to them in age, but I'm not so sure. Perhaps when I get my ambition out of the way – even if I don't achieve it – I wouldn't mind giving up then. Mind you the house isn't very big and we'll have to move. But I don't think you're really settled enough at the beginning of a marriage to have children. You ought to get over the business of getting married first."

Anne couldn't have made her position clearer, but there were some writers who just would not accept that she was telling the truth. One told the readers of a weekly magazine for women that Anne was scared of having children because of repercussions from the operations she had had for an ovarian cyst three years earlier. The same writer suggested that the princess had been pregnant in 1974 and that the Queen and the Queen Mother had been overjoyed. The writer dismissed this incident with a bland quotation from an unnamed source that a baby "wasn't to be", thereby leaving the readers to draw their own conclusions as to what had happened. Anne was unable to do anything about these unsupported allegations and innuendos.

There was further speculation a few months later when she was admitted to the King Edward VII Hospital for Officers in London for a forty-eight hour stay, causing immediate front page headlines: "Princess Anne Pregnant?" and "Anne Joyful on her Big Day". Once again it was a false alarm. No indication was ever given as to why she had been admitted to hospital, other than for a routine check-up.

In the run-up to the Olympics, Anne was selected for the official British team to compete in the European Championships at Lumuhlen, West Germany, along with Janet Hodgson, Sue Hatherly and Lucinda Prior-Palmer, the first all-woman team ever selected to represent the nation, and the first British team ever to have a member of the Royal family. It would also be one of Britain's best-ever performances. Lucinda Prior-Palmer got the individual Gold, Princess Anne won the Silver and the team also achieved a Silver.

With such good results behind them, it was now almost a foregone conclusion that Anne and Mark would compete at Montreal. Their concentration on this one ambition was broken temporarily in March by a family matter. It was announced from Buckingham Palace that Anne's aunt, Princess Margaret, was to separate from her husband, Lord Snowdon. The Queen's sister, who had herself been prevented from marrying Group Captain Peter Townsend because he was divorced, was now to become a divorcée herself. The publicity would have rebounding and knock-on effects for the Royal family. An analysis of modern Royalty which could now allow a divorce within its ranks highlighted a total change of course which was approved by the Queen herself in consultation with the Church and political leaders. Princess Margaret had long been getting a bad press over her marriage, and particularly over her friendship with the socialite and gardener Roddy Llewellyn. The previous autumn, there had been some fairly open accounts of Princess Margaret's visit to a hippy commune in Wiltshire where Llewellyn lived from time to time. The popular press had interviewed members of the commune at some length to make the most of what was an entertaining Royal story. In January 1976, Princess Margaret flew off to her island hideaway of Mustique, owned by her old friend, Colin Tennant, who had by now made a fortune developing this tiny playground for the rich. Princess Margaret showed little concern for the growing scandal and took Roddy Llewellyn on holiday with her. She seemed to be under the illusion that, out-of-sight, she would be out-of-mind. But the *News of the World* got hold of a photograph of her and Llewellyn and splashed it across the front page. Lord Snowdon, perhaps rightly, complained with unusual openness that he had been made to look a fool once too often. The Mustique trip was the last straw; he wanted a divorce. He was also visiting the lady he would eventually marry. The Queen, presented with a situation that was now attracting feverish and constant press attention, had little choice but to agree.

Princess Margaret, by her own actions and a failed marriage, had finally put an end to the Rule of Court which had been so strongly upheld by her grandmother Queen Mary: that divorce in the family could never be. Queen Mary had always refused to allow any divorcée at Court, not even in the sacred Royal Enclosure at Ascot. For Princess Anne, the effects of her aunt's divorce would be twofold. First, she would find herself having to undertake a far greater volume of Royal work because the aura of scandal around Princess Margaret, not to mention her emotional state, would mean a very definite curtailment of her public duties, some of which would be passed to Anne. Secondly, Princess Margaret's final and total severance of the "no divorce" rule within her family would put greater pressure on Anne and Mark. This was the greatest crisis the Royal family had faced since the Abdication. It signalled the start of a gloves-off approach by the popular press which Anne would have to endure whenever her own marriage came into the spotlight.

If all this wasn't enough as Princess Anne headed towards achieving the greatest ambition of her life, she suffered a further setback. With barely three months to go before the team selection in July, she was taken to hospital after a bad fall during horse trials at Durweston, Dorset, on April 22. Captain Phillips was also riding in the event and was already out on the course when he heard on the loudspeaker system an appeal for a doctor after his wife's horse had stumbled at a fence, crashed to the ground and then rolled back on top of her. Mark galloped back to the scene and found Princess Anne still unconscious; he knelt beside her and covered her with a rug and then helped carry her, still out cold, into an ambulance for the seventeen-mile journey to Poole General Hospital. After seeing his wife comfortably installed in a private room, Mark was surrounded by newsmen who had chased the ambulance to the hospital. "Falling off is an occupational hazard," he said. "It is a risk you take every time you go into a competition; I don't see why it should upset her at all. She's come off dozens of times. She will obviously have to take it easy for two or three days but she should be back riding soon." In fact, Anne's injuries were rather more serious than that. After a thorough examination, the hospital announced she had a hair-line fracture of the vertebrae, which according to the consultant physician, could mean three months of pain, and out of the saddle a lot longer.

It was almost a re-run of the year Anne had been laid low by the operation for an ovarian cyst; on that occasion she defied the doctors and astounded her trainer and family by getting up from her hospital bed to enter the European championships. She was about to do the same again. One fall wasn't going to halt her Olympic aims. For one thing, she knew it could well be her one and only chance of representing her country. The increasing work-load being put on her by the Palace would eventually curtail her eventing and the prospect of starting a family – which, according to the press, the nation expected – loomed ever closer. Ann faced the injury at Durweston with determination to beat it. She still suffered pain for which she received intensive physiotherapy but, sure enough, by the time the moment came when the team choice could be delayed no longer, Anne and Mark were among the five named to go.

For Anne, it would be the pinnacle of achievement. For Mark, it was tinged with disappointment. Although he considered he had done enough in the final trial at Osberton, where he performed well on his two horses Persian Holiday and Favour three weeks before the team was due to go, he was named only as a reserve. He felt cheated but didn't show it. There would be no sign of resentment on his part as he joined his wife, who was to ride Goodwill, Hugh Thomas on Playmar, Richard Meade on Jacob Jones, and Lucinda Prior-Palmer on Be Fair. But, in the Olympic circles, there were conflicting views: some were publicly quoted in their belief that Mark's two horses stood more chance than at least two of the selected entries.

Mark stayed out of the controversy and, with Anne, he joined the rest of the team on an economy flight to Montreal. They were shown no favours when it came to accommodation in the Olympic village, which was no surprise to them or their team-mates, but raised a few eyebrows in the press both in Canada and at home. The British team-manager, Colonel Bill Lithgow, was moved to point out that "Her Royal Highness herself wanted to be regarded as an ordinary member of the team and that's exactly what she is."

Security was always going to be a major headache. The Canadian hosts were on edge after the massacre at Munich four years earlier when a terrorist gang murdered eleven Israeli athletes. There had also been special links with Scotland Yard and the Royal Protection Unit over Princess Anne following the bomb and terrorist atrocities in Britain over the preceding few months. Anne found the village accommodation excellent, though she was shadowed by security men and her own private detective twenty-four hours a day. Once again, she reasserted her style of no pretence, and even had a smile for the photographers who were even more in evidence than the posse of security men.

It was a pity, after all they had been through, that the Olympic Games were something of an anticlimax. Sitting on the sidelines, Mark watched his team make a disastrous start. Hugh Thomas's horse went lame and Lucinda Prior-Palmer's pulled a tendon and the British team was eliminated. Princess Anne on Goodwill had a spectacular fall in the cross-country, which was announced over the public address system and left Mark and the Queen, who was also at the Games, waiting anxiously for news. Anne was advised to retire, as she was technically ruled to be unconscious, but she refused and remounted and crossed the finishing line in a total daze. No medals, no disgrace either. More importantly, Anne had won the hearts of Olympic watchers around the world and had proved once again her stamina and determination. Though she would never reach the same heady heights again in eventing, Princess Anne's sporting life was by no means over.

During that year of the Olympics her public image improved. Followers of Royalty were beginning to say she wasn't a bad sort after all, and the stories about Her Royal Haughtiness and Princess Sourpuss were being disregarded. There had also been an unusual show of public reaction at the Durweston trials in April, when Anne had suffered that bad fall. As photographers and newsmen dashed to the scene to get their pictures of Anne lying unconscious on the ground, they were attacked by spectators who were trying to protect her from the prying lenses. Heated exchanges between pressmen and public occurred and one photographer was punched on the nose.

Similar public sympathy was aroused in the month following Princess Anne's return from Montreal. With the massive coverage of Princess Margaret's marriage break-up still a matter for continuous public consumption, German newspapers came out with a run of astonishing stories suggesting similar problems for Anne and Mark. Captain Phillips had gone to Hamburg to take part in horse trials on August 18. According to the story in *Bild Zeitung*, Germany's largest selling newspaper, Mark then angered his wife by failing to meet her when she arrived at the airport at 10 pm on August 21, a task that was left to their

85

close friend, Siegfried Broemel, who drove her to the Hotel Heidschnucke. Mark was nowhere to be found and Anne went straight to bed. According to the *Bild* story, he returned at midnight, somewhat the worse for drink and discovered that Princess Anne had locked him out. When she refused to let him into their suite, Mark is said to have kicked the door until it opened. The following morning they left the hotel without taking breakfast and without talking to each other. Anne, said the report, was terribly put out by the incident and at the horse trials later that day refused to applaud her husband during his round, and declined to accompany him to a press conference. Buckingham Palace immediately took the unusual step of denouncing the German story as absolute nonsense. The Palace, mindful of Princess Margaret, added with a note of bitterness: "Foreign newspapers seem to think that the British Royal family are fair game for sensational stories."

SIX

The Farmer's Wife

Princess Anne had obviously decided that, once the Olympics were out of the way, they would move into a new house and start a family. Obviously? Well, it seemed to be quite carefully thought out, and even before they went off to Canada, they'd found the house they wanted.

They toured around looking at properties: they visited an especially expensive and magnificent mansion. This was it, Anne said to the estate agent showing them round. They would take it, she said without a passing glance to her husband. What Princess Anne meant, said Mark ushering her towards the door, was that they would go away and think about it. They did, and they didn't buy it.

Mark's only source of income was his Army salary of less than £5,000 a year. He must have known that his mother-in-law had intended to help him out, as a first-time buyer. But was he sure as to the extent? Anne didn't seem to bother and was making appointments to view extremely expensive homes. The next one they saw was called Highgrove, an estate in Tetbury, which had just been totally refurbished and came with a lot of land. Mark thought the land was expensive and the house was too close to the road, and they both thought it did not have a great deal of charm. They were not to know that four years later Prince Charles would buy it for a million pounds, have it remodelled inside and have some charm added, to provide his first home in his marriage to Princess Diana.

For some time, Mark had been discussing with Anne the possibility of leaving the Army to concentrate on a civilian career, which would both embrace their love of horses and provide them with an income – in other words a working farm where they could also train and breed horses and he could run a riding academy. There were a number of reasons why he felt it would soon become necessary to leave the Army. For one thing, he might be forced to do so: the Service was about to jettison 12,000 men in stringent cuts. He also wondered how much longer he could go on neglecting his Army duties to escort his wife on her various official duties. Thirdly, the restrictions placed upon him by his marriage to Anne would clearly hamper his career in the Service; he could not, for example, be considered for any overseas posting, or one that involved going into a danger zone. The alternative to his job as an instructor was one of penpushing in London, and he didn't want that either. Princess Anne shared his disappointment that he would never be able to do what he wanted, to proceed up the ranks and command a squadron. So the alternative was to leave and go farming, with a house which was suitably countrified yet within commutable distance of Buckingham Palace.

The decision was really made for them when Lord Butler, an elder statesman of the Conservative Party, offered them Gatcombe Park, deep in the Cotswolds, which he had inherited from his first wife's father Sam Courtauld in 1947. He had not used it much and the property was dark and rather shabby after a number of tenants. Anne and Mark went down for a look around and knew instantly it was what they wanted. The Queen bought it for them and paid half a million pounds; a further few tens of thousands would be required to make it habitable for a modern young couple. Lord Butler's description ("it's not too vast, just a nice little farm") was hardly met with agreement elsewhere. Mr Neil Kinnock, for example, exploded with rage and said: "I don't know which is worse, the Queen for being wealthy enough to give it to them, or them for having the neck to take it." Various MPs reacted with unsurprising speed and tabled a motion in the House of Commons to state that fifty homes for the needy would be a worthier investment in those days of public expenditure cuts.

Yes, it was a nice little farm. With the fine Georgian house went seven hundred and thirty acres of farmland and woodland, surrounded by some of the loveliest countryside in England. There were a twelve-acre lake, a full and complete range of farm buildings and four cottages. The house itself was not lavish, but a comfortable home, a typical country gentleman's residence with ten bedrooms, two sitting-rooms, a library, staff quarters. It was originally built in the 1770s by Edward Shepherd, a sheep farmer. It was remodelled in 1820 by the then owner, Sir John Soane, who commissioned George

Basevi for the work, and it has since remained largely unaltered. It is a handsome grey house, with a moulded cornice and balustraded parapet. On either side, there are one-storied wings and it appears larger than it really is. A superb conservatory was added in 1829, giving further width to the property's overall appearance. Although, by the time Anne and Mark bought the place, the interior was in a bad state of repair and required total refurbishment, the scope for magnificence was obvious from the description written by Sir Nicholas Pevsner who said: "The entrance hall gives on to the main staircase which is partly screened from it by a pair of tall Doric columns. The east side contains the dining rooms. The library is beyond in a single-storied wing, with book cases evidently designed by Basevi. Behind this is a kitchen with domed roof. The west side has two drawing rooms and the conservatory beyond. Good stone vases in the grounds which are splendidly landscaped. The stables are built around a polygonal yard with an embattled wall facing the buildings."

One report said it was an eighty-two-roomed mansion, which it certainly was not. Another said that the Queen would be paying for the very heavy remodelling cost, when in fact Anne and Mark took out a mortgage on the property to do that. The bad press had, once again, hurt the princess, and it annoyed her intensely when people lumped her Civil List allowance with income she and Mark might have from the farming venture at Gatcombe and the money they would spend to set it up. Not a penny, she insisted, of the Civil List money had ever gone on her private life or her private interests. She was always happy to explain that the greater part went on maintaining her office, the establishment that supported her public job: secretaries, ladies-in-waiting, overnight expenses and all kinds of incidentals. Her other life, now, would be that of a farmer's wife and in her off-duty time she would try at Gatcombe to live, as she herself put it, "what they laughingly call a perfectly ordinary life". She would say that if, for instance, she did not have a public life she would not want to live in a house the size of Gatcombe. But opting out wasn't an option; and, while she faced these responsibilities, she felt that the house was not over-large for the purpose.

The speculation over his finances gave Mark cause for considerable anguish. Those closest in his circle of friends knew, from conversation, that above all he wanted to be the provider in the household, and not dependent on his wife or mother-in-law. That was why he built up his farm and equestrian activities into a fully fledged, commercial venture from which he could earn sufficient to illustrate his independence. It was for this reason that Mark had begun to extend his riding to become an all-round competitor, so that he would not be restricted just to eventing. He required additional success in the show-jumping ring as part of his long-term aim to set up equestrian tutorship along with training, horse rearing and farming.

For two years he had been trying his skills at show-jumping, which brought a constant stream of derision from his most ardent horsey critic, Harvey Smith. But in July, 1977, he achieved his best result so far when he rode his horse Hideaway to victory in the Matthew Norman Clockmaking Stakes at the Royal International Horse Show. What made his success so much sweeter was the fact that he knocked Smith into second place. In the preceding months he had put up with a lot from Smith. First, when he was invited to take part in a Benson and Hedges Championship, Harvey said of him: "If he was Captain of the Good Ship Lollipop and not Princess Anne's husband, I wonder if he would be in it. Perhaps somebody in show-jumping is after a knighthood. I could name a hundred riders who should be invited ahead of him." And a few months later, when Mark was selected to appear in another major event Smith growled: "Damn disgrace".

Diversionary activity, however, was already to hand. With the Olympics out of the way and a new house to move into, Princess Anne in her tradition as a Very Organized Person was now moving on to the next role in life. Sportswoman, housewife, princess, woman of the world ... she had done that, been there. Now she could enter the realm of motherhood, and she would organize it exactly so that the birth of the Queen's first grandchild would come at the end of her Silver Jubilee Year.

1977 was a year of celebration and pleasant surprises for the Queen, organized largely by her son and heir, the Prince of Wales, to celebrate her twenty-five years as Queen. The news in April of Princess Anne's pregnancy came as a great joy to her. Anne for the moment would have to curtail her riding competitions. There was now plenty to do, anyway, without eventing. The busy engagements connected with the Jubilee had given the entire family a full calendar of events. The popularity of the Royal family was at its height that year, with the Queen and Prince Philip travelling the length and breadth of Britain. The Queen's State visit to Australia in February was met with less enthusiasm: the republicans were out in force, waving banners which declared "Anarchy not Monarchy". Princess Anne and Mark had a better reception when they went to America in June, visiting Washington and Maryland where she unveiled a statue of Queen Anne, in Centerville, Queen Anne's County. Prince Charles also had a merry welcome when he went to Beverly Hills to attend a Variety Club charity dinner with the stars of stage, screen and Hollywood who had paid $2,000 a ticket. Incidentally, 1977 was also the year Prince Charles met a shy young girl called Lady Diana Spencer for the first time since childhood.

Meanwhile, the rebuilding of the desolate interior of Anne and Mark's new home was well under way and Mark was for ever nagging about the cost. David Hicks, who had married Mountbatten's younger daughter Pamela, was a specialist in the restyling of period houses and drew up ambitious plans for the property. The bedrooms were to be restored to the front of the house and a self-contained nursery and flat built from the maze of staff rooms on the top floor. In the end, because they were on a limited budget, Hicks's plans would prove to be too expensive and only part of the work was carried out, to keep the cost within the £35,000 that Mark Phillips had borrowed on mortgage for the renovation work.

The improvements would be followed avidly by newspaper readers the world over; Anne and Mark were still the young stars of Royalty and, although Prince Charles had made his mark, he still didn't provide the same romantic appeal – or controversy – nor would he until Lady Diana came on the scene.

The stable block also required attention. The existing accommodation for the horses was old fashioned and in poor repair and Mark himself designed a new stable block which would cost almost £100,000, which they raised by the sale of two of their horses, coupled with the insurance money Anne received after Doublet had to be put down. The new stables would include what was described in the newspapers as a swimming pool for horses and, once again, the jibes came thick and fast. There were accusations that Anne was using her Civil List money to subsidize their private work. She denied this with some ferocity. They had built the stables with their own money and, as for the swimming pool, she offered to open the doors

91

to anyone who cared to search the place. They wouldn't find one, said Anne, because there wasn't one. What they had put into one of the horse boxes was a sunken floor which could be filled with eighteen inches of water to bathe horses with sore feet or legs. And the controversy of Gatcombe wasn't over yet. In the summer of 1977, Mark Phillips talked to his neighbour, Captain Vaisey Davis, about the possibility of buying a couple of fields from him. To his surprise, Davis offered to sell him the whole farm, all five hundred and thirty-three acres of it. Anne and Mark were in turmoil. They could see the valuable prospect of merging the two farms into one 1,300-acre estate but now had no money to buy. Mark began talking to several financial institutions with the idea of their buying the farm and leasing it back to him. The negotiations were well advanced when Anne mentioned their plans to the Queen over dinner. The Queen immediately insisted that she should buy the farm and rent it to them. In October, the Queen became the owner of Aston Farm with her daughter and son-in-law as the tenants. Commentators quickly dashed to their calculators and discovered that the Queen had now invested more than three quarters of a million pounds in her daughter's future. With the money Anne and Mark had put in themselves, it came to more than a million.

So it was with some derision that Mark's comments about being "just a young couple with a mortgage" were treated by the tabloids. The *Daily Mail* caught the mood of the moment and used the quote with front page banner headlines when it reported some months later that Mark had signed an equestrian sponsorship deal with British Leyland. It would pay him £60,000 over three years for which he would ride in competitions five horses which would be known as the Range Rover team. Mark pointed out that, at the time, it cost £3,000 a year to keep one horse in training. They had no other income to finance their horses since the farm was taken as a separate entity, a business with controlled and audited accounts. But there was no question that this young Royal couple had been immensely fortunate in their acquisitions when others their age were struggling to make ends meet. Mark's own explanations hardly matched public condemnation and ill-feeling towards them. At the time, British Leyland was in dire financial straits and of course the repercussions were instant. The Labour MP and Royal critic Dennis Skinner, who was always ready with a quote, described the deal as "bloody staggering", in which he was naturally joined by Willie Hamilton who weighed in with: "It really shows the insensitivity of these people ... some people say Mark and Anne haven't much money. They are rolling in it. They are grubbing around for anything to keep them going. They are parasites." And there are no prizes for guessing which word in that little quotation would be used in the headlines the following morning.

Support for Mark came from an unexpected source. Derek "Red Robbo" Robinson, the militant bogeyman of the age and shop steward at Leyland, said it made commercial sense and he welcomed it. There would be further sponsorship deals involving much greater payments when, as we shall see, Mark got down to the business in earnest.

In the middle of all this, Anne was progressing towards motherhood, and her advice to prospective mothers afterwards would be: Never have a baby and move house at the same time. Fortunately, with her domestic staff of six, some of the more arduous tasks were eliminated as Princess Anne reached the time of her confinement.

She had been celebrating their fourth wedding anniversary with a family dinner party at Buckingham Palace on November 14. It was also Prince Charles's twenty-ninth birthday, and everyone was hoping that her baby would be born that day. There was no sign of the infant's arrival, however, and they retired for the night. At 3 am, the contractions started and Mark Phillips drove his wife through the bitter cold night in the family Rover to St Mary's Hospital, Paddington. Readers of that day's *Evening Standard* would soon learn that the princess was put into a spartan twelve-foot by twelve-foot room, with cream paint and floral wallpaper, which cost £55 a night and contained no special concessions for its Royal occupant, apart from a picture of a horse, which had been especially hung on the wall, and a vase of twenty lemon and peach roses, a gift from the staff.

The baby boy who would be christened Peter was born at 10.46 am on November 15 and the birth in hospital established an abrupt departure from Royal tradition. All previous Royal births, with the recent exception of the confinement of the young Duchess of Gloucester, had been at home. The crowds who normally gather outside Buckingham Palace on such occasions now surrounded the hospital from around 7 am onwards. The nursery was already prepared at Buckingham Palace, where the princess would live temporarily upon her return from hospital, and Miss Mabel Anderson, who had been appointed a nursery assistant by the Queen at the time of Princess Anne's birth, was called into service once again. Mountains of gifts and baby clothes had been pouring into the Palace ever since the princess's pregnancy was announced. The new baby was also welcomed by massive and warm press coverage and Mark told reporters: "Well, it's nice to think I've done something right for a change." Auberon Waugh wrote in predictable terms: "Princess Anne has given birth to a centaur ... the best thing is surely to enter him for Eton and Fred Winter's stable at Lambourn and decide which is more suitable nearer the time."

What did raise a few eyebrows was the wording of the announcement of the baby's birth, traditionally a typed message hung outside Buckingham Palace. It read simply: "Her Royal Highness the Princess Anne, Mrs Mark Phillips, was safely delivered of a son. ..." This meant that for the first time in history the grandchild of a ruling sovereign was born without a title. There was an angry response from George Hutchinson, writing in *The Times*: "At the risk of appearing churlish in this particular week ... I now put forward a word of criticism not of the Princess but of the designation with which she has been saddled: The Princess Anne, Mrs Mark Phillips. Princess Anne is not, she cannot be, Mrs Phillips. By virtue of her royal birth she is Princess Anne and as the daughter of a duke she is Lady Anne. Mrs never. I have never understood why this abuse, this inaccuracy, has been allowed by the Palace."

Behind Hutchinson's words lie the deep-rooted conviction of Captain Mark Phillips that he would not accept a title. It would be too strong to say that this had caused an argument between himself and his wife's family; let us say they had discussed it at length and Anne and Mark would not be pressed into it. He knew it would mean the Queen's grandchildren would be born without title, other than the prefix The Hon, and that's the way he wanted it. If having a title meant the kind of public scrutiny he had endured since his engagement, then he would do his best to avoid it for his children. He gave in on the question of accepting a family Coat of Arms, which consisted of a horse and spur with a winged lion. Mark had made no secret of the fact that he thought Anthony Armstrong-Jones was a snob for accepting the title of Lord Snowdon when he married Princess Margaret. So did a lot of Snowdon's friends, and Mark didn't want that to happen to him. Among his horsey set, he was plain Mark Phillips. In the Army, he was nicknamed The Chief and would always make a point of being among the men. Once, on Army manoeuvres, he stopped his Landrover and waved to the troop carrier behind to pull into a pub car park for refreshment. Mark walked into the bar and ordered a pint for himself, his favourite drink incidentally, and one all round for his companions. The flustered owner of the public house, recognizing his famous customer immediately, offered him a more relaxing atmosphere and carpets, in another bar. No thanks, said Mark, he would prefer to stay with his men. Although a similar story might well be told about Prince Philip or Earl Mountbatten, the difference was that neither would allow lowly comrades to forget the rank of the Royal personage. Absolutely no liberties would or could be taken. Anthony Armstrong-Jones was quite an ordinary chap when he met and courted Princess Margaret, but, under Prince Philip's tutorage, he began to take on a Royal aura himself for which he would eventually be ribbed by his "ordinary" friends. It was, one of them told me, rather amusing to watch the transformation. As a photographer, he had been quite a casual sort of person, in speech and dress. But as he became more Royal, his speech was slower and the words more thought out, he adopted a certain haughtiness for which his wife was renowned and there appeared in his sentences the "one" syndrome. The *Guardian* was among those who recorded more than a "tinge of disappointment that plain, honest Mr Armstrong-Jones should have a title thrust upon him". The *Sunday People* recorded a stronger passing of the Royal mister: "Tony Armstrong-Jones had one very big claim on the sympathy of the British people, he had no handle to his name. He was in fact one of us ... now he has lost his most precious asset, his birthright." In his defence, it would be argued that Snowdon accepted the title for the sake of his children (his son received the title Lord Linley) but there was more than an indication that he at first enjoyed, for example, joining his wife on a Caribbean holiday and travelling in the sealed-off luxury of the entire first-class cabin of a BOAC jet which caused the airline a £5,500 loss of revenue. Captain Mark Phillips wanted none of that. He had seen how his wife's aunt and Lord Snowdon had declined into media subjects, and how even good friends had jeered at them behind their backs.

The importance of what happened to Princess Margaret and Lord Snowdon must not be understated. As we have already seen, Anne would become the Palace workhorse, taking on more and more of her aunt's public duties. Also, as interest in Margaret's matrimonial problems began to subside, even greater press attention would be deflected towards Anne and Mark in the increasingly competitive atmosphere of Fleet Street.

Anne was obsessively strict about allowing Master Peter, as he was called, to get too much media attention. She would make a point of shielding him and was determined not to let the cameramen too close to her new son. She wanted to see him ensconced in as normal a life as possible. (Whether she will achieve this aim is another matter. The likelihood is that, as he reaches his teens, Peter, too, will be drawn into the limelight and become part of the Royal circus.)

The birth of Peter gave Anne herself a chance to reassess her life and indeed she seemed to come to terms more with the fact that she was really two people: a Very Public Person and A Farmer's Wife and Mother. The latter role, which the onset of motherhood crystallized for her, slowed her down. At Gatcombe in the privacy of her own home she was able to resort to jeans and wellies and a more casual style. She and Mark, by dispensing with some of the more personal formalities of being Royal, discovered that they could lead a fairly average life, as she put it, and see private friends in natural surroundings. She felt that commentators on Royalty invariably underestimated how much members of her family lived an existence *outside* the Palace. She went on record as saying that insofar as there is an "average life", a common denominator, "we" see a great deal of it. The trouble, as always with Anne's statements on such matters, was that she sounded somewhat condescending.

Her engagements were kept to a minimum after Peter's birth, though not for long. Various overseas visits were already in the pipeline for 1978 and her official duties at home would soon be mounting up again, to an average of one hundred and fifty a year. She really did try to keep her child's early upbringing in her own hands, though Nanny Mabel Anderson was running the nursery and would still do most of the chores.

The birth of Master Peter also coincided with a change in life-style for his father. A month after he was born, Mark Phillips announced he was leaving the Army to become a full-time farmer and planning to take a one-year course in farm management at the Royal Agricultural College in Cirencester.

Anne had not lost sight of her riding interests and within two months of Peter's birth was back in the saddle to join the local hunt in a three-hour gallop across the Wiltshire countryside. By April, 1978, she was back in competitive riding and, by July, was in serious competition in Germany. The arrival of a baby had not dimmed her hopes of joining the British team in the 1980 Olympics in Moscow. In the meantime, she was having a brief respite from critical press attention, which had been diverted by a flurry of sensational stories surrounding other members of the Royal family, chiefly events involving Princess Margaret, and the arrival of a newcomer, Baroness Marie-Christine Von Reibnitz, a divorcée and daughter of a former Nazi SS officer, who was preparing for entry into the Royal circle.

In February Prince Andrew celebrated his eighteenth birthday which entitled him to draw £17,282 a year from the Civil List, much to the wonderment of the usual critics. His elder brother, Charles, having let slip the casual remark that thirty was a good age to get to take a bride, was for the rest of the year being married off to all and sundry.

Princess Margaret was now temporarily off the list for Royal public appearances and good works. Apart from being ill with hepatitis, her quickie divorce was about to end her eighteen-year marriage to Lord Snowdon. She made history as the first to be divorced at the heart of the Royal family since Henry VIII dispensed with Anne of Cleves. Privately, other senior members of the Royal family saw this as possibly the greatest crisis the Monarchy had faced since the Abdication and a carefully discreet conference was called by Prince Philip on the Queen's instruction, with the Prime Minister and the Archbishop of Canterbury, after Princess Margaret offered to retire from public life. The Queen herself thought her sister's departure from public duty would cause immense damage and it was considered best to let her go on. They did, and in the summer her Civil List income was duly increased in the annual awards to £59,000 year.

It was hardly with the best of timing that Prince Michael of

Kent had applied to the Queen for permission to marry the divorcée, Baroness Von Reibnitz, formerly Mrs Tom Troubridge. However, it was perhaps on the basis that all the problems should be dealt with in one go that the Queen granted permission for the marriage, seven days after Princess Margaret's divorce. There were still some thorny questions to be resolved, since they could not be married in church; he was Church of England and she was a Catholic. A register office wedding is not available to members of the Royal family and eventually they settled on a civil ceremony in Vienna at which hardly any members of the family were present. Also Prince Michael had to renounce his rights of succession to the Throne.

Surprisingly, the Royal family's popularity with the British people did not suffer; just as the TV ratings went up when JR was shot in *Dallas* or half the *Dynasty* cast was massacred, the nation eagerly awaited the next instalment. Sales of the mass circulation newspapers enjoyed a sudden upsurge. A poll conducted for *Woman* magazine showed the Royal family's popularity at its highest since the period immediately after the Coronation. The Queen and Prince Charles topped the poll with 73 per cent and 68 per cent respectively. Princess Anne remained firmly in the lower regions of the popularity stakes. Although Princess Margaret had been pilloried, she scored 29 per cent in the voting. Princess Anne was only one point higher.

Yet, strangely, Anne and Mark had been mainstays in what King George VI used to call the Family business. The lack of public warmth and affection towards either of them was largely due to what Prince Philip described as "dontopedology" which means opening one's mouth and putting one's foot in it. To the mass followers of Royalty, they seemed a bit of an oddity, toffee-nosed, spoilt and constantly liable to extract comments like "Who do they think they are?" It would be some time yet before they would shake off this image; a good PR man could have done the couple a world of good.

Mark had obviously decided that the family needed cheering up: just after Christmas, as that awful year came to a close, a reporter discovered him in a joke shop buying some rather unusual items to jolly up the Royal winter holiday. His shopping list included crapalot teabags, Dr Windbreak's Fart Powder and sexy sugar lumps that released contraceptives when the sugar melted. When the reporter inquired of Buckingham Palace as to the purpose of Captain Mark Phillips's purchases, he was told that "he has a good sense of humour and enjoys a joke like everybody else." The unanswered question, of course, was: did the rest of the Royal family enjoy his sense of humour? But perhaps he could be allowed some frivolous moments. As the new year began, he was studying at agricultural college and Anne was contemplating her next move on the sporting front. She was still hopeful of competing in the 1980 Moscow Olympics but her performances had not been her best since the birth of Peter and the months of family trauma. Perhaps she should call it a day. The additional work she was getting from the Palace, along with the mounting list of charities with which she was connected, made increasing demands upon her time. With Mark now studying hard on his intensive one-year course, there were enough pressures on them without the tension of competition on the eventing courses. Still, they both carried on and both harboured the ambition for another appearance in the top team but the headlines "Anne takes a tumble" and "Crash goes Anne" give an indication of the frustration she herself must have felt as she failed to get back into winning form.

Their marriage was back under the microscope. At the root of it, said an article in *Woman* magazine, was the anguish of Mark who hated being "a kept man". More so than most husbands, he perhaps over-compensated by refusing to be the one to back down in an argument. He would always remember the advice of his brother-in-law, Charles, that he should "not let Anne get away with too much".

Whatever the press said about them, it was largely speculation. The débâcle over Princess Margaret marked a further decline in relations with the press and television and saw the arrival of a new era in the way in which reporters tackled Royal stories. Any semblance of kid-glove treatment had disappeared. Anne and Mark were very vulnerable to these attacks, and the author recalls that they were certainly considered "fair game" by popular journalists. As yet, neither had done a great deal to endear themselves to the public and when there was a story published about them, more often than not, it would be critical. On the surface, at least, they appeared to have everything and published examples of "giving back" were few.

SEVEN

Joy and Fury

The Royal family is managed in the same way as a major, multi-million-pound business, of which the Queen herself is the head and Prince Philip the chief executive. Behind the scenes is a massive organizational and management team whose responsibilities cover the vast range of services to the Monarchy, in addition to managing the Queen's estates, the Royal archives, art treasures, property, and personal holdings; in all, an undertaking which would require a book on its own to explain fully. The public face of Royalty, the appearances of various members of the family at thousands of engagements annually, their involvement in State occasions, in Commonwealth activities and even the public part of their holidays, is considered by the Queen to be an important and vital part of the Royal establishment. Without it (or with consistently bad publicity which could alienate public sympathy) the Monarchy would surely go into decline. Each member's performance is assessed annually, quite informally, and Prince Philip is charged with the task of commenting on any aspects which have brought displeasure, or where behaviour might be adjusted.

As she reached thirty, Princess Anne began to change her image. It didn't happen overnight, and it seems to have been a deliberate and planned move towards a more acceptable public face. Princess Anne has never admitted she embarked on such a course, but a certain mellower and softer approach was noticed, and she was not on quite such a short fuse. She was still entirely capable of telling reporters to Naff Off, and there were plenty of other examples of her occasional outbursts of expletives over which the Queen would enlist the aid of the unshockable Queen Mother "to have a word with Anne about her language". The Queen could not always master her daughter's fiercely independent attitude. On one occasion, now legend, the Queen turned to lady-in-waiting Lady Susan

Hussey and said angrily: "Can you do anything with her? I can't."

During 1979, Anne's travels had taken her thousands of miles. She had been to Portugal, Germany, Thailand, the Gilbert Islands, New Zealand, Australia, the Bahamas for its 250th anniversary, and Canada, the latter on behalf of the Save the Children Fund. Captain Phillips had accompanied her on only four of those overseas visits, and it would become increasingly difficult now for him to be at his wife's side, because of his own business commitments. Indeed, that year of 1979 would be the last in which Mark participated to any great extent in her duties. His involvement would become less and less, leaving the princess to journey the world with Palace officials and her ladies-in-waiting as company. The decision was made for them: he had his business, she had hers. It was as simple as that.

It was at the start of that extremely busy year that one of the Palace advisers made the point that there was a substantial and widening gap between Anne's press and public image and what was deserved from the work she was actually doing. At the time, one Royal observer said the directive that Anne should try to do something about this came from the Queen herself; but an inquiry at Buckingham Palace brought the response from the Queen's assistant press secretary, John Haslam, that, if any such decision was made, it would have come from the princess herself.

The relaunching of Anne started there. Within not many months, the results would begin to show as her popularity rose and her position in the Royal top ten moved slowly but surely upwards. This new openness was marked by a surprisingly frank and revealing interview with Kenneth Harris for the *Observer* which went a long way towards trying to explain some of her past feelings. She was asked, for example, if she regarded herself as a wife and mother who also happened to have a public career, or did she think that being a princess came first? "There is a sort of constant battle with priorities," said Anne, "but I think it's possible to get them balanced. There are moments in your life when it's more important to be a mother than it is a princess but you can afford to adjust the priorities for that occasion because your public life is going to go on well, for ever, as far as you're concerned. Whether I'm getting the balance right is too early to say. I've been a princess all of my life but I've become a wife and mother only comparatively recently."

Princess Anne was also frank about her husband's position when she was asked if he had adjusted to the role of Royal husband and consort. She said: "Yes, I think there is a special difficulty. After all we normally still think of husband as number one and wife number two whereas in the case of a Royal female who has public duties to perform it's rather the other way around. How does he cope? There has got to be a problem there hasn't there? Even if you don't let it worry you, it's there. My father had a naval career and had to give it up. My husband had an army career – he didn't have to give it up but he could see that he would never be allowed to serve with his regiment to the extent he felt he should and do the service he really joined to do, so in a way, yes, he had to give it up too. That in itself is a difficulty. Doing what he's doing now creates a special kind of difficulty; while people would say that being an army officer is a career, most people don't regard our farming as a career. Nowadays it certainly is. When you consider that farming is the most capital intensive industry in the country – not just a pleasant pastime – you can't play around with just a couple of fields."

And on the question of her image, the princess was once again honestly open: "I think it would be unnatural if I didn't resent it somewhat but I'm also resigned to it. One of the reasons I don't worry about it is that it's an image only in certain sections of the popular press ... mind you I know I'm a bit impatient and say things at the wrong time, but not without provocation."

As her popularity in the country rose, it was matched by her list of engagements, and soon she would be averaging between two and three hundred a year which was a daunting workload and one which would mean that she and her husband passed like ships in the night. Whatever time of day she finished, Anne would, however, try to get back to home base and start out afresh the following day. But even that could never be guaranteed. She was also having to adapt to a certain loneliness, and she would at times rely heavily for support on members of her staff. Perhaps that is why her personal detective, Peter Cross, who was at her side for ten months during this extremely busy period rather got ideas above his station and thought that he and the princess had developed a "special" relationship. He would have ample time to reflect on those months; he was subsequently sacked for over-familiarity and, as we will see, some years passed before he was able to sell his story. The *News of the World* published his startling allegations in 1985, relating to his time as Princess Anne's bodyguard.

But the whispers started much earlier, from around the time he was taken off the Royal Protection Squad. Those early rumours were spread largely by Cross himself as he tried to peddle his gossip; he also told many of his friends, his wife and his girlfriends that his relationship with Princess Anne was more friendly than a working one, which most who knew him found hard to believe. However, there was without doubt more than just a crumb of familiarity on the princess's part; the blame could not entirely be placed at Cross's door, though he can be accused of breaking trust in his revelations.

One of his incredible claims would be that Princess Anne herself rang him after he had been sacked to tell him of the birth of her second child Zara in May 1981, but four years would elapse before the *News of the World* ran his story.

Princess Anne became pregnant again when all chances of riding for her country in the Moscow Olympics vanished. First, she was out of form and, anyway, she had never found a really good horse to replace Doublet. Thirdly, Prime Minister Margaret Thatcher pulled the British teams out in protest over the invasion of Afghanistan.

She and Mark told the Queen of the impending arrival of her second grandchild during a party at the Ritz Hotel to celebrate Princess Margaret's fiftieth birthday. Most of the family were there with friends, and somehow the news of Princess Anne's pregnancy leaked out and flashed round Fleet Street. That put the Phillipses in a quandary because they hadn't told Mark's parents. They were on holiday in a cottage in the west country, out of touch by telephone, and eventually the local constabulary was charged with the job of carrying a message to Mr and Mrs Phillips senior, asking them to get in touch urgently. Within the hour, Mark's mother was in a local telephone box to her daughter-in-law. "What is it?" she asked breathlessly. "Thank goodness you called," replied Anne. "I just wanted to tell you I'm pregnant."

It was going to be a busy few months ahead. Prince Charles had recently bought Highgrove House for a million or more, much to the disgust of the usual chorus who berated one of the world's richest young men for such an obscene display of wealth. What could he possibly want with such a huge mansion, he being a bachelor? The newspapers were already solving the problem by arranging his marriage to Princess Marie-Astrid of Luxemburg, one of the few suitable princesses left available to him. Clearly, Charles did not agree with their selection of a wife and, doubtless bored with the constant references to his bachelorhood, decided it was perhaps time to make his own arrangements. In February, therefore, he announced his engagement to Lady Diana Spencer, shy and nineteen, extremely attractive and the perfect partner in every way. What a vintage year it would be for Royal watchers and the Buckingham Palace press office. There was a Royal twenty-first birthday (Prince Andrew's in February), a Royal engagement, a Royal birth, a Royal marriage and, incidentally, to complete the circle, a Royal death. Princess Alice, Countess Athlone, died in that year a month before her ninety-eighth birthday. It was also the year someone fired blanks at the Queen during the Trooping of the Colour. "Life must go on," she said determinedly. Marcus Sarjeant who fired the gun was jailed for treason.

It was while she was carrying Zara that Anne made the oft-referred to comment that being pregnant was the occupational hazard of being a wife; and that pregnancy was a bore. Long before Zara was born, she and her husband had arrived at a sensible approach to the way their children would be reared. They were both aware that being in the public gaze could, if they let it, influence the way they brought up their children. "That would be unfair to the children themselves," she would say. "You must do what you think is best for your child ... I read about the controversy Labour politicians get involved in when they send their children to private schools ... That's part of what freedom of choice in this country is about. When a Labour politician is known to be sending one of his children to private school one half of the country says 'Fair enough' and the other half says 'you shouldn't'. Some people might say about us 'Why don't they get in touch with reality and send them to state schools' ... others might say 'why are they in the state system when they can afford to have their children educated privately?' ... I think you have got to be completely objective, consider the personality of your child and try to work out what's going to be the right thing for him or her. The child must come first." Of all the Royal children closest to the Queen, Peter and now Zara would never be pushed into the limelight by the parents. Indeed, the reverse would be the case and they would be seen only at major family events.

The birth of Zara on May 15, 1981, an eight-pound one-ounce "noisy girl", according to her father, was marked with a press fanfare and Captain Phillips, who was present at the birth, standing by in white overall and mask, was front page news when he made an off-the-cuff remark to a Sunday newspaper: "Yes, I was present at the birth but I wouldn't recommend it to other fathers." Esther Rantzen and others were ready with instant quotes. Poor old Mark. There was always someone waiting in the wings to have a go, it seemed.

Anne's confinement and subsequent cancellation of some of her engagements gave an opportunity once again for Princess Michael, now well and truly married into the family, to try to take over public duties of a more vital nature. She had also been carrying on something of a campaign to get her husband an income from the Civil List. She is said to have complained to the Queen about the size of the room allotted to her and her husband when staying at Windsor for Christmas. Similar stories were plentiful. The most acid came allegedly from the lips of Princess Margaret, whose incisive and cutting responses were back to earlier form; it is said that, when asked what she would give her worst enemy for Christmas, she replied "Dinner for two with Princess Michael."

And now there was Diana-mania. Every day for months, Lady Di adorned the tabloid newspapers and even the "heavies" got caught up in the tailwind; no one could ignore her. From the day of her engagement, she was removed to safe keeping, to remain under the protective wing of the Queen Mother. Here was a new phenomenon: an inexperienced girl whom the public could closely identify with, because she had the appearance of being a working girl who loved her job caring for children; and who wasn't good on horseback, who smiled sweetly towards every camera, who waved when the cameramen shouted "Wave, Di", who didn't swear when the press got excited, and who seemed without a petulant bone in her body. Her only aim, it seemed, was to please. For almost twelve years, Anne had been the *young* Royal. Did she slightly resent the speed in which Lady Diana went straight into the limelight that she had held for so long? The massive interest in the future Queen and her good press even took the Palace press office by surprise, and there was more than a touch of jealousy on Anne's part. Diana felt Princess Anne looked upon her with some disdain, like the headgirl looking down upon first-year arrivals at school was how she put it to one of her friends. It was no secret either that Anne, who was always a stickler for doing her homework before attending any function or meeting so that she actually *knew* what she was talking about (instead of reading some speech prepared by another person), questioned Diana's ability to be able to carry off that role. In those early days Anne once referred to her as "The Dope". Anne was no intellectual genius; but she knew more than most that Royal women have to be, above all else, *tough*.

Princess Anne had always insisted that she herself was not a fairy-tale princess. But that is exactly what Lady Diana was to become. The stuff that dreams and fairy-tales are made of: a glass coach, a wedding dress which was a confection of satin lace and shimmering mother-of-pearl, several hundred million television viewers dazzled around the world. The gorgeous bride nervously mixed up her husband's names and called him Philip; afterwards Prince Andrew roared "She's just married my father."

Anne got back to work, and it was at this point that the press began taking her more seriously. Diana's arrival had taken the heat off her and, for a time, the focus of press attention would be upon Anne's work for charities and the Save the Children Fund.

Captain Phillips went to Australia to ride in a three-day event at Melbourne. Suddenly, the Australian press came out with the story that he was having a "close relationship" with a television personality. And since most people knew that journalist Angela Rippon was writing a book on Mark, she immediately became the centre of attention. Angela had spent almost a year in the regular company of not just Mark, but Anne as well, on the research for a comprehensive biography, *Mark Phillips: The man and his horses*, which was published in April, 1982. The story was published in Australia, and picked up by the British press from whom it had been fed in the first place.

It is always easier to follow up an article which is highly sensitive for legal reasons when it has been published abroad first, particularly in this case since the built-in innuendo was sufficient, almost, to constitute an action for libel.

The story said that Anne's marriage was on the rocks and Mark had been sent to Australia by the Queen to think things over. In fact, he had received the invitation to Melbourne seven months before. Angela Rippon herself recalled the shock of seeing the story in print. "I felt sick," she said "and so did my husband Chris. He knew there was no truth in it and fortunately he's used to picking up newspapers and reading lies about us. Two days later I had to speak to Mark Phillips on the telephone and I was acutely embarrassed. He took very much the line that Chris did; that people were telling lies for filthy lucre. He felt it was one of the most evil things that had ever been written about himself and Princess Anne. My friends told me it was the most potentially damaging thing that had ever been written about me which would have threatened my own marriage and my professional credibility. Mark was philosophical about it but the whole thing was a carefully worded pack of half-truths, innuendoes and lies."

Angela had gleaned a lasting impression of life at Gatcombe which she saw as charming, relaxing and comfortable. It was an atmosphere that was infectious; on informal occasions when friends visited, most wore slacks or casual clothes. Even the butler had been seen in blue jeans. Angela wrote: "Captain Phillips and I would be talking in his study and the princess would come back from shopping or taking Peter to school. She would pop her head round the door and say 'Like a cup of tea?' If it was the butler's day off, she would bring it herself. I took it as a great compliment that they invited me to stay at the house, rather than at a hotel, and treated me as a welcome guest. They were marvellous hosts. I'd have dinner with them and then we'd watch television together. It was all very relaxed."

Running an eventing team of international status is an expensive business; running a successful team is cost-intensive. To remain in a position where he could obtain sponsorship money, which was his lifeblood, Mark had to be successful. He was now running a stable of more than a dozen horses and was personally involved in their training and schooling. Seven were leased to the Range Rover team, and everything looked fine as he started that season of 1981. Princess Anne, after the birth of her daughter, was also back in the saddle and riding in major competitions on the Queen's promising horse Stevie B. But long before the season was out, more than half Mark's team of eventers had to be taken out of competition through injury or resting. And what had promised to be something of a landmark in his eventing career was, that year, a dismal disappointment.

His income was necessarily supplemented by other activities connected with the horse, such as teaching small groups of riders at pre-organized sessions, not just at Gatcombe but in various parts of the world. He was already recognized as ranking among the world's best riders. "I've sacrificed half my life to competitive riding," he said. "I don't smoke. Hardly drink. I seldom go to the theatre or night-clubs and when I come home at nights, I often fall asleep in front of the television. I have been lucky and moderately successful but the only way I could continue was with the help of a sponsor. I have no great private income and I have to run Gatcombe Park totally as a commercial enterprise."

Anne herself, at the end of that busy year, was preparing to go abroad for what was now intended as an annual mission for the Save the Children Fund. The cameramen were still camped outside the door of her new sister-in-law, Princess Diana. It was noted at circulation conferences on the *Daily Mirror* that a good front-page picture of her would always improve that day's sales substantially. Mike Molloy, then editor of the *Mirror*, dubbed it "their daily dose of Di" as if the British public was addicted to her, which they certainly seemed to be. Consequently, there was not a great deal of coverage for Anne when she left for a gruelling tour of Nepal, and with the pressure off she went about her duties with a warm, sunny smile, endless enthusiasm and breathtaking energy. As *Woman* magazine recorded a few weeks later, "we saw the affectionate side of her nature that we had forgotten existed."

This visit was the first of many that showed Anne in a new light. She was never eager to promote herself in any boastful way. John Cumber of the SCF noted, for instance, that whenever the cameras were out of sight Anne would be in amongst the children in the Nepalese clinics. She said Greetings in their native tongue and saucer eyes lit up. Five minutes later, they were in her arms, jabbering happily. In Katmandu, her tiny cavalcade of three cars and a motorbike rider became a familiar sight as she visited local dignitaries. Then it was off to the more remote areas and into the foothills of the Himalayas where her party had to make an hour-long hike to reach a mother and baby clinic. It was an outpost of the Fund's field work, and a visit that its staff and patients alike would remember for ever. Mothers with sick babies walked for two days or more, with infants in their arms, to reach the clinic. It was facts such as these which made a lasting impression on her, one which would influence the extent of her work in future which would soon take on expansive and generous proportions.

Anne returned to London to find that the press fever over Princess Diana had subsided not a jot, which did not altogether please her. She would show herself as not entirely patient with this continued torrent of adulation which reached new heights early in the new year with the news that Charles and Diana were expecting their first child.

Later that year Princess Anne was visiting the United States when Princess Diana gave birth to Prince William, and she promptly hit the headlines. She was asked in New Mexico: "Your Royal Highness, any word about Princess Diana?" to which she replied "I don't know, you tell me." When told that Princess Diana had given birth to a son and asked for her reaction to this she replied testily: "That's my business, thank you very much." The interview was captured by television cameras and made such a bad impression that Buckingham Palace was moved to take the unusual step of issuing an explanation, that earlier Princess Anne had been *mis*informed that Princess Diana had had her baby and on this occasion she could not be certain that what she was being told was true.

A seasoned follower of Royalty, Dennis Bardens, a correspondent of the Press Association, found Anne's attitude sufficient cause to challenge the princess and in an article he wrote for *Majesty* magazine came as close as anyone has done to giving her a rap on the knuckles. Bardens posed the question: "How comfortable is Princess Anne riding on the Royal roundabout? As the Queen's only daughter there is naturally much interest in the part she plays in Britain's social life and fulfilling State duties. In the Queen's absence, she is Counsellor of State, charged with receiving ambassadors and with reading and signing State papers. Her itinerary of official engagements is one of the most comprehensive in the Royal calendar ... yet she is subject to rather more criticism than other members of her family." Bardens went on to ask if there was any substance to the impression that the press did not give her a fair deal. "The first point that needs making," he wrote, "is that receiving as she does the privileges, the financial support and social status inherent in her rank, she ought not to begrudge to any degree the public interest felt in the Royal family and herself in particular. Putting it simply it goes with the job. No doubt it can be tedious to have to answer questions but the same people who fail to co-operate with the press are the first to grumble if the facts are not published. Princess Anne has had many brushes with the press and has been known to draw upon a vocabulary expressive, explicit and certainly inappropriate or unexpected from such a quarter. I can understand Princess Anne's annoyance (and Captain Mark Phillips's fury) at allegations that their marriage is foundering ... apart from these speculations it seems to me that the press have merely reported what they saw or how witnesses reacted ... there is absolutely no doubt that many Americans recently thought her rude and offhand." Anne could not ignore such reactions which were particularly unfortunate since the US had declared its support for Britain over the Falklands War.

The week before Princess Diana's safe delivery of a son, the British Task Force recaptured Port Stanley, to the relief of the wives and mothers of 6,000 troops who were carried in thirty ships to that tiny outpost of colonialism, and the face of the Queen appeared on every front page, typifying the feelings of those mothers. Her second son Prince Andrew would be returning safe from the war.

On the night of Friday July 9, 1982, an appalling breach of security at Buckingham Palace allowed an incident which, had it been included in the plot of a novel, would have been edited out as too unbelievable. The Queen awoke to find an intruder sitting on her bed.

The Queen pressed the panic button at the side of her bed, but it went unanswered. Michael Fagan meanwhile had smashed a glass ashtray and cut himself, thus dripping blood over the bedclothes.

The Queen spoke to him softly, chatting to gain his confidence, and then, under the pretext of going to fetch him a cigarette, she managed to summon the attention of a footman who detained Fagan while police arrived. Prince Philip was not in the Palace at the time.

The Queen was justifiably furious. Fagan proved harmless. But it might have been a terrorist who broke in ... and there were plenty of them still abroad in London.

The break-in at the Palace was kept secret from the press but not many hours passed before a reporter from the *Sunday Mirror* learned of the story. He took it to the then editor, Bob Edwards, who simply refused to believe it. Edwards was nervous about Royal "exclusives" anyway, after running allegations that, before their marriage, Prince Charles and Lady Diana had met secretly on a parked Royal train, which brought denials in the strongest possible terms from Buckingham Palace. A man in the Queen's *bedroom*? He anguished with his executives, and in the end he refused to run it. It was left to the *Daily Express*, then edited by Christopher Ward, to break the story of the decade.

Less than two weeks later, eleven of the Queen's Household Cavalry were killed by IRA bombs in Hyde Park and Regent's Park; seven horses also died and fifty people suffered alarming injuries. On July 19, the Queen's personal bodyguard, Commander Michael Trestrail of Scotland Yard, resigned after a male prostitute tried to blackmail him. The *Sun* came dashing to the aid of the Queen, to alert her to the errant ways of the man who was in charge of her security.

Princess Anne was in Canada at the time of the Fagan intrusion. She learned of it when her mother telephoned, as she did to all her closest relatives in case they should hear it on the radio. Anne hurried to her mother's side, as soon as her public duties permitted. While the Queen put on her usual brave face, she was deeply affected by the Fagan incident and psychologically the memory of that night would take years to dim from her mind. Princess Anne and the Queen have always been the closest a mother and daughter can be, except perhaps on those occasions when Anne has been in one of her moods. But now they became even closer. The Queen wanted Anne to be the one at her side, and apparently found difficulty in discussing it in any real detail with anyone other than her daughter. In the remaining few days before the Royals began their summer holidays, Anne gave up as much time as she could to stay with the Queen, and joined her as well at the family's summer home at Balmoral.

It was Anne's presence that helped give the Queen her outwardly untroubled attitude; and she would need all the strength and support she could muster as one crisis or another confronted her. Not the least of her concerns was the aftermath of the Falklands War, over which Mrs Thatcher had been heavily criticized by some factions. It had strange echoes from almost thirty years before, when, instead of Mrs Thatcher, the Queen was seeing Anthony Eden twice a week over the Suez crisis. What remained after this war was an inquest which the Queen herself felt was unpleasant, particularly for the many who had lost husbands, boyfriends, or sons. She would have to wait until September before welcoming her own son, Andrew, home.

Some time later, Princess Anne was asked if she found it difficult, as an only daughter, to retain a close relationship with a mother who was also the Queen. Anne replied: "I think you have got the question the wrong way round. It's much more difficult to remember that she is the Queen rather than my mother. After all, I've known her longer as a mother than as Queen, and that's the way I regard her. Only the formalities of our work bring us down to earth."

That year of 1982 had already been one of the busiest and most active in Princess Anne's working life; but in the remaining two months, she would undertake the most extensive, and one of the most dangerous, tours she had ever tackled. The Save the Children Fund would take her to Swaziland, Zimbabwe, Malawi, Kenya, Somalia, Djibouti, North Yemen and, a secondary trip, into the worst of all danger zones, Beirut. It would be a difficult and uncomfortable journey, travelling more than 14,000 miles in three weeks by air, road and boat, through changing temperatures that took her through intense, unrelenting heat, an assortment of insect bites, torrential thunderstorms and alternating dust and mud in central Africa.

She would face a thousand outstretched hands wherever she went, and had to prepare herself for the total contrast of State banquets in the cities she visited with poverty, starvation and disease in the bush.

Those who tried to belittle the princess's efforts, by suggesting that she ignored children waiting in the rain to see her, would soon be overwhelmed by the sheer achievement of that tour, as it unfolded through Africa, a great land of despair. The days were long: up and moving by 7.30 am and often not retiring before midnight. It was as if Princess Anne was saying once again to the trailing pack of pressmen who were having some difficulty keeping up with her action-packed schedule: Stick that in your typewriter and print it. But of course it went beyond that: this was Princess Anne's work. She had found yet another challenge, and nothing had ever made such an impression upon her as the vision of black Africa that was now before her. And above all she was *interested*. "You can always tell when someone is showing a polite, superficial interest," said one of the SCF field organizers in Swaziland. "This is very different. Princess Anne has a deep knowledge of our work. She understands the specific problems in individual countries."

Even if it messed up her time-schedule, she insisted upon hearing all the details of the field work, warts and all. In Swaziland, where polio and typhoid are rife, she visited an immunization centre. She would never forget it. "There we were in the middle of nowhere, no doctor just two nurses and a handyman who is a well-meaning dogsbody," she said later. Anne also went to the Project Zondle which served meals to 14,000 people a day. Her experiences here, in this rather craggy African kingdom, were a dusty foretaste of the remaining days of her tour, in which she would be roughly transported along the miles of potholed, bumpy tracks that led to the charity's various projects in the remotest parts. Before leaving the capital Mbabane, there was a sudden rush of enthusiasm among the press when a Swazi woman revealed that, during a period of mourning for their recently departed King Sobhuza II, whose death at eighty-three left his nation in a state of nervous apprehension, there should be no sexual intercourse permitted for two months. Naturally concerned about this surprising and unexpected little tale to be relayed back to the news desks of Britain, reporters cornered bewildered Swazi girls and showed great interest in their sex lives. It hardly mattered; the story was untrue, anyway. It was a momentary diversion for a tetchy bunch of pressmen who had been manhandled by the overly protective African police and kept at bay by various resident British officials.

Later, as they all moved on to Zimbabwe, the princess agreed to a photocall beside the extremely photogenic Victoria Falls. It was a historic site and a popular one in the Royal family albums. The falls have long-established Royal associations. They are named after Queen Victoria; the Queen Mother (as Queen Elizabeth) was pictured there with her two daughters in 1947, Prince Charles flew over them in 1980 at the time of Zimbabwe's independence. The princess agreed to pose for a few minutes at a given point provided that she could afterwards

113

be given a few moments peace and quiet to relax and take her own photographs unhindered. Wherever she goes in the world, Princess Anne has always taken her own photographs to show to her children.

But even by agreement that "arranged" photocall would not be completed without some animosity creeping in. When Anne duly took her position overlooking the falls, she went to a spot which differed from the one the photographers had agreed with the organizing British officials and, consequently, they went dashing through nearby bush. In the end, the photographers refused to take the picture until Princess Anne moved to the prearranged position, which she did. She stood there, unable to raise the requested smile. After a couple of minutes she asked frostily: "Can I go now ... please?" and then a moment later: "Do I have to move or are you going to?" A voice from the assembled photographers indicated that the choice was hers and she strode away with an exasperated roll of the eyes.

The rancour remained. The press blamed the patronizing attitude of the British officials surrounding the princess. That same day Princess Anne visited the Batonka tribe, one of the most backward and primitive tribes in East Africa. There, apparently, she was offered, as is tradition for honoured guests, a calabash pipe filled for smoking by the Batonka womenfolk. It is the custom that the women and their female guests pass the pipe around. Princess Anne accepted the smouldering, foul-smelling smoking aid though politely declined actually to take a puff at it. That evening, as stories were being written on the verandah of the Victoria Falls Hotel, discussion occurred among reporters as to what the pipe contained; someone alleg-edly in the know suggested that the Batonka women have for centuries grown and smoked their own type of marijuana, known locally as dagga. Indeed, a television crew had already filmed and recorded an intriguing little item of "news" that the princess may have unwittingly been offered a smoke of pot. In humorous vein, reporters as one began to write their own versions of the episode and filed immediately to London. The British officials arrived on the hotel terrace for drinks some time later. At first, the princess's spokesman treated the story with equal humour, but soon the implications began to dawn on him. Soon a native official was wheeled out to confirm that the pipe contained nothing more exciting than locally grown tobacco, quite harmless and unsinister. Once again the wires were hot as reporters rushed to retract their original copy prior to publication.

Then it was back to reality. The following day, in Zimbabwe, the princess came upon a SCF unit where children were so crippled by disease that they pulled themselves along by their fingers, dragging their bodies behind them. From there, the Royal party went to Malawi, and saw a deeply depressing treatment unit for a group stricken by a rabies epidemic. In Somalia, Anne walked through a camp of 40,000 starving refugees. And so it went on. One heart-rending sight after another. By now she had captured the total admiration of the press pack, not to mention the folk back home following the drama of the tour, increasing day by day in its coverage through television and newspapers.

The princess and her entourage had completed only half the schedule when, in early November, she received an urgent communiqué from the Foreign Office in London advising her to abandon the tour and return home immediately. The continuing hostilities between Ethiopia and Somalia were boiling up again and Foreign Office intelligence had warned of possible dangers. She refused point blank. "Damn them, I'm going on," she said. On November 8, she set out on a five-hour drive along dirt tracks to visit the Boroma refugee camp five miles inside the Ethiopian border. Startling, shocking pictures of human suffering, highlighted by her visit, were sent round the world, thus pointing the way to a massive and long-lasting relief effort in which Princess Anne would be followed by many, notably the pop singer Bob Geldof.

As if that wasn't enough, Princess Anne rejected further warnings that she should cancel her visit to Beirut. The day before her arrival, sixty-two people had been killed in a bomb outrage close to the point where she would be travelling. It only gave her further determination. The duration of her visit to the strife-torn capital, where civil war had killed hundreds, was extended by several hours which she spent touring refugee camps, medical centres and some of the worst-hit areas. It was courage indeed, and now Fleet Street was tagging along, open-mouthed and respectful.

Organizers of the Save the Children Fund were delighted with the impact of Anne's tour, as she was herself. Headlines and photographic coverage around the world had alerted a previously unaware public to the plight of the impoverished,

115

disease-ridden conditions under which vast numbers of the population of black Africa were living – and dying. The SCF tills were jingling with contributions and Princess Anne could rightly claim some of the credit. "I think it is fair to say," she admitted in an interview with *The Times*, "that I probably attract slightly more attention than the average." Others would come in her wake and, as famine tightened its grip in Africa, the greatest charitable operation in the history of mankind would be mounted.

The Princess Anne factor had at last come into its own, but Anne rightly predicted that the benefits of her tour would be seen only in the long term. "Achievement is very difficult to pin down. Hopefully it will turn up later when we want to start new projects or other governments ask us to help them when they have got a particular problem in the field in which we specialize." Indeed it would.

The tour enabled her, as President of the Fund, to see what was going on in the field. It also had the effect of giving great heart to those there, on the ground, working for the children in such remote and uninviting parts of Africa. The spin-off was the publicity.

Anne had lost nearly half a stone in weight. Perspiration in the heat was obviously one of the causes. But also she seldom ate a complete meal during the tour; she would pick at her food. Her sole drink for most of the time was Coca-Cola. Back in the bosom of the family, and with Christmas just ahead, Anne was able to recover her health in readiness for a further SCF tour, which was already being planned. Four months later she was off again. In April, accompanied this time by Mark, she paid an official visit to Tokyo to attend a gala performance of the Royal Ballet and other official engagements. On the way back, she stopped off in Pakistan where she toured SCF field hospitals and refugee camps close to the Afghan border. Security was rigid, not just because of the conflicts from which hundreds of mothers and their children were fleeing in Afghanistan; in the week prior to the princess's visit seven of the Fund's workers in Ethiopia had been kidnapped by the Tigrai People's Liberation Front and naturally tension was running high.

The Fund had been providing aid to Pakistan in ever increasing ways since 1980. Now, there were more than two and a half million people in that country alone under their regular

116

care. They draw their health workers mainly from the local communities; in that area of Pakistan at that time, there were 7,000 women who had been trained in basic health and hygiene care to run the Fund local community care programme. Just thirty actual Fund workers ran that vast number of helpers, and Anne was able to see for herself the great logistical problems with which the SCF was confronted.

Anne had attracted worldwide interest to the Third World. She would now be treated with greater respect by the press. But she had not entirely melted the hearts of all her critics. One, for instance, posed the question: "Try and find a photograph of Princess Anne close to a sick or dying child. You won't find one, because there aren't any."

To that criticism, incidentally, Princess Anne has always said "You have to stay remote, otherwise you'd crack up." She has also admitted that she actually isn't too keen on children, and insisted: "You don't have to like them to be interested in their welfare."

Another writer on the tour pointed out that she personally didn't have to suffer too greatly on these trips because there is always good food and water brought in for her even to remote villages. Showers and the creature comforts are always laid on, and she has the best of the transport that is available. Quite often she is rude and uncooperative particularly with media people and the stories are legion among photographers of how badly she treats them.

Clearly, Anne's differences with the press had not been wiped out.

EIGHT

Family Differences

Whereas Princess Anne had been the first television princess, Princess Diana became the first international Royal cover girl. She led the way in fashion, hairstyles and hemlines, stockings with seams, off-the-shoulder ball gowns ... plus a public informality that broke the previous boundaries of Royal mystique. Princess Anne had never been a leader of fashion. Seldom were pictures selected on the basis of what she was wearing; more generally it was because of what she was doing.

Once in Australia, for example, she was criticized for wearing the same dress she had worn on a previous visit four years earlier. "Oh, it's older than that," she replied wearily. Princess Diana on the other hand, could do no wrong. She had been, with the aid of some expert grooming on deportment, public appearances and general presentation, made into the slim-line star of the House of Windsor, outshining everyone – even the Queen, in a different way.

She had also discovered the tensions and pressures of a Very Public Life. Like, Anne, Diana would become painfully aware that public tantrums on the ski-slopes or beside the polo field were doggedly recorded by an ever-faithful band of notetakers. Conferences in national newspaper offices to discuss the day's events would always include any activity which was to be attended by Diana or Anne or both. But Princess Diana had stepped into a vacant Royal role – that of a glamorous young woman around whom the fairy-story could be woven – and, by the merging of fact with fantasy, she arrived at the eye of any camera as a beautifully sculpted dream-princess. Diana came from an aristocratic family outside the mainstream of Royalty; indeed her parents were divorced and both remarried, a fact which fifty years earlier would have totally precluded her as a suitable bride for a future king. Diana had that magical Cinderella touch, denied to both Princess Margaret and Prin-

118

Marje Proops was invited into the Phillips' home for the first fireside chat they granted to a journalist.

A topping gesture at the Olympics. Mark, who had been disappointed by the selectors' decision to cast him in a reserve role, assists his wife (*below left*) with last-minute preparations.

Just another team member: Anne flies out to Montreal on an ordinary economy flight, dressed in the casual uniform of the British contingent.

A face in the crowd: Anne, surrounded by her fellow Olympics-competitors, is pictured taking photographs for the family album. Was she snapping her mother performing the official opening?

With several members of her family anxiously watching, she begins the gruelling cross-country on Goodwill. Hopes turned to disappointment when she had a bad fall. She recovered and courageously completed the course, but was judged to be technically unconscious through concussion.

When the Queen purchased Gatcombe Park for Anne and Mark, fifty MPs tabled a motion deploring this display of "obscene wealth" for a young married couple.

Nowadays Anne and Mark are rarely seen together on official duty. On their way (*right*) to a Thanksgiving Service at St Paul's Cathedral during celebrations for the Queen's Silver Jubilee.

Pregnant with her second child, Princess Anne (*left*) is photographed in a casual off duty moment at Badminton Horse Trials in April 1981, with her son, Master Peter, holding the hand of her personal bodyguard. The scandal of the alleged familiarity by Peter Cross, a former guard, was to cause her pain and embarrassment.

Traditional family group, gathered for the christening of Zara. The photograph, by Lord Lichfield, was issued in conjunction with Princess Anne's thirty-first birthday on August 15, 1981. (Front row: The Queen, Princess Anne with Zara, Mrs Anne Phillips. Back row: Major Peter Phillips, Captain Mark Phillips and Prince Philip.)

The princess lost no time in getting back to sport and work after the birth of Zara. Anne at Burghley (*left*) with Mark. Angela Rippon at Badminton (*right*) with Mark. They were working together on a book when scurrilous rumours of an affair between them hit the press.

During a mammoth African tour for the Save the Children Fund in 1982, Princess Anne poses for cameramen at Victoria Falls. Seconds after this picture was taken, she stormed off after a row with her press attendants.

Nyash Mvaimvai (in wheelchair) presents Anne with a poem called *The Tree*. She was visiting a centre for handicapped children at Jairos Jiri, Zimbabwe, in November 1982.

(*Below*) She inspects a guard of honour in Swaziland. This was the most extensive, arduous and dangerous tour she had yet made on behalf of her beloved Fund, travelling more than 14,000 miles in three weeks, and rounding off the trip with a visit to the danger-zone of Beirut. She returned home a stone lighter.

This photograph received worldwide coverage. Anne's courage in visiting
the suffering rallied unprecedented charitable support among the
international community.

Princess Anne's descriptive vocabulary when dealing with members of the press hit the front pages in April 1982, at Badminton Horse Trials. She implored a group of photographers: "Why don't you Naff Off?" and to make sure they understood her meaning, added: "Shove off! Why don't you grow up?" Later she was all smiles when she beat her husband in the dressage.

At Balmoral (*below*), she is captured in a more coy and charming mood with the Queen at a highland gathering.

cess Anne, who were rather haughty, in keeping with old-fashioned Hanoverian attitudes. This Cinderella also possessed some of the famous Spencer temper and was capable of letting fly verbally, and occasionally with her fists, at her husband. She once told a Canadian reporter that the things the press wrote about her really hurt, sometimes. "I then get the feeling that I don't want to set foot outside the door." The reporter naturally took a note of everything she said and promptly printed it, thus adding to her frustration.

If Diana was looking for advice on how to handle her life at that particular time, she would not look to Princess Anne for any heart-searching guidance. Although they weren't unfriendly towards one another, there was no great show of affection either. Princess Anne, worldly and experienced, for a long time regarded Diana with some indifference. They had nothing in common. Anne was by now the epitome of a professional Royal, who was equally tough in her sport, and could kick and punch with the best of them. She had no time for fools; was impatient with sycophants and hangers-on; refused to mix with the so-called upper-class set and only enjoyed the company of a small group of real friends. Although she enjoyed parties, and would dress up and join the fun on occasions, such as the grand family Christmas gatherings, Anne was not a great attender of society events. Her work and her sport commanded too much of her to fritter the spare hours in the company of flatterers whom she did not wish to be with. She enjoyed relaxing at Gatcombe, or at horsey events, in casual clothes which she couldn't wait to change into after a long round of formalities. Nor did she treat with disdain any of her engagements, though occasionally her staff were given a hard time if the schedules did not run according to plan.

Diana, on the other hand, still loved shopping, carefree young friends and a café society existence. Anne regarded the continuing press adoration of the new princess as a lot of fuss about nothing and there was every indication that it irritated her. Consequently, there was never a great social exchange between Anne and Mark and Charles and Diana. Initially, they seldom got together as a foursome and the latter rarely went as a couple to any of Anne's and Mark's popular and homely barbecues in which Anne excelled as a hostess.

It had also become clear that Diana and Anne differed in their attitude to their respective children. When the Prince of

Wales took his princess to Australia early in 1983, Diana insisted that Prince William should go with them; she simply did not want to be parted from him so soon after his birth. She set a new precedent of not leaving a Royal infant in the care of staff while on an overseas tour, and the attendant publicity, about the two future kings travelling together over such a huge distance, took some weeks to subside. However, the happy family group made tremendous photographic coverage, was warmly welcomed in Australia and went down as one of the most successful Royal visits to that country.

Princess Anne, on the other hand, has always and definitely kept her children in the background. Seldom have they been seen with her when engaged in official duties. Even when she was off on her travels promptly after the birth of Zara, she appeared unconcerned that her children might go for weeks without seeing her. That is not to say she cares for them any less; indeed she undoubtedly tries to compensate for her absences and spends as much time with them as possible. She does not show a great deal of outward affection in public, but she adores them none the less, and they her. That is why Princess Anne tends to treat Gatcombe as her great fortress of homeliness; nowhere else can she be the person she really likes to be: a caring, casual, loving mother and farmer's wife. Both she and her husband agree that their time outside is so dictated by gruelling schedules that at home, in off-duty hours, they relax. Neither are great disciplinarians, but their children have been brought up to the realization that they have to obey orders, as has been demonstrated by an occasional witnessed spanking. As they grew older, Anne impressed upon them that it was her job that separated them so frequently and they understand this. However, when she is away, in remote parts of the world, she 'phones home frequently and sends postcards. Her aides have experienced her wrath when she has been unable to get through on the telephone at the appointed time. She speaks to the children for anything up to half an hour at a time, although when Peter went to boarding school, she – like other mothers – was not encouraged to telephone him during term-times.

Diana has tended to try to keep her little sons away from the huntin', shootin' and fishin' for which Royalty is famous. Diana has never been keen on hunting and doesn't like shooting at all. Anne and Mark, however, have been unapologetic about taking Peter on shoots. At the age of seven, he was pictured wearing earmuffs at a pheasant shoot, and carrying his own toy pistol. His father hurled a recently shot bird towards him and Peter caught it and threw it unconcernedly into the air. Princess Anne, knowing full well the row it could cause among the anti-bloodsports lobby, merely scowled at advancing photographers and said defiantly: "I shall be disappointed if that isn't on the front page tomorrow."

The contrast between Anne and Diana was naturally well detailed in the Continental press. Diana was shown in the women's-interest magazines as a devoted and suffering mother who had regular conflicts with her nursery staff over her desire to have her children with her at all possible times; and Diana with one infant in arms and another curled around her left leg became a familiar sight. But in many walks of life there were increasing numbers of working wives, even one-parent women, who had to face the prospect of leaving their children continually in the care of others. That was the situation chosen by Anne. In consequence Diana became cast, particularly by the French and Italian magazines, simply as a housewife who also had the opportunity because of her Royal status to become an extravagant clothes-horse. It was an interesting contrast: Anne the Worker; Diana the Megastar Royal Mother.

But as one member of the British paparazzi, Mauro Carraro, was heard telling a mystified American reporter: "The British press daren't have a go at Diana yet because she's the darling of the public. But they will, mark my words. They will." Mauro, a master of the long-Tom lens that can capture a Royal indiscretion half a mile away, *was* right, as the state of the Princess of Wales's marriage became an object of unkind and humorous speculation.

For Princess Anne, however, there was at last a new mood of congratulatory respect. James Whitaker, of the *Daily Mirror* and veteran of countless skirmishes with Buckingham Palace and dozens of overseas tours with his quarry, reckons he started the "let's be nice to Anne" vogue simply because he was bored with writing nasty things about her, though in hindsight he might agree that the soothing, massaging hand of someone important at the Palace might also have had something to do with the new attitude. Certainly as that year of 1983 progressed after her African tour and visit to Pakistan, the headlines were favourable. The *Mail on Sunday* published a glowing account of

121

her work under the headline "The Blossoming Princess"; the *Sunday Times* ran a piece which it entitled "The denaffing of Princess Anne", the *Daily Mail* talked of "Anne's Miracle Transformation" and *Woman* magazine recorded "Princess Anne is reaching parts the other Royals don't," noting that the previous year she had travelled officially to eleven foreign countries – including danger zones like Beirut and Northern Ireland – each one packed with official engagements and an overloaded work schedule. At home, she had given twenty-one official audiences of top-level importance; she had attended thirty-six receptions, lunches or banquets; she had officiated at four meetings; and had carried out a further one hundred and seven official visits up and down the country. Apart from that, she was personally involved in the planning arrangements for all her duties and there were many hours of behind-the-scenes work at her suite in Buckingham Palace, answering mail, giving interviews and generally being personally associated with the running of her office.

The *Mail on Sunday* made an interesting observation when, in 1983, she joined her husband on a private visit to Australia. Writer Richard Sears asked: "Is Princess Anne's character that of a chameleon, changing only when she flies abroad? Does she have to escape the establishment restrictions of Britain ... to show she is warm, brave and caring? Must she go to the opposite side of the earth to prove on Australian TV and radio that she has a brain which flashes as quickly as a dragonfly, a droll turn of self-mockery and a sense of humour that makes professional comics happy to fall about?"

Her friends at home had been well aware of these attributes for years, but somehow or other Anne had never managed to get them across to the home-viewing public. It took television personality Michael Parkinson to extract these qualities. She and Mark agreed to appear on his chat show, on the proviso the television company made a £6,000 donation to the Save the Children Fund. The result was a relaxed, witty and intelligent encounter in which even the monosyllabic Mark Phillips came over sensibly. Anne arrived in Australia to the usual refrain of press criticism, that she was wearing an old suit, and looked frumpy. But she was, in truth, in the mood of an over-worked wife on holiday and the Australians soon noticed her carefree and jocular air. At a restaurant in Sydney, she had invited the world-famous entertainer Victor Borge to dine with her and

Mark. During the evening, she was heard singing along. "I love music" she said to Borge, "but I was forced to give up the oboe because my teeth got in the way." Anne collapsed with laughter. Mark yawned. "Wake up," she said prodding him. "Or go and join that man at the other table who is nodding off."

She was cheerful and charming with Parkinson, was co-operative in a radio phone-in, and was almost apologetic when it rained during a picnic and barbecue some friends had arranged for her. "Don't worry," she told them, "we're quite used to getting a little wet and muddy at home." The "new" Anne was so clearly evident to Australian Royal watchers that in Melbourne, Dr Anona Armstrong from the department of psychology at Melbourne University, studied the appearance Princess Anne made on television and came to this conclusion: "She already has charming characteristics. What has happened is that the lack of official duties has brought her real personality to the fore. Behaviour can be influenced by a tendency to imitate people you are with ... so when Anne is on formal engagements she will behave formally, but when she is not on duty she can let herself go."

But the old Anne was still there. She responded to one question about praise for her professionalism, niceness and dedication: "I hadn't noticed I'd undergone a miracle cure. Perhaps the press feel it necessary considering the trips I've done in recent years." Some believe that her new improved image was the result of a heart-to-heart with the Queen a couple of years earlier.

In 1984 her list of official engagements would be increased dramatically to just over five hundred. It would be her busiest year so far in public service and would include six overseas trips. On only one of them would she be accompanied by her husband.

In January she flew to the United States, visiting Houston and New Orleans as president of the British Olympics Association during the run-up to the Olympics that year in Los Angeles. Two weeks later, she was in Yugoslavia for the winter Olympics at Sarajevo. After five days in those cold and icy conditions, she travelled 9,000 miles to the dusty, dry heat of Africa to begin a tour of Morocco, the Gambia and Upper Volta.

In preparation for what was to be her most ambitious tour yet for Save the Children, she had to undergo a series of potentially dangerous injections against meningitis, rabies and hepatitis. The vaccine for hepatitis B is considered by some medical experts to be almost as dangerous as the disease itself. But all the vaccinations were vital as the arrangements would take her to some of the most poverty-stricken regions of the world in what was surely the most risky tour of duty ever undertaken by a member of the Royal family. There was also the unspoken risk of bringing one of those killer diseases back into the heart of the Royal family itself.

The following ten days were packed with sights so horrific, they would be likely to remain in the princess's memory for the rest of her life. The irony of so many of these visits is that they begin with a lavish welcome from the wealthy. Before setting off, the princess dined with the Moroccan Royal family in all their palatial splendour.

In the Allatentu leprosy camp in the Gambia, she touched the withered stump that was once a man's hand and walked among men, women and children, some with no arms, some with no feet, some blind, some who could only crawl in the dust. In Basse Sante Su, she walked through the shanty town where hundreds sleep in the streets and where Save the Children Fund field workers perform up to three hundred operations a day in a dilapidated health centre. On through a four-hour drive over rough roads to a village of mud huts where SCF volunteers run a clinic. The following day in the Upper Volta (now Burkino Faso) there was a certain unreality to it all when she was welcomed to the country at a reception at a local hotel and later, with dinner given by the British Ambassador. Not many miles away, twenty-four hours later she discovered hundreds, perhaps thousands, of starving people in the heart of the country and saw some of the worst sights of her tour. Children, she noted, with old faces who were not long for this world; cattle and livestock with their bones protruding through their skins and vultures hovering above awaiting their downfall. At the hospital in Gorom Gorom, she found emaciated children with pot bellies crawling with insects. The roads ended at that desert town, and the onward journey was rough and ready, by Landrover to the town of Dori three hours' drive away. As she arrived at what the locals called a hospital, three children who had just died of starvation were being laid out. Outstretched hands begged for food. Tears do not do for a princess whose purpose it is to draw attention to the plight of others and to encourage the field workers of the Fund who, in anonymity and adversity, soldier on regardless of a world largely ignorant of their work. That night, unable to sleep through the heat and sheer concern for the awfulness of the situations she had seen, Princess Anne was up before dawn and ready for the next stage of the journey, a three-hour drive to Sebba, which was described as the most desolate village on the tour and then a five-hour trek to a deserted airstrip where she picked up a plane to take her back to Ougadougou.

Officials of the SCF had been amazed and delighted by her stamina, energy and caring, and on her return forty MPs tabled a Commons motion to pay tribute to her courage. Even old adversaries in Fleet Street were moved to a warming display of congratulation, best summed up, perhaps, by Jean Rook in the *Daily Express* who likened her to a "latter day Florence Nightingale, Curie, Queen Victoria or a member of the SAS".

What Princess Anne had now successfully achieved was virtually unknown in the traditions of Royalty. Her visits to these deprived areas of the world were made in her capacity as a working President of the SCF, and her Royal status took second place. It hardly mattered to those she was visiting anyway, because few in darkest Africa really knew who she was, and even some of the locally recruited volunteers working for the Fund were merely aware that she was someone of importance. Rank and status, she observed on her return, mattered little. What was important from the Fund's point of view was that her Royal position often gave her immediate entrée to presidents and other government heads who might never be persuaded to discuss their country's problems with mere working members of the SCF. In the Upper Volta, for instance, she discovered no less than eighty relief agencies at work in varying ways, and so it was important to bring the SCF efforts to public attention. She was well versed in all aspects of the Fund's work in most of the regions of the world where it operates.

She could talk to the people with influence, demonstrating a knowledge acquired from experience. Princess Anne could hold forth on the difficulties of distributing powdered milk; on how mothers using it could not be expected to know how much to give their babies; on how to educate people not to mix it in polluted water. She could talk about the importance of village

125

food banks, or water schemes, or the need for locally trained health workers. And at the same time, she was able to co-ordinate other support, such as aid from the National Union of Townswomen's Guilds of which she is patron. Above all, the publicity surrounding her efforts for the Fund sparked off community action in Britain, quite spontaneously. Shortly after her return from Africa, she received a cheque from two school-boys who had cycled from Land's End to John O' Groats.

The Anne Bandwagon was rolling for the Save the Children Fund and, at their London headquarters, thankful Fund officials gleefully weighed the ever-mounting bundle of press cuttings. Communities were responding well with help. The Fund would build on its success; and for the princess that could only mean more work and more time, which she was happy to provide.

By now, Princess Anne had acquired a formidable list of organ-izations with which she was personally connected. For instance, she was Colonel in Chief of eleven British, Canadian, Australian and New Zealand Regiments; she was President of the British Olympics Association; Patron of the Riding for the Disabled Association; Chancellor of the University of London; President of the British Academy of Film and Television Arts and the St John's Ambulance Brigade, and Commandant in Chief of the WRNS. She held a position of one kind or another with seventy-five organizations, each expecting and usually receiv-ing individual attention.

To handle the ever-mounting workload, she had a per-manent staff of four at Buckingham Palace to organize her crowded calendar. Their salaries came out of the Civil List allowance which had increased to £120,000 a year.

Each day brought a new round of meetings. In one mem-orable quote to a visitor to her office she recorded, "You are the 139th person I have met today." The office staff who deal with her arrangements, correspondence and tour organizations are in constant touch with Anne herself. She has the final word on everything, and holds regular planning conferences to be sure she knows what is expected of her. Often there is research to be done for her speeches. She likes to have a general knowl-edge of any particular situation she will be confronted with.

She does not, however, always link names and faces, as the stars of a famous TV soap opera, *Coronation Street*, discovered when she asked unashamedly "And who are you?" (She apologized later: "I haven't got the time to watch a lot of television.")

She has three detectives, who work in shifts round the clock to maintain a guard, and one sleeps under the same roof as the princess wherever she might be. There is also a panel of six ladies-in-waiting, selected for their cheerfulness, companionship and organizing ability, from whom a choice is made for one, or sometimes two, to accompany her. Again, several women are necessary to keep up with Anne, and their duties for the following day's activities begin on the afternoon of the previous day, when they read themselves in to the programme ahead. Their hours are long, often starting at dawn to supervise preparations, and ending when the princess has retired, perhaps after midnight. The following day, the "duty" lady-in-waiting is required to write "thank you letters" to the previous day's hosts. All, at sometime or another, have to face the temper, tantrums and tears of their boss, but the job is certainly not without its lighter moments and the amusement is usually sparked by Princess Anne's deadpan sense of humour. Once when they had landed in Africa and were about to be confronted by a guard of honour, Anne whispered to her lady-in-waiting: "Good God, his flies are undone," and they both had to bite their lips to stop bursting into laughter as Anne inspected the men. Of her ladies, Anne is specific in her requirements. "They must be good at chatting, and making people feel at ease, which helps me really. It's no good if you get someone turning up in the morning looking like death, ratty and bored. That's no help at all. So it is important that they should be capable of being interested in the people we meet." The people they meet, Anne is quick to remind her travelling companions, have perhaps been planning her visit for months; what she consistently tries to do, sometimes with difficulty, is to put on a show of individuality so that organizations or groups she visits are left feeling that she actually *was* interested and only they matter.

Apart from the pure logistics of arranging her diary so that she can attend three or four "bookings" in one day, there is also the transport to organize. Quite often, Anne will drive herself, or is driven by her detective in her personal car. On other more formal occasions, there is a chauffeur-driven limousine at her disposal. For longer journeys, a helicopter is brought into service and for overseas trips, within range and where

127

scheduled air services are not suitable, aircraft of the Queen's Flight are available. Because of the amount of travelling she undertakes, she is a frequent and popular user of the Queen's Flight. That prerogative does not come as a right. The use of the Queen's aircraft is strictly monitored by the Queen herself; if Princess Anne's staff require to book the use of a helicopter or 'plane, it has to be done officially through the Secretary to the Queen's Flight. The Royal "batting order" is brought into play if there is overbooking, and in those cases junior members of the family have to make alternative arrangements. The Royal aircraft, particularly those for longer journeys, are fitted out to make travelling less wearisome; and since they usually carry few passengers there is plenty of room for manoeuvre. Quite often it is necessary for a member of her staff to go on ahead of the princess. On tours for example, all accommodation is checked, as are the people who will be presented; right down to personal details such as a private rest room for the Royal visitor wherever she stops. Not the least of the concerns for Palace staff these days is the question of security, and the checks that have to be made in that area provide a continual headache for the Royal Protection Squad.

Anne's programme is carefully mapped out and her personal arrangements well taken care of. But things can go wrong. On a cold day, for example, she was due to take a helicopter and then a 'plane to attend the re-dedication ceremony of the frigate HMS *Amazon* in Devonport. With the snow falling heavily, the helicopter which was to have landed at her own pad in Gatcombe Park was ruled out and Anne was urged to consider cancelling. "No," she insisted. "We'll drive." And at the wheel of her Reliant Scimitar and with her detective in the passenger seat, she set off from Gatcombe just before it was cut off by snow drifts. She drove twenty-five miles to RAF Lyneham, Wiltshire, in appalling conditions, to board an Andover of the Queen's Flight to Exeter. "What sort of transport have we got?" asked Anne upon arrival at the airport. The helicopter from there to Devonport had also been cancelled and, with her own approval, a police Range Rover drove up to take her through the snow to Devonport, where she arrived at the local drill hall just twenty minutes late. The *Amazon*'s Commander John Ellis, announcing her arrival, pointed out that the princess would have called a sleigh into service had it been necessary. Anne has many fans among the top brass in the services, as well as the men in the ranks, and tries to visit the British Regiments she is connected with at least once a year.

Three weeks later, she was back among service people, whose hospitality and enthusiasm for her presence she always enjoys. It also gives her a chance to mess about with the Army hardware: firing new guns or driving a heavy duty transporter. On this trip to Germany, she was visiting the 14/20th King's Hussars of which she is C-in-C. And once again she was soon at the wheel of their newest "toy". Wearing a specially tailored khaki suit, she was shown directly to the driving seat of a 750-horse-power Chieftain tank, and with a look of sheer pleasure roared off across the North German plains.

By the middle of 1984, it seemed that all the good things to say about Princess Anne had been exhausted. Princess Diana was waiting, in privacy, for the birth of her second child, expected in September, and the spotlight was once again turned upon Anne and Mark and that good old chestnut, the state of their marriage. It couldn't have come at a worse time for either of them. Things were actually rather strained, as it was, largely through pressure of work. For the first few months of the year, as we have seen, Anne was up to her eyes in engagements. Mark was similarly busy with his horses and the work on the farm. In July, Princess Anne had travelled to America for a short round of engagements in the dual role of President of the British Olympics Association and President of the British Academy of Film and Television Arts. Ironically, the story broke on the day she was in Hollywood meeting two other famous adorners of front pages, whose various marriages have provided ample tabloid scope: Elizabeth Taylor and Joan Collins.

Harry Arnold's front page story in the *Sun* sounded convincingly authentic when he wrote: "Princess Anne's marriage to Captain Mark Phillips is causing deep concern to the Queen and Prince Philip. The gulf in the couple's marriage has now widened to the point where they lead separate lives. The Queen sympathizes with the fact that her daughter and son-in-law are bound together by a loveless union ... but has ruled they must keep up appearances in public." The basis for this latest allegation seemed to be the fact that when they both visited Los Angeles later that month for the Olympics, *they would be staying in separate hotel rooms*, Anne at the Huntingdon Sheraton in Pasadena, Mark thirty miles away at the Holiday Inn in Hollywood. Buckingham Palace refused to be drawn into the scandal-mongering and Mark Phillips took the unusual step of answering press inquiries himself; he angrily explained the reason for separate rooms. It was simply that both he and his wife were involved in busy separate schedules. She had her work and he had been hired by Channel Ten of Australia to join their commentating team covering the Olympics. Under the terms of his contract, Mark pointed out, he would have to stay in the same hotel as the rest of the twenty-eight-strong team. Meanwhile, most of Princess Anne's engagements were centred around another part of Los Angeles and, as Mark insisted, anyone who knows the appalling traffic situation in the great urban sprawl of Los Angeles would know that a joint hotel arrangement would be hardly feasible. For the record, Mark said that it was "absolute nonsense" to talk of a marriage split and his mother, when questioned, said waspishly: "It makes me dreadfully angry. Why don't people just leave them alone. They are a happy couple really." But it didn't end there. When Princess Anne arrived back in London, to the renewed interest of cameramen, it was now being claimed the Queen herself had intervened and "ordered" the couple to put on a show of togetherness. Sure enough, Mark was at his wife's side for her next three engagements and an air of tetchiness between them was noted when Captain Phillips got lost in the crowd at the Berkeley Square ball which brought the reported response from his wife when he eventually found her: "Where the hell have you been?" It was also noted by certain scribes that Princess Anne did not dance with her husband once and, when they left at 1am, she went to her apartment in Buckingham Palace and he made the long drive back to Gatcombe Park.

Princess Margaret added further to the increasing blur between fact and fiction when it was announced she was to make a once-only appearance on the radio soap opera, *The Archers*, playing herself. Meanwhile, Prince Andrew showed his anger to the press when he, too, went to Los Angeles. He sprayed a crowd of cameramen with white paint, causing considerable damage to equipment and clothes. Buckingham Palace accepted claims for compensation and paid up without a murmur. What got totally obliterated in the continued publicity about her private life was the real reason why Anne had gone to America in the first place at the beginning of July. In a four-day tour, covering 14,000 miles, she attended twenty-four fund-raising events on behalf of the British Olympics Association which brought in more than £35,000 in donations. In Texas, for example, rich oil men paid up to $1,500 a head at a dinner where Anne was guest of honour. One billionaire pushed forward to tell her personally: "This evening has cost me $20,000 but honey you're worth every red cent." The praise heaped upon her by the British athletes was largely unreported, as was her extremely effective support for the British film industry whose most recent efforts were bolstered by Anne's arrival in Hollywood wearing her other hat as president of BAFTA. Reginald Collin, BAFTA's director, with Anne on that trip, recalled: "You should have seen her promoting British films and television. On one day, we started out at 8 am and finished at 1 am the next morning. That was seventeen hours, eight engagements and two speeches. When I tried to sit down for a couple of minutes she'd say. 'What! You're not getting tired, surely?'"

When Anne came back to the film city for the Olympics proper a couple of weeks later, the eyes of the world, through the media, would be upon her for all the wrong reasons. Britain's star decathlon gold medallist, Daley Thompson, didn't help an already delicate situation by his off-the-cuff jesting in front of worldwide television cameras. Having appeared wearing a T-shirt emblazoned with the question: "Is the world's second best athlete really gay?" he was questioned about a conversation with Princess Anne. Daley said: "She told me I was a damned good-looking guy," but quickly added: "That was a joke." And when asked if there was a woman in his life with whom he would like to have babies, he said: "You have already mentioned the lady and I hope the children are white." Not content with that piece of alleged jocularity, Daley then answered, when asked if he was surprised that Princess Anne went to talk to him, "Not when you are as close as we are." Press uproar followed. The *Daily Mirror* said Daley scored a gold for being the greatest athlete in the world and a lead balloon for his "stupid wisecracks". A hasty conference of the British Olympic officials was called to consider sending Thompson back to Britain in disgrace; but Princess Anne stepped in to save the day and insist she was not offended by his comments. Palace press secretary, Michael Shea, prepared an immediate statement that "Princess Anne wants to make it clear that she finds it totally and absolutely absurd that anyone should think anything said by Daley Thompson after his brilliantly outstanding achievement was offensive in any way." Privately, however, after almost a month of batting off inquiries about the Phillips's private life, Shea would have preferred Mr Thompson to have kept his mouth firmly shut. It was left to the controversial runner, Zola Budd, to record the feelings of some of her fellow competitors when she wrote in a newspaper article: "Today I met Princess Anne; what a lovely person she is. I always thought Royalty would be a bit remote but she was so friendly. She spent all morning with the athletes and officials ... she also spent time with us at the house where we are staying, ate with us and even came to the training track with us. I had a long talk with her ... she was telling me about her own Olympic experiences; she knew exactly how we are all feeling at the moment and the excitement and worry. She promised me all that is forgotten once the moment of competition starts ... it was like meeting someone you have known for years, rather than a member of the Royal family."

That line of Zola's – "someone you have known for years" – is a telling summary of what has happened to the British Royal family during the course of the Queen's reign. The lives of the most active Royals have become an open book. In bringing forward to public view the human face of the Royal family, which the Queen set out purposefully to do, the appeal of a centuries-old Monarchy has suddenly accelerated, as its very popularity ran out of control.

In the 1950s and early 1960s, the Monarchy took on a rather boring tone. It has been refurbished, in a more human way, but without taking into account advances in world technology – such as instant colour television that could bring the Royal family into everyone's homes at the flick of a switch, the effect of the Fleet Street circulation wars, and the addiction of the public to Royal stories. During the early 1970s, the Palace press department seemed able to contain the flow of detail about the daily lives of the Royals. Then the scandals surrounding Princess Margaret and the trials and tribulations of Princess Anne changed all that. Past constraints and the tiresome observation of politeness and protocol in dealing with the Royal family were finally and completely dispensed with by the bottom end of the media. The family, which had made itself into a fascinating saga, would find the pressures increasing, although (as John Pearson rightly perceives in *The Ultimate Family*) many of its members have proved surprisingly accomplished actors in the designated roles, increasingly assured in the modern art of self-projection.

In September 1984, Prince Henry (Harry) Charles Albert David, second son of the Prince and Princess of Wales, was born at St Mary's Hospital, Paddington. When she'd had Prince William, Diana had left the hospital looking tired and dishevelled. Now her exit was a carefully stage-managed affair for which a Hollywood producer could not have written a better scene. She spent hardly any time at all in the maternity wing once the baby had arrived, and emerged on the hospital steps looking radiant and immaculate, dressed in red. Every woman in the land who had had a baby, and most of those who hadn't, marvelled at her appearance, her confidence and her glowing beauty. She looked like the Holy Mother, to be captured on celluloid a thousand times and flashed in marvellous natural colour in hundreds of millions of homes that night.

But, behind the scenes, there were rumblings that the Palace press office chief, Michael Shea, knew – and warned – might spoil the show. The date of the christening was, like all Palace events, arranged well in advance to avoid clashes with any public duties that members of the Royal family might have. Everyone was *well aware* weeks before that the christening had been fixed for December. Michael Shea was therefore horrified to discover that Anne and Mark Phillips had arranged a shooting party at Gatcombe for the same day, and were steadfastly refusing to cancel it. He knew there were already stories filtering through of Princess Anne's jealousy of Princess Diana. Indeed, it was not without some significance that neither Princess Anne nor Mark Phillips had been asked to be a godparent to Diana's children. All kinds of excuses were subsequently proffered to explain their absence from the christening, but they had taken the view that, if they weren't to be godparents, there was no point in their attending. The Queen was told, the shoot went ahead, and Princess Anne sent her two children to the christening with the nanny.

It was only after the resulting publicity that the Queen apparently gave them all a talking-to. A few weeks later, there was a public "reconciliation", once again with the hand of Shea somewhere in the background to make sure that the cameras were present to record the declaration of peace. The Prince and Princess of Wales and Princess Anne and Captain Phillips would be seen chatting together in great accord in a hostelry near Highgrove. And so ended another exciting episode.

It wasn't only Anne who could become impatient with Princess Diana. Both Prince Philip and Princess Margaret were enraged that she chose the solemn occasion of the State Opening of Parliament to show off her new hairstyle, which had never before seen by her audience, and had been carefully coiffured by Kevin Shanley (who incidentally was subsequently sacked as a Royal hairdresser for selling "The Secrets of Diana's Hairstylist" to the *Sunday Mirror* for an eight-week serialization for £50,000). The new Diana look was so stunning that she completely stole the show. All eyes were on the princess, when they should have been looking at the Queen as she performed her ancient ritual before the joint Houses of Her Majesty's Government, which she does with all the finery, pomp and severity that befits such an important Royal duty.

NINE

Hurtful Allegations

Rumours of intrigues and rows surrounding various members of the Royal family as well as the IRA bombing of the Conservative Party conference at Brighton, virtually submerged Princess Anne's next important trip for the Save the Children Fund which would take her to India and Bangladesh. Press interest only came alive after the assassination of the Indian Prime Minister Mrs Indira Gandhi.

Princess Anne had arrived in Bangladesh to discover that the past work of her charity was already taking shape. The immediate effect of her presence brought joy to the local official of the Fund who had been negotiating for the building of a new nutritional centre for which they were being asked £200,000. No amount of pleading had been able to cut the amount to a more manageable figure. The day after Princess Anne arrived, the cost was reduced to £40,000. She also saw the results of the British connection at work in Bangladesh where her Townswomen's Guild donations of £750,000 were being put to use for the building of other much needed health centres. Further, she was able to see volunteer helpers from the staff of British Airways, pilots and stewardesses who had adopted an orphanage there. Some of the pilots were knee deep in human excreta digging latrines, while stewardesses were painting walls.

In some of the areas she had visited, there had been no rain for ten years and the people were dying of starvation through harvest failure, but the reverse was the case in Bangladesh, where the monsoon had burst the banks of the Jamuna river, devastating local life and killing hundreds. In these areas, the SCF aid was just as desperately needed as in the dust plains of Africa. On Wednesday, October 31, the princess was heading into the foothills of the Himalayas on a dangerous drive to a school for Tibetan refugees when rumours began of a tragedy

135

in Delhi. Later that night, one of the party approached her with the news, whispering as in fear of being overheard, that Mrs Gandhi had been murdered. In London there were hasty consultations between the Foreign Office and Buckingham Palace on the question of whether Princess Anne should be brought back from the volatile area immediately.

Foreign Office officials rightly predicted that there would be widespread violence and reprisals against the Sikh community who were held responsible for Mrs Gandhi's killing by Sikh members of her own bodyguard who had fired thirty-seven bullets at her. Anne still had eleven days of her tour left but it was agreed that it could not continue. She was flown to the Indian capital for the funeral. She represented the Queen, and had to borrow suitable clothes from British Embassy staff since on this occasion no mourning dress or hats had been packed in her luggage. She joined Prime Minister Margaret Thatcher and other heads of State at the funeral pyre, where she would remain until Mrs Gandhi's son, Rajiv, raked through the ashes. Three hours later she was being flown home to safety aboard an Andover of the Queen's Flight, perhaps contemplating the apparent ease with which world figures, such as Mrs Gandhi and Lord Louis Mountbatten, were dispatched from this earth.

Behind her, she left a seething press corps who would long remember the Indian trip for other reasons than Mrs Gandhi's murder. When the princess's tour was abandoned, reporters and photographers began making their way to the local airport in a minibus, hoping to get to Delhi. On the way, their Indian driver suddenly stopped their vehicle, got out and ran away. James Whitaker, of the *Mirror* recalls: "It was, without exaggeration, a life or death scene. There was every chance that if we had been left up country, we would have been seriously injured by marauding Indians who had lost control following the assassination." Another reporter, Steve Lynas, flagged down the Royal convoy and asked if the press could travel to Delhi in the Royal plane. The answer was a firm No. The princess's lady-in-waiting, Shan Legge-Bourke, intervened: "You can't leave them here, especially the girls," and eventually she secured the use of one of the Royal party Range Rovers to take the journalists on to Delhi. Whitaker adds: "While we were begging and arguing, the princess just sat there, taking no notice whatsoever, oblivious to our plight." And another encounter ended in acrimony.

136

Before she left, Anne promised her SCF workers that she would return as soon as possible to continue the tour. In the meantime she was lured to the Middle East where oil-rich Arabs with millions in small change wanted a touch of class for an equestrian circus. They promised her a rather miserly £20,000-donation to the Fund if she would take part in the show at Dubai and Abu Dhabi. It would not have been politic to refuse or offend, though Anne insisted that Mark Phillips should be invited, too. The Arabs were pleased and Mark was paid £11,500 to co-star with her in a horsey extravaganza that made the Arabs' donation to the SCF look like peanuts.

For Anne and Mark it would be a welcome opportunity for a few days of togetherness. It was the first overseas engagement on which Mark had accompanied her for almost eighteen months. After weeks apart, through his work commitments in Australia and New Zealand and her traumatic Indian adventure, they were virtually inseparable. A luxurious guest palace had been laid on for Anne but she insisted on remaining with her husband who had been allotted accommodation at a local hotel, which required some delicate negotiations by her staff to avoid causing offence to the hosts.

When it came to the equestrian events, Anne and Mark discovered that the Arabs, for whom horsemanship is treated with pride and importance, earnestly expected a competitive show to excite the sheiks and sultans of Saudi Arabia. The seriousness of the event became clear to Princess Anne when she learned that a Dubai hotelier, Khalaf Al Habtoor, had spent £50,000 to buy five horses to ship to the Gulf especially for Anne to ride. But, the obvious dripping and drooling wealth of the place must have been a stark, if not positively obscene, contrast to the Bangladesh she had not long left. On their arrival, Anne and Mark were assigned a £130,000 stretched golden Rolls Royce with six doors for the duration of their visit; there were three extraordinary banquets and three lavish lunches laid on, with food and flunkeys everywhere. At the horse show, they found the dignitaries lounging on huge sofas laid out under awnings to shield them from the sun, and where Princess Anne took her place of honour beside an Arabian prince, Sheik Hasher Maktoum, while Mark joined a parade of saluting competitors. The opening ceremony had all the trappings of a mini-Olympic Games as parachutists from the United Arab Emirates floated down to earth in front of them, to the strange out-of-place sounds of brass bands and pipe music.

Anne acquitted herself well in the riding and won a silver cup in the dressage. She certainly earned the fee. For as Mark noted, the horses brought over for the event were both untried and unfamiliar to them. Mark was openly nervous at times as he watched his wife take her place in the arena. In the wings, he was whispering encouragement and, when she had done her stuff, she rode directly to his side to hear his comments on her ride. It matters to them both that they constructively criticize each other's performances.

Anne must have thought she had sold herself short for £20,000 for the Fund. It was also British Week in Dubai and a hastily assembled list of engagements was put together for Anne to attend, with Mark constantly at her side. On the final day, she called on the president of the UAE, Sheik Zayed, who was holding court at a local palace of some opulence. He pressed the princess to remain a while in his country which seldom saw British Royalty. "I will call your mother," he told her, "and ask her if you can stay longer." Anne, not wishing to offend, said: "It is not as simple as that . . ." The sheik replied "I will only let you go if you promise to come back." Anne promised, but could not promise when.

First, she had a more pressing promise to fulfil, which was to return to the land of poverty she was forced to desert so rapidly when Mrs Gandhi fell to the gunfire. And, in her life of contrasts, here was another one. In February she flew to Calcutta, where she saw with her own eyes some of the world's worst urban poverty, the "city of dreadful night", according to Kipling, and now the territory of Mother Teresa. From there she went to Orissa, one of India's poorest states where the SCF operates a sterilization clinic, and on into remoter areas where the Fund runs hostels for migratory tribal children. She is very supportive of the field workers and, when she sees a project that requires cash, she knocks on doors when she gets back home until she gets it. She is now able to converse with the SCF doctors and nurses and local volunteers in a manner which shows a great knowledge of many relevant subjects and, from her travels she can now boast, though she never would, that she has become something of an authority on the Third World. She is good at raising local morale, gingering the less-caring of politicians. Those doctors who have never met her and who talk down in a patronizing way about their work soon discover they are conversing with someone who knows as much about the Fund's problems as they do. Once she was asked if she would ever consider a full-time career with the Save the Children Fund. "I have actually thought about it," she admitted, "but I think really I would only last about a year. What I saw, for instance, in Upper Volta made me realize I would not have the stamina to do it for much longer than that." Fund organizers saw her usefulness in other directions. While in India, Princess Anne personally received an anonymous gift of £50,000 and in a few short weeks she had secured £70,000, enough to buy some badly needed relief and finance long-term projects in India and Bangladesh. What she brings in is clear profit. The princess costs the Fund nothing as President; her lengthy overseas excursions are funded through the Foreign Office which pays the basic costs provided the princess undertakes a number of official engagements en route, such as calling upon statesmen or joining an export drive on behalf of British industry. Some of the organizational costs still have to be met from the princess's Civil List allowance. Because of the Foreign Office contribution to finances, locally based diplomats occasionally try to dictate to the SCF where money should be directed in their areas, or what the princess should be shown. The Fund has become past-master at tactfully rejecting this attempted interference, and where tact fails Anne herself steps in.

Her stamina, physical fitness and capacity for carrying on where others are ready to rest have now become legend among Fund workers who have accompanied her regularly, though she does occasionally groan at the thought of attending an official banquet or function, where few of the guests speak English, and which after a heavy day of rough travelling might well prove to be totally unproductive. She does not work hard because she feels simply that she has something to prove; she has done that. Anne is ever aware of her father's edict that the Royal Family must be seen to be earning its keep; further, she has herself used the example of Princess Margaret who never sought to be a "career" Royal, settled more for the niceties of life and suffered great unhappiness as a result.

The SCF is well aware of the princess's value. No charity, they appreciate, could afford the advertising and publicity that accompanies her involvement. If she were a figure-head princess, just along for the ride, it would not be the same. According to one senior Fund official, apart from the recent phenomenon of the pop star Bob Geldof, she had become the best-known charity head in the world.

Anne was full of praise for Geldof who had just swept through Africa rattling the conscience of the western world to the plight of the starving in Ethiopia. There was a mammoth response to Michael Buerk's tragic BBC film. Geldof's incredible and unprecedented fund-raising, through Band Aid, Sports Aid and a variety of spin-off activities, was an operation which, by its very nature, would be difficult to repeat. As *The Times* noted in a comparison, Princess Anne was "less mercurial, but a steadier and no less stern breeze who is likely to be blowing brisk resolve into the Save the Children Fund long after Geldof has returned to full time rockery". Further, Geldof had also discovered the great hurdles of bureaucracy, corruption and politics that confront any major charity effort in these parts; he was able to break down the barriers, temporarily at least, through his avalanche of world-wide publicity and anger. The SCF, meanwhile, had to consider the *long term*.

No sooner had Anne returned from India than plans were already in hand for another great tour of some of the worst areas of Africa in a trip that would take her to Tanzania, Mozambique, Zambia and end up in the remote refugee camps in the border regions of Sudan. She would also head-up in London a series of seminars on "Prospects for Africa", which would involve politicians, academics and representatives of other major charities in an attempt to co-ordinate thought and deed in tackling the great problems which Geldof and Buerk had brought, through the medium of television, into the living rooms of a slumbering public. Now her work was receiving the acclaim deserved. Edward Heath summed it up for the author thus: "She has shown herself to be one of the most active Royal patrons of all time, tireless in travel, fearless in facing hazards in countries overseas which are often starved by drought or riddled with disease, and uninhibited in showing understanding of children's problems wherever she finds them."

Princess Anne continued to utilize her public engagements in Britain to further the cause, wherever she could. While addressing a conference of freight operators at Brighton, for example, she moved quickly into the role of charity collector and obtained donations of services from a world-wide courier company who promised to deliver medicines to any SCF project anywhere in the world free of charge. At a conference of tax officials, she was able to extract a substantial donation from the Inland Revenue Staff Federation, and only nine of the 700 present walked out in protest at her presence.

One of Princess Anne's long-standing interests has been the Riding for the Disabled Association which has benefited substantially from her patronage over the years.

On St George's Day, 1985, she made her début in horse-racing when she decided to ride at Epsom at a meeting in aid of the RDA. She had been showing an increasingly competitive interest in race-riding for some months, and had been riding out, at stables owned by David Nicholson, a neighbour in Gloucestershire whom she had known for some years and who had ridden steeplechasers for the Queen Mother.

Other friends, such as Virginia Holgate and Maureen Piggott, joined her in the race on April 22. She took Nicholson's huge bay colt, Against the Grain, and finished fourth. It gave her a taste for another area of riding in which she had yet to prove herself and, before long, racegoers at Goodwood were surprised when the unnamed jockey riding Little Sloop in the 3.25 was revealed, twenty minutes before the off, to be Princess Anne. She started at eight to one and finished sixth out of seventeen runners. Nicholson was delighted with her performance and, as we now know, it was the start of a new career which would receive praise from all quarters of the sport, including such critical and witty observers as the writer and racing enthusiast, my friend and ex-colleague, Jeffrey Bernard, who described her as looking extremely comfortable in the saddle of a racehorse, more comfortable in fact than most people look in an armchair. Mark Phillips was apparently also pleased with his wife's switch from the more demanding sport of eventing. As she headed towards forty, it would become a matter for speculation among her horsey friends as to just how long she would continue to flirt with danger and the dramatic falls she had encountered on the obstacle courses. Mark summed up his feelings, with which his wife did not necessarily agree: "I think women who have had a baby become less courageous as riders. I've noticed it before." Did that include Princess Anne? "She's a woman isn't she?" said Mark, pointedly. But when she emerged the following year to become a

141

major competitor in flat-racing, he would be there on the sidelines giving the support which she always sought from him.

For many months, there had been bubbling under the surface in Fleet Street the story which, in the words of one Royal reporter, was "waiting to be written". It broke in huge headline type in the *News of the World* on Sunday, September 15, when Princess Anne was due to appear in a cross-country ride at Badminton to raise cash for the Riding for the Disabled Association. Anne might well have preferred to have stayed in the confines of Gatcombe Park that morning. In true style, she ignored what she knew would be whispered gossip behind her back and carried on with her commitments.

Out in the open for the first time were the allegations which her former bodyguard and ex-sergeant in the Royal Protection Squad, Peter Cross, aged thirty-seven, had been touting around newspaper offices for the past three years. Cross, it will be recalled, had been attached to Anne's entourage as one of her personal detectives towards the end of 1979 and had remained on that posting until September 1980, when he was suddenly removed and sent back to a uniformed job in ordinary police work at Croydon. He finally left the police force January 1981, and went to work for an insurance firm in London. A year or so later, he first began to try to sell his story. He claimed that he had been sacked from his job because of a "special relationship" he'd had with Princess Anne, and he approached both the *Sun* and the *Daily Star*. His asking price was £600,000 but there were no takers.

In the meantime, Cross, a married man who lived with his wife Linda and their two children, had started an affair with a girl named Gillian Nicholls who worked with him in the insurance company. According to his wife, it was not the first time he had indulged in extramarital relations during their marriage, nor would it be the last. Mrs Cross eventually asked him to leave, and they were subsequently divorced. Miss Nicholls was by now living with Cross in Farnborough, but in August 1985, instead of marrying Miss Nicholls, the ex-policeman ditched her and secretly married his latest love, one Angie Plant, a dental nurse. Where women were concerned, it had become clear to all who knew him that Mr Cross possessed a certain lustfulness for which he could not be trusted. One way or another, a disgruntled Miss Nicholls found herself in

the offices of the *News of the World* where she was being offered
a fair degree of recompense for spilling the beans, and out came
the story: "Jilted lover tells for the first time about The Princess
and The Royal Minder."

The story was being told *not* by Cross, but by his ex-girlfriend,
and in this way the *News of the World* could put a toe in the
water and test the reaction without too much fear of castigation
for running the confessions of Cross himself. Miss Nicholls
claimed Cross *had told her* that he kept up an "amazing secret
friendship with Princess Anne" for almost two years after he
had left her service; that she telephoned him regularly at the
insurance office and that she had, for example, telephoned him
on the night her daughter Zara was born.

The jilted lover went on to make extensive claims that Princess Anne telephoned their office regularly, using the name Mrs
Wallis, that she met Cross for tea at Gatcombe Park and
elsewhere, and that Cross was in love with her. On some
occasions Cross was on the telephone to the princess for an
hour. Of course, all hell broke loose among the tabloids as the
author himself well recalls, being Night Editor of the *Daily
Mirror* at the time. The *Star* and the *Sun* both told how they
had been offered Cross's story but had refused to pay his price.
Reporters from both newspapers reckoned Cross had gone into
detail about the "relationship" which had developed because
he was gentle and caring; but some of the things he told them
were unprintable, even allowing for bad taste. There was a
week of follow-ups and other speculation until the following
Sunday when the *News of the World* did it again. They repeated
all the allegations made by Miss Nicholls but, this time, it was
Peter Cross himself who had "decided to come out into the
open". Using an expression well known to writers of such series,
Mr Cross now wanted "to put the record straight" and for the
next three weeks that newspaper's readers would be able to
discover how he would set about that task, bearing in mind the
massive coverage the story had already received. He began: "I
well remember the first evening Princess Anne and I began to
confide our real problems to each other ..."

The "evidence" was all rather one-sided, based largely on
Cross's own account of what took place (or didn't), and the
only corroboration came from his wife and girlfriend recalling
what Cross had told them, although confirming that Anne had
telephoned. But nothing that was published during those weeks

proved that Princess Anne's "special relationship" with him was anything more than that of an extremely busy woman who at times felt very lonely and depressed because of the pressures and solo nature of her work, and who was also capable of finding charm and sympathy a worthwhile characteristic in a servant.

It wasn't the written words that upset Princess Anne and Mark so much as the between-the-lines innuendo of the articles. Their friends knew only too well that, although they both put on brave faces at public functions, they were deeply hurt. Phrases like "somehow we were sitting together on the backstairs [at Gatcombe] which led from the kitchen up to my room ..." (there is a room set aside for the duty detective who must sleep in the house when Princess Anne is at home) and "her arm, I noticed, was leaning against my knee ..." did not require a great deal of imagination for anyone to be tempted into reading more into a situation than in fact existed. Perhaps there were a number of long conversations with him and perhaps Princess Anne had, like many other Royals, relied upon her detective and constant companion rather more than she should have done. After all, he was with her for almost a year, was often the only person with whom she could speak immediately after the tension of a public engagement, and all at a time when her husband was himself taken from her side by his own work and studies. Cross had the effrontery to write "everyone wants to know if I was in love with Princess Anne or just flattered that she should enjoy the friendship of her bodyguard. The answer is, Yes I was genuinely enamoured." As if anyone was really interested in *his* feelings for *her*, he continued to take himself so seriously as to suggest that Anne had spoken to the Queen about him and had told her that "I was doing well and that she enjoyed my company." Later in the articles, he also claimed to have met Princess Anne secretly after he had left her employ.

Buckingham Palace, the Queen, and everyone connected with the Royal household simply refused to comment on these startling claims other than to say they were beneath contempt. Since there was no outright denial some writers subsequently suggested that perhaps there had been moments when the princess relished the feeling of being a carefree, ordinary woman who actually enjoyed the company of this vain man well experienced in the art of discreet flirtation. It was left to Mark

Phillips, in an impromptu interview at Tetbury horse trials, to express his anger over the "hurtful stories and fantasies".

But the story was up and running, world-wide, on all the agency tapes and headlines in most countries which had the slightest interest in the British Royal family. Into the fray stepped Cross's, "long-suffering wife, attractive dark haired Linda, aged 37 who lived then with her two daughters in Mitcham, Surrey". In that second week, September 22, she exclusively revealed in the *Sunday People* that her husband was a "two-timing cheat". Mrs Cross said her husband had done some rather rotten things over the years. "He is a very convincing liar and now I don't know what to think over his friendship with Princess Anne." However, she would also confirm that Princess Anne had telephoned the Cross household on many occasions, to the point where it was a regular occurrence to hear one of her children shouting out: "Dad, it's Princess Anne on the phone for you," a situation which Mrs Cross alleged continued long after the detective was removed from her service. Mrs Cross, like Miss Nicholls, would say that Princess Anne telephoned Peter Cross to tell him of Zara's birth, that she phoned him on her brother's wedding day and also once while on tour in Canada. Cross always took the calls on the bedroom extension, and they weren't just brief chats.

There were occasions when the princess may have had difficulty in locating him. At the time he was working for Anne, Cross was apparently having a "torrid affair" with an Iranian girl called Mina with whom he shared a flat in London on his off-duty days. His wife found out and put his clothes into plastic bags, left them on the doorstep and requested his departure from the matrimonial home. The girlfriend, however, soon tired of Cross and turned up on his wife's doorstep one day and asked *her* to take *him* back, which she did ... until he met Miss Nicholls.

Not to be left out of the action, the *Sunday Mirror* weighed in with the Secret Life of the Sex Mad Minder, revealing claims by a former girlfriend that he had an outrageous sexual appetite and had indulged himself in seven extramarital affairs in recent years. All of which prompted discussions with editorial executives at the *Daily Mirror*. The editor, Mike Molloy, used the leader column to ask questions of another sort. "It is a betrayal of trust and abuse of his position as Princess Anne's bodyguard that makes the behaviour of Peter Cross repugnant. He had touted around a pack of innuendoes, veiled allegations and smears about his time with the princess, demanding in return a huge payment. He has condemned himself showing not only that he is despicable, but that he was quite unfit to be a Royal bodyguard . . . yet this man was picked by Scotland Yard and the palace to guard Princess Anne. Eleven years ago, there was a terrifying attempt to kidnap the princess . . . she can consider herself fortunate that she wasn't being protected by Peter Cross at the time."

The condemnation of Peter Cross was fairly universal, though by this time he was laughing all the way to his honeymoon, having called at the bank on the way. So were the newspapers happy. That period of sensational allegations pushed up circulation figures by as much as ten per cent. Whether or not Princess Anne truly had any affection for him, we shall never know because only one side of the story has come out and that from a man whose words must be treated with extreme caution.

As each day went by, for almost three weeks, the media pressure on Princess Anne, not to mention her husband, was intense. Yet the Queen had given instructions to courtiers and press officials at the Palace to stay out of it. There was no public show of support for Anne and Mark. Privately there was a great deal of support from her family, and Anne needed it because this was one of the most galling and potentially embarrassing situations of her life. But, as with most things that do not involve constitutional or Church issues, the Queen was prepared to make them ride out the storm, knowing from personal experience that it would all be over eventually and that the Monarchy, in any event, was perhaps attracting more sympathy than criticism through it. This was the first lesson to be learned from this unsavoury episode.

The second was the realization that perhaps Princess Anne was vulnerable after all. Could it really be true that someone had found a chink in the armour of this Royal toughie? The question of her feelings, if any or none at all, towards Cross, was not the issue. She had been consistently battered. Those awful three weeks of September had left her drained and tired. For once, it *had* been a strain. She laughed it off in public, of course, but probably with a feeling of deep bitterness, and, more importantly, it had forced her on to the defensive, which was definitely against the grain.

146

She had always been seen as an overwhelmingly self-assured person, but perhaps never too sure about herself as a woman. In other words her sex appeal, compared with that of, say, Princess Diana, is not something of which she is especially confident. Those who have met her in the flesh will know that Princess Anne is in fact strikingly attractive, with apple-fresh skin, a high waist and, despite her athleticism, a delicate bone structure. Close observers now might detect a more adventurous approach to clothes, hair and make-up. She began to appear in more stunning dresses; her hair was experimented with and styled to show-stopping effect; even her make-up looked as if rather more care and thought had gone into the selection of tones and colouring. It would not be in the least inaccurate to suggest that her new boldness stemmed from the post-Cross publicity, when she had to fight off the slightest sign of self-consciousness as she pursued her public engagements.

As she pushed this disagreeable interlude to the back of her mind, she emerged as a woman even more determined to be a *caring* person, fighting some of the injustices of this world, in a warmer, less remote way, yet evidently with even greater and relentless determination than before. Perhaps, strangely, she became more beautiful also.

In November she boarded an aircraft of the Queen's flight to begin her twenty-four-day tour of Africa. Her schedule was gruelling.

Tanzania
Sunday November 17, leave London.
Monday November 18, arrive Dar-es-Salaam; official reception and meet local dignitaries.
Tuesday November 19, fly to Mbeya to visit hospitals; meet SCF officials.
Wednesday November 20, visit rehabilitation centre; fly to Songea.
Thursday November 21, fly to Zanzibar, visit hospital and meet local officials; reception.
Friday November 22, Ngorongoro crater to view wildlife.
Saturday November 23, fly to Mozambique, official reception.
Mozambique
Sunday November 24, fly to Inhambane to see SCF projects and meet SCF field workers.
Monday November 25, tour health centre in Maputo; meet local dignitaries.

147

Tuesday November 26, visit Quelimane then fly to Lusaka.

Zambia

Wednesday November 27, official reception; visit Cheshire Home and hospital in Lusaka.

Thursday November 28, fly to Mwinilunga to visit local hospital, meet local officials.

Friday November 29, fly to Chipata, visit local hospital; fly to copperbelt and tour local industry.

Saturday November 30, meet local businessmen, visit copper mine, fly back to Lusaka.

Sunday December 1, fly back to Dar-es-Salaam.

Sudan

Monday December 2, fly to Sudan; local reception committee.

Tuesday December 3, visit Hospital in Khartoum; meeting with local SCF.

Wednesday December 4, fly to Niyala, visit SCF workshops and lunch with field workers.

Thursday December 5, fly to Umbala to visit refugee camps, driving over rough terrain.

Friday December 6, driving again, this time to Zalingei camps; fly back to Khartoum.

Saturday December 7, fly to Gedaref relief camps.

Sunday December 8, return to Khartoum; local reception and farewell dinner.

Monday December 9, visit war cemetery and memorial for brief ceremony. Return home.

Tuesday December 10, arrive Gatcombe Park to be reunited with husband and children.

It was an ambitious tour, with forty-five official engagements as well as SCF projects. She travelled thousands of miles by air and road and, once again, in the last week of the trip, into dangerous and remote areas stricken with disease and suffering. A fact-finding mission to the devastating famine in Sudan, Africa's largest country, was her main priority. The scale of the disaster was enormous. In the six months before Anne's visit, the SCF had poured seven million pounds into the country, but it was a drop in the ocean. Millions were facing death.

She travelled from Khartoum to the western province of Darfur 600 miles away to see the refugee camp at Umbala where 20,000 people of skin and bone had gathered from neighbouring Chad since June of that year. The SCF had built the camp and set up clinics and begun feeding and immunization programmes. It was, as one worker put it, a scene of immense tragedy, the results of the worst famine of all time. In that camp alone, 9,000 people were suffering from severe malnutrition and, while the princess was there, deaths were running at six or more each day, but even that statistic was a vast improvement when compared to the situation before the SCF operation began.

At Christmas the previous year, the SCF had sent out two emergency teams with three plane loads of supplies. From that beginning, they began feeding 1,500 children a day, and, as word spread, the numbers increased to 50,000. Then, 100 were dying each day. Anne was able to see how her Fund workers had at least contained the vast problem. Even then, hunger was still widespread and, just before she arrived, a train carrying wheat was ambushed by two hundred women.

Anne went out among the crowds of desolate people who despite their agony knew she was for them a figure of hope. In the heat and dust, with temperatures in excess of 100 degrees F, she strode around in cotton headscarf, blouse and jeans. Naked children ran forward crying, "Amira, Amira" (Princess, Princess). She spent a night in a small mud hut, sleeping on an iron bedstead with a mosquito net. Her sleep was short; she sat up half the night talking to her field workers about the problems they faced, and the importance of anticipating the next crisis which would not be long in arriving.

The next morning, she went back to Khartoum, and then took an Andover of the Queen's Flight in a journey east, virtually to the border of Ethiopia. From the small town of Gedaref she drove for three hours over bumpy tracks to the refugee camp at Safawa. Although the worst problems of the Ethiopian tragedy were now under control after the massive world-wide relief operation, the SCF camps still had thousands of refugees under their care; their pitiful condition is not solved quickly. Continuing malnourishment and rampant diseases, such as cholera, meningitis, diptheria and whooping cough, present a constant threat; the lack of ample medical supplies is just as much a difficulty for the SCF as the arrival of food. They all know that, even if the worst is over for the moment, the next famine is never far from the horizon. What Anne learned from this tour was that if the SCF was merely to maintain its level of relief in these worst-hit areas of Africa, a

149

major cash commitment would be required. And at the end of her tour, she was at lengths to point out that if the relief agencies had the resources to move into these areas *before* the crisis, similar disasters could be averted in the future. Who would listen? The politics of the region dictated the future of relief work and, just as Geldof discovered, there was never a high degree of co-operation. Sure enough, within three years there would be signs that, in spite of the massive aid programmes injected into Ethiopia and Sudan, another disaster was looming.

Anne had seen on this trip how relief agencies can produce a startlingly quick improvement to the plight of millions of stricken people. What the SCF knew was that, in her, they had a Third World campaigner who is able to bring instant public focus to the areas that need help.

The press corps which followed Anne around the African tour gave her a suitable accolade for the courage and energy she had once again displayed, though there was one sour note. At Umbala, an eleven-year-old girl who had been bitten by a poisonous snake required a blood transfusion to save her life. The half dozen or so reporters and cameramen, who arrived at the pitifully poor camp in Northern Sudan, had hardly had a chance to look around the mud huts in which they were to spend the night, when the call came in for volunteers to have their blood tested, in the hope of finding a match for the sick child. The journalists, men and women, rolled up their sleeves and were happy to co-operate, particularly when they were told that the snake bite had destroyed the blood's clotting process and, without fresh blood, the child would bleed to death. The Royal party, who had arrived ahead of the journalists, had already had their blood tested but had produced no suitable donors. The journalists lined up in a hot, fly-blown hut. One of them recalls the incident vividly: "Princess Anne was in the hut immediately next door, and she took not the slightest bit of notice. We could see each other, for goodness sake. We were thousands of miles from home, supposedly on the same side, united in a cause to do good and she didn't even glance in our direction."

The blood tests finally revealed that three of the journalists, including Mike Woolridge of the BBC, had the right blood and each gave a pint. The following day, Princess Anne went to the hospital ward with the press in tow to record the event,

In the mid-1980s, Princess Anne began the shift from eventing to racing. She made her debut on a special occasion for Riding for the Disabled in 1985. Here, at Folkestone the following year, she displays the same determination with which she had tackled her earlier sporting activities. Soon her appearances at race meetings would become so regular that she was relegated to the sports pages.

Princess Anne is patron of many service associations, as well as being Colonel-in-Chief of several regiments. In February 1985, she visited two of them in West Germany, the 14th/20th King's Hussars, and the Worcestershire and Sherwood Foresters. She drove a huge Chieftain tank and fired the latest Army weaponry.

Informal family gatherings at horsey events: well wrapped up against the April cold at Badminton (*below right*); in pensive mood at Windsor Great Park (*right*); and walking the show-jumping course at Gatcombe (*below*). Zara shows an interest, though perhaps not the same enthusiasm as her mother, in competitive riding.

The arrival of two sisters-in-law took some of the media pressure off Princess Anne. At the Christmas family gathering, the cameras focus on the Princess of Wales (*above*) after a church service at Balmoral in 1984. At Royal Ascot (*below*) Anne takes Sarah Ferguson along.

A favourite in showbiz circles as president of the British Academy of Film and Television Arts, Princess Anne meets Jimmy Tarbuck, Henry Cooper, Ronnie Corbett and Terry Wogan at a star-studded dinner at which she was presented with £15,000 for the SCF and St John Ambulance Brigade, May 1987.

In her official robes (*left*) as Chancellor of the University of London, a post she was awarded in 1981 against strong competition. She brushed aside embarrassed glances from theatre managers (*right*) at the Royal Première of the film *Absolute Beginners* in April 1986, when Patsy Kensit and Mandy Rice-Davies were presented.

Contrasting moments, formal and
informal, but forever in the public
eye. (*Left*) She greets King Juan
Carlos of Spain on the occasion of
the first visit of a Spanish monarch
to Britain for eighty years. (*Right*)
She finds company with her father
in a stroll through the enclosure, at
Epsom for the Derby in 1987.

Three generations of the House of Windsor, plus Princess Michael, laugh at the 1988 Derby. A man in full morning dress dashed onto the course below them, flung off his clothes and headed for the winning post in a bet for charity, before being caught by a policeman. The Queen noticed him first, and pointed him out to the others.

In more sombre mood, sisters-in-law, the Princess of Wales, the Princess Royal and the Duchess of York, attend the Poppy Day ceremonies at the Cenotaph in Whitehall. At the same time, IRA bombers struck at the memorial service in Enniskillen. The Royal family are in constant danger of terrorist attack.

The Princess Royal spends less money on her appearance than her glamorous sister-in-law, the Princess of Wales, but when the occasion merits she can look just as fashionable. She has admitted that as she gets older she has become more "adventurous", and in these photographs (*right* and *below*) she proves her point in dramatic outfits and swept-back hair.

Mark, meanwhile, looks pensive at a press conference. Criticism of his business activities has not deterred him from his aim to achieve millionaire status in his own right.

one of them having written a little placard, placed on the child's bed, proudly proclaiming: "BBC Blood, Mike Woolridge." The cameramen desperately wanted Anne to go up to the child; instead she walked down the opposite side of the ward and they got not a single picture of her with the girl they had saved. Nor did Anne in any way acknowledge their assistance.

TEN

Friends and Rumours

Public interest has a habit of moving rapidly from one key member of the Royal family to another, as if they were on a merry-go-round of media megastars. Occasionally one falls off, to be surrounded by flashbulbs and television cameras and radio mikes held two inches from the nose. The ups-and-downs of Anne's turn under the public microscope had finished for the moment. Cracks in her facade after the talk of scandal had been quickly papered over by her acts of goodness. As she weighed the press cuttings, praise may have won in terms of column inches against criticism. Anne was philosophical. You can't win them all. And so as the world's Best Loved Family gathered around the seasonal table to hear Prince Philip's assessment of their performance the previous year, a new star was bubbling towards the surface. Her name was Miss Sarah Ferguson and 1986 would be her year, giving the Princesses Anne and Diana another brief but well-earned rest from the limelight.

Miss Ferguson was the subject of rumour for weeks and correctly so; on March 19 her engagement to the Queen's second son was announced, and suddenly there was a new bright and breezy personality to capture the front pages around the world. It was perhaps not before time that Princess Anne's younger brother had decided to settle down. Unlike the discreet romances of the elder brother Princes Charles, Andrew's wild oats had been sown aplenty and publicly. He took not the slightest trouble to cover his tracks during his affair with the former soft porn actress, Koo Stark, and ended that romance only when his father pointedly remarked that she was getting more publicity than he, and was hardly suitable for Royal status. She was American, anyway, and there were still none-too-pleasant memories of the last lady from the other side of the pond who had entered the charmed circle. Could anyone really imagine Koo as the Duchess of York? Anne once observed to her brother. In later months, the young prince lost his bathing trunks while cavorting on a Caribbean holiday where he met model Vicki Hodge and others who were not unforthcoming in their reports to Fleet Street on what they all got up to. Vicki, I recall, spent a long time on the telephone to one of my colleagues, giving him chapter and verse.

Unlike Princess Diana, who had a history but not a past, Sarah Ferguson had both. Her history was that she was related to the Royal family through Princess Alice, a cousin of Sarah's father. Her past, not unnaturally for a bachelor girl of twenty-six, included a couple of fairly high-profile romances which included a live-in period with a racing driver. But once that was printed and out of the way, Fergie would, initially at least, become a popular new member of the clan. Where she differed from Princess Diana was that she lacked any coyness; she was bold and upfront with the press and what the public seemed to like about her was that she was an ordinary working girl, who spoke normally, was easy to identify with, and had something of a devil-may-care attitude. She looked a perfect match for the handsome, harmless and not overly bright – though at times extremely arrogant – young prince.

Princess Anne was not unhappy about her brother's choice, either. Although Miss Ferguson commanded a great deal of press attention, she would not be quite so adoringly portrayed as Princess Diana. Despite her alleged indifference to anything that appears in newspapers, Anne nonetheless reads her press cuttings and likes to remain in the foreground. That is a fact, whatever her defensive friends and press spokesmen may say. It is important to her that her *public* work is well recorded and well received.

Her *private* life is another matter.

She and Mark took the children skiing in the French Alps at the start of the year for what was billed in the *Sun* as a second honeymoon to get over the harm done to their marriage during the Peter Cross business, which had almost driven them apart. Mark seemed to agree with that assessment of the trip when he said in another "exclusive interview" shortly after his return that it was a "wonderful holiday. We haven't had a holiday like it for nine years. We had a fabulous time." And then that little matter which, it seems, is never far from his thoughts, jogged his memory. Money. Smacking his back pocket, he said:

153

"But when we do something like that the money has to come from here." Normally, his family holidays at the Queen's homes at Balmoral or Sandringham or Windsor, or trips around the coast on the Royal yacht, come free. This one, he'd had to pay for himself. The fact that his mother-in-law's portrait is on every coin and banknote does not entitle him to spend more than he can earn. He seemed to be telling us once again that he was hard up. That, he insists, is why he has to travel the world. To earn his family's living. "You can count on one hand the number of weekends I spend at home," said Mark. "I don't see half as much of the children as I should."

He has not changed a great deal through the years of his marriage to Royalty. He is more confident and worldly now, through experience; a likeable, agreeable and modest man who still embarrasses quite easily. He is still slow in his responses. But he was never nicknamed Fog by Princes Charles, supposedly because he is thick and wet. That is a story that has been so often repeated that it became seen as fact, which it wasn't. He is still slim, a six-footer without a trace of fat or middle-age spread as he heads towards the 1990s, and that has not been easy. Fitness is his key to success at work. In spite of his rather diffident nature, Mark Phillips is a tough nut to crack; he has a firm expert control over his horses which on at least two occasions has earned him complaints for ill-treatment which he has always denied. Mastery of a strong eventing horse, he points out, does not mean cruelty. He has retained his abilities as one of the world's finest horsemen. All the diffidence evaporates once he swings into the saddle. He has the authority and confidence of a man who knows his job. He still finds television appearances daunting, and, after all these years, entering family gatherings and the presence of his parents-in-law still gives him a hint of butterflies. But he relaxes when Anne is around; she is always the ice-breaker in any difficult situation, except, of course, those which she has created herself.

After the togetherness of that skiing holiday, Anne and Mark looked ahead to another year of the frequent separations which result from their work. If German newspapers were to be believed, it would be quite a different story. They came out with the news, followed up in Britain by the *Sunday People*, that after the skiing holiday Anne was expecting their third child; the Queen had been told and the birth was due in late summer. There was not a word of truth in this, but Buckingham Palace left Fleet Street in a turmoil by simply responding with the words: "No comment." The author recalls, that weekend, reporters were frantically trying to fulfil their news editor's wishes and come up with a story with confirmation. The palace stayed "mum". But to show how ludicrous it was, Princess Anne took over, and the following weekend booked herself a horse and went racing!

The princess already had in her diary eight trips overseas for that year, and Mark was pencilled in to join her on only one of them. His diary would take him to Jamaica to run an equestrian teach-in; a similar task at Gleneagles Hotel, in Scotland, where he would be the tutor to a group of fifteen consisting mostly of women on a four-day course at £295 per head; and later in the year he was off to Australia, New Zealand and Japan. All this was over and above his tasks on the farm and the organization of his own Gatcombe Horse Trials which had now become established as an important event in his year.

The trials at Gatcombe were started in 1983, and Princess Anne wasn't at all sure whether she liked the idea of thousands of people invading her sanctuary where she can relax privately, without fear of intrusion. But she finally agreed. For Mark, it would be another source of sponsorship income which he felt was badly needed to help support his business. The first year of the event attracted 20,000; in 1986, 40,000 would pass through the gates. The sponsorship cash from Landrover was further supplemented by Daks who also supply his clothes; but the biggest sponsor of his Gatcombe Trials has been the International Distillers and Vintners Company, makers of Croft Original Sherry, who had put up more than one million pounds in the four years to 1986. They also chipped in towards the cost of building the fences, which subsequently carried names such as Bodega Butts, Sherry Rack, Cellar Steps and Croft Casks.

His farm at Gatcombe is a sizeable operation, running 150 beef cattle, 500 or more sheep and 850 acres of cereal. He was never short of something to do, nor were there many opportunities, he admitted, to be at his wife's side during her public engagements. This prospect would become even less likely in the immediate future; plans were already well advanced by mid-1986 to build a Captain Phillips Equestrian Centre at the Gleneagles Hotel at which his presence, 350 miles away from Gatcombe, would be regularly required.

Anne's own engagements continued to mount and that year's overseas trips began in March when she was booked for what appeared on the surface to be a fairly routine, even pleasant, visit to Rio de Janeiro for a Royal Gala Performance of the Sadlers Wells Ballet. It turned out to be a hazardous nightmare. By some remarkable intelligence work, undercover police in Brazil discovered that a murderous, drug-trafficking gang were planning to kidnap Princess Anne and hold her hostage in exchange for their imprisoned leader, Jose Carlos dos Reis, who was serving a thirty-year sentence. The Brazilians knew that Reis had followers who were entirely capable of carrying out their threat. He had a large gang living in the slum areas of Rio, which were to be visited by the princess, and there had already been several attempts to get Reis out of prison. The most spectacular occurred when his gang flew into a maximum security gaol by helicopter and tried to airlift their leader away, but the attempt ended in a shoot-out with guards and police. Meanwhile, the police got wind of the plot to kidnap Anne and the proverbial "ring of steel" was thrown around her, upon arrival in Rio. Her guard was doubled, her schedules and engagements altered (much to her annoyance, incidentally) and for the entire visit she was surrounded by men with mach-ine-guns.

Furthermore, top brass in the police force suggested that someone should be used as a decoy, to travel everywhere in the official car laid on for Princess Anne, and that she would travel behind in a plain and unmarked Jaguar. The idea was put to the British Ambassador, Mr John Ure, and his wife Caroline, who is of similar age and build to the princess, immediately and bravely volunteered to act as the decoy. John Ure said: "This gang had committed some very large-scale crimes and the threat to Princess Anne was very real indeed. We could not afford to take any chances." The greatest risk would be at the airport, where fifty armed police surrounded Caroline Ure and Princess Anne while the car switch was made. The princess, when told of the threat, didn't bat an eyelid, but she did insist on a news black-out until she was back in London so that she could personally tell the Queen.

She returned to England in time for a major family event, the sixtieth birthday of the Queen, on Monday April 21. Princess

Anne has become, in many respects, a copy of the Queen. Capable of stunning beauty or conversely a dull and dour appearance, her looks and mannerisms can be surprisingly similar. Her work load is almost as heavy as the Queen's, and on official duties she is likely to retain that same air of aloofness, just apart and slightly superior to most people around her. Princess Anne has also followed her mother in breaking new ground, going down paths previously untrodden by Royalty.

But, unlike the Queen, Anne has on many occasions let dignity slip, and even her most regular critics in the press can forgive her for that. The media like it when Princess Anne gives them a new line. Her current determination during that year was to get recognition as a top woman jockey in major race meetings, and also to become the first Royal to win a race. All her spare time, now, was devoted to that aim and, as with her previous ambitions in the eventing world, she would achieve a certain fame. It became such a regular occurrence to see Anne racing, that her picture was eventually relegated from the front end of the newspapers, where it had first appeared, to the sports pages at the back. At the *Mirror*, her racing engagements were always on the day's news schedule for coverage. But after the novelty had worn off, I would put her picture on the news pages only if she fell off, or won! Her goal actually to win a race was achieved after thirteen attempts on August 5, 1986, when she galloped home a clear winner by five lengths on a horse called Gulfland. She actually smiled for the cameramen. She kept on riding, and almost a year later won the coveted Dresden Diamond Stakes at Ascot on Ten No Trumps.

That summer also, the now-familiar television production for a Royal wedding came and went, with all the usual pomp and ceremony, the glass coaches and the Give-Us-A-Kiss-On-The-Balcony scene. Sarah Ferguson, now Duchess of York, became part of the Performing Monarchy, which has to turn out, in ever increasing numbers, for these star-studded events, closely observed by five or six hundred million viewers. The totally public atmosphere of Sarah's wedding was the most spectacular yet, a far cry from the private ceremony of the Queen's wedding thirty-nine years before.

During the period approaching the prince's wedding, weeks in which Andrew's and Fergie's previous lives and paramours were scrutinized and examined for public consumption, Princess Anne also became the focus of salacious gossip and rumour. This time, certain newspapers were attempting to link her romantically with the actor, Anthony Andrews, whose fame started with the television series *Brideshead Revisited*. Mr Andrews, called Tony by Anne and Mark and Julie by some of his actor friends, had been the subject of rumblings below the surface for several years. In fact, the mutual friendship between Anthony Andrews, and his wife Georgina, and Princess Anne and Mark Phillips, began in 1982. Georgina, the daughter of Dr Leonard Simpson, the Harley Street specialist who is also chairman of the family store group known for its Daks clothes, had lent Mark her horse Blizzard through a third party. Until then, they had never met. Then at the Downlands Horse Trials in Liphook in March 1982, Princess Anne, Tony Andrews and Georgina Andrews were rebuilding a fence when a photographer came over and began taking pictures. As Georgie explained to Nigel Dempster: "For some reason, I stepped aside and Tony said, 'Why did you do that?' and that's when the rumours began. Princess Anne is marvellous. She never mentions these silly stories about her and Tony."

The rumour would not go away. It intensified as the years went by, particularly as stories filtered back from Gatcombe that Tony Andrews had been a guest in the house during Mark's absence, that he and Anne dined alone there while their respective spouses were away, and that on those occasions he sat at the head of the dinner table, as if he was master of the house and even ordered the wine. (This was doubtless true. Since Anne seldom drinks wine, it is quite likely that he would prefer to choose his own.) By then, the Andrewses ranked among the Phillipses' closest friends. They are one of the few couples they actually stay with on trips abroad. One of the few times Anne and Mark were together during the Los Angeles Olympics was when they stayed with Anthony Andrews at the house he had rented while filming in Hollywood. The Phillipses have a small group of real friends. Those who come to dinner at Gatcombe regularly can be counted on two hands. Jackie Stewart and his wife Helen are frequent guests, and often join them at horsey events; similarly Anne and Mark have stayed at the Stewarts' home in the hills above Lake Geneva, Switzerland, where they are undemanding guests who like to be treated as friends rather than 'Royal' visitors, though in all company Anne is referred to as "Ma'am". Their friendship goes back to the time Anne and Jackie Stewart shared the Sportswoman and Sportsman of the Year titles in 1971; after that, they were constantly meeting at sports events, which threw them together, and the association developed to include Mark and Helen. When Zara was born, it was Helen whom Anne first thought of as godmother.

It is this part of her life that Anne protects with passion; this is *hers*. It is *private, keep out*. And because her friends are loyal and trustworthy, only rumour and speculation leak from behind Gatcombe's closed doors. Her guests are often the Barbour-and-green-wellies set. Diana Maxwell and her husband Patrick Helmore, whose daughter married pop singer Bryan Ferry, also have Anne and Mark to stay at their Northamptonshire home, particularly during the Brigstock Horse Trials. Others you might find on any night dining around the Gatcombe table include David Nicholson and his wife Diana, who are another no-nonsense couple and near neighbours. David too, has had to put up with innuendo about his friendship with Anne, though everyone knows they are friends simply because he was her trainer, and they've known each other far longer than that. Another of Anne's confidantes is Lady Leonora Lichfield, former wife of the Queen's cousin, photographer Patrick (Lord) Lichfield. She also is godmother to Zara. Daughter of the fifth Duke of Westminster, wealthy and intelligent, she is a part-time lady-in-waiting to Anne, though with three children of her own, this aspect of their association tends to be somewhat limited.

Others in the Gatcombe circle naturally come from the 'horsey' set. Major Malcolm Wallace, an official of the British Equestrian Association, and his wife, Caroline, have long been friends and have a country cottage near the Phillips's home. Two old flames, Richard Meade and Andrew Parker Bowles, both former escorts of Anne before she became engaged to Mark, live within visiting distance and, with their respective spouses, Angela and Camilla, are also regular dinner guests. Bowles and his wife are also friends of Prince Charles and it was Camilla who is reputed to have been a matchmaker between Charles and Princess Diana. They all enjoy the relaxed informal atmosphere at Gatcombe. In the daytime, everyone wears jeans, and for the staff it is a constant battle to keep the place tidy, littered as it often is with riding boots, dogs, children's toys and the paraphernalia of an upper-class, but uninhibited family home.

At informal gatherings, Princess Anne has been seen wearing a simple kaftan, with her hair down, and as one of her friends put it "totally unlike the public image of the princess". More often, though, when there are guests of twelve or more, it is the order of the day to dress for dinner, and this is especially the case when the Queen comes to stay. Then, the butler and the rest of the staff will revert to formal etiquette, and convention, and out comes the Georgian silver which was a present from the Queen.

Princess Anne expects, and gets, total discretion from her intimate friends. She cannot stand social climbers, does not like so-called glamorous stars who would travel halfway round the world for an invitation to the table of a Royal, and sees any uninvited attempts to break into her circle as an unwarranted and unwanted intrusion. It is perhaps because of this closeness that neither Anne nor Mark seem to have any particular anxiety when they are observed alone in the company of someone else while abroad, or at home for that matter. But others cannot resist laying feelings not only of anxiety but even of guilt on them, from the outside. There was much made of Mark's luncheon with a blonde in Canada; Kathy Birks was advising him on business and public relations and her name would crop up again with more sensational claims a year later. Nor would the Anthony Andrews story go away, and after a summer-long spate of innuendo and gossip Anne was fuming.

In September, she chose a banquet hosted by the Associated Press to deliver a massive broadside at the press in front of an audience which included those most powerful of media men, Rupert Murdoch and Robert Maxwell. If they had heard from their staff that the princess was the most outspoken and ferocious of all the Royals, she certainly lived up to it that night. The ticking-off was accompanied by her acid wit, and therefore remained good humoured, but those present could hardly escape the message in the fifteen-minute speech which she wrote herself and which came straight from the heart. She said: "This summer I suffered severe aggravation from the amount of unadulterated trivia, rubbish and gratuitous trouble-making that appeared in all sections of the so-called media in response to a perfectly normal family occasion [Prince Andrew's wedding]. My reaction was to forget about them

160

immediately but the sheer volume of repeated stories, half-truths and lies has an effect on the subject matter as well. I would like to be able to read a newspaper or magazine or watch the news on television without having to make constant translations and adjustments for exaggerations and sometimes lies." She went on: "These articles may not amount to slander but they get close to it sometimes and I am tempted to suggest the re-introduction of the Norman Law where a slanderer not only had to pay damages but was also liable to stand in the market place, hold his nose between two fingers and confess himself to be a liar. Alfred the Great in the ninth century took a stronger line. Persistent slanderers had their tongues cut out." She referred to other ancient customs of locking slanderers in the stocks and pelting the offender with rotten fruit and vegetables. (Perhaps it is a cherished dream of hers to see certain Fleet Street writers so treated!)

Then, as an afterword, she said: "I have been told that women members of the Royal family should not make jokes, because they do not come out in print," and went on to compare many stories about the Royal family to an estate agent's brochure. "There is a lot more I would like to say on this subject," she concluded, "but I don't have the guts."

Guts she certainly displayed in making that speech to an audience whom she knew controlled most of what appeared in the press and on television daily. There was a great deal of sympathy towards her remarks, though some present felt that she was encouraging more controls on the media, and likened her view to that of the Prime Minister, Mrs Margaret Thatcher, who gets equally cross when matters of which she does not approve are revealed by journalists. The dilemma editors of the competitive popular newspapers face – as the Royal family realizes, surely – that public interest lies, not in their official duties, but in their personal lives, their looks, their deeds, their fashions, their habits, their holidays, their children and, yes, their affairs. Definitely their affairs. They are all people of high profile, and it is these aspects of their lives that their adoring public unashamedly read with avid, unquenchable interest. Worthy though Anne's work is, and important though the Queen's duties are, they are not the stuff of popular appeal nor happenings with which readers can readily identify.

The trouble comes when personal matters concerning the Royals are over emphasized or even made up. The "close friend

161

told me" syndrome is now easily identified in Royal reports and some of this is due to Buckingham Palace itself. Whenever these stories are written, Palace press staff are contacted for their reaction *prior* to the story appearing (in British newspapers at least; the same cannot be said for overseas publications). But the Palace has virtually given up trying to deny or confirm anything to do with what they view as tittle-tattle, and rely now on the standard "No Comment".

Often there is a rearguard action to try to quell the effects of bad publicity, but usually this occurs *after* the event. When the *Daily Mirror* revealed, for instance, that Princess Michael's father was a former Sturmbahnfuehrer in the SS, the Palace press spokesman admitted the story was true but said that the princess did not know about her father's past. The next day, Princess Michael was given expert advice by executives of TV-AM on how to cope with a highly embarrassing situation when she appeared on television biting her lip and brushing away a tear: "I honestly did not know," she said. "It is something I shall just have to live with." Perhaps Princess Michael did not know; Buckingham Palace almost certainly did, since it is never possible for a member of the family to marry without the antecedents of the entrant Royal being examined. However, it did the trick and Princess Michael was praised for her brave approach to an agonizing ordeal.

She didn't quite get the same response a few months later, when the *News of the World* delivered a body blow by publishing a highly documented and authenticated report of her liaison with Warren Hunt, of the (then) incredibly wealthy Hunt family of Texas who once tried to corner the world's silver market: Royalty as Soap Opera indeed, since the Hunts were the original models of the long-running television saga of the Ewings in *Dallas*! The Palace press department offered no comment on dirty journalism, and promptly pushed Prince and Princess Michael back into the limelight to ward off the damage. They turned up at Wimbledon for the tennis, hand in hand and yearning for a sympathetic reception; which they got. The crowd stood in ovation. But Princess Michael would, after a suitable lapse of time, retire gracefully into the background of the Royal circle. Once again, the Queen rightly felt displeasure at disclosures concerning a member of her family, and Princess Michael – dubbed Princess Pushy by the *News of the World* – would eventually feel the draught.

Princess Anne, in her speech about the press, ended with the words: "Whether the media reports my activities or approves or disapproves doesn't make any difference to me." But there are some who would argue that this statement could not be taken literally. The princess *does* care what is said about her; more importantly both the Palace and the media *should* care about wanton reports of all those surrounding the Monarchy. Inventive and speculative journalism is never a good substitute for lack of facts, and everyone in Fleet Street knows that. The trouble is that inventive and speculative journalism is quite often brought into play when there is "No Comment". This generally applies to the type of story that sells more copies and of course, even a comment from the Palace would not necessarily end salacious reporting.

Clearly, relations between Princess Anne and the press had reached a particularly low ebb in that winter of 1986/87. Anne did not feel in the least co-operative towards the needs of photographers, unless she was on official business. This is perhaps best demonstrated by two anecdotes, now legend. Fleet Street photographer, Clive Postlethwaite, by sheer chance happened to board the same Inter-City express early one morning when Anne was travelling from Stroud to London where she was to attend among other things a Mansion House banquet given by the Worshipful Company of Carmen of which she is Master. Postlethwaite couldn't believe his luck, to find a member of Royalty travelling on an ordinary train, in a fairly grimy carriage, albeit first class. Biding his time, he waited until the train started before taking the action every picture editor would expect of him. He moved in, camera held high and at the ready and began taking his pictures. Princess Anne exploded in anger and, according to Postlethwaite, told him what to do, in two short words: "F... Off!" He maintained that Princess Anne shouted at the top of her voice and other passengers apparently looked on in amazement. As he walked away, the Royal detective with Anne grabbed him and had him imprisoned in the guards' van until she had left the train. Postlethwaite said that the detective later apologized for man-handling him. The photographer said he was "quite shocked" by the incident, though few would have any sympathy for him.

Another story of difficult relationships comes from Jayne Fincher, daughter of the famous photographer Terry. She is one of the more charming, diplomatic and gentle of the press pack who follow the Royals. Not a paparazzi, but one who has a good working contact with Buckingham Palace and who always obtains proper accreditation on tours. She seldom takes a picture that would upset any member of the family and is a particular favourite of the Princess of Wales. Princess Anne knows Jayne better than most photographers and, when Anne flew out to the United Arab Emirates in February to visit Qatar, Kuwait and Jordan, Jayne was the only accredited photographer on the tour. She had made her own travel arrangements and was particularly keen on providing good and delicate coverage since the Fincher family is well known in those parts, particularly to King Hussein. Every day in Abu Dhabi, the Arab hosts sent a Mercedes to collect her and she was treated by them as part of the Royal party. The only person who did not acknowledge her presence, she says, was Princess Anne herself. "She didn't even say good morning. And that got embarrassing, because I was included in all the official lunches and would often end up sitting opposite her at the table. One day I went to cover a private picnic in the desert which was attended by only 15 people. After I had taken some pictures, an Arab made me take off my shoes and ushered me into a tent where a meal was being served. I tried to say no, but he insisted and I ended up a couple of feet away from Princess Anne. We had to eat the food with our fingers and I was dying to take a photograph of Anne doing this. Her secretary [Lieut-Col Peter Gibbs] just glared at me fiercely as if to say 'Don't you dare'. In the end I didn't but I'm actually not sure the princess would have minded. She certainly doesn't mind having her picture taken when she's on duty." But what left a sour taste with Jayne Fincher was the lack of any kind of acknowledgement from the princess, whom she was close to for almost a week.

These were minor skirmishes that demonstrate the extremes of both patience and impatience on both sides. But Fincher makes the point that most Royal followers now fully appreciate and understand: when Anne is *on* duty, she will work the press to her best advantage. When she is *off* duty, she wants nothing whatever to do with them and perhaps no one can blame her. Grudges are not held for long and, even within a period of "Hate the Press", she was capable of skilfully diverting the publicity to one of her own causes.

She caused a stir, for example, when she visited three gypsy camps in Buckinghamshire. It was a mission on behalf of the SCF to uncover the health and conditions of the children of travelling people. She chatted to many of the gypsy families. The council gave them a site but expected thirty families to use one toilet, they complained. Every time they had a bath, said one gypsy mother, they had to carry the dirty water away in buckets to a cesspit two hundred yards away. The conditions, Anne agreed, were appalling. She entered the dangerous area of politics in her implied criticism of local authorities in their failure to provide adequate sites and facilities for the 50,000 travelling people in Britain, and it was an interesting exercise to observe the response. While Anne's missions to draw attention to the miserable plight of children in far-off lands brought praise, the reverse was the case when she and the SCF made the point that children of the gypsies in Britain were entitled to good health, welfare and education. The people of Buckinghamshire thought her remarks were inappropriate. They accused her of attempting to get "cheap publicity", and one newspaper further inflamed public opinion by suggesting that she might like to allocate a couple of acres at Gatcombe for occupation by the gypsies, and all the mess that goes with them.

At the same time, her brother Prince Charles was mounting his own campaign against Inner Cities and decay and poverty in urban areas. Both were to appear in a television documentary which would emphasize to the British people that, while the needs of children abroad were enormous and widespread, there were also problem areas at home. Whether they both consciously set out to enter this fraught arena of debate is possible, but unlikely. However, it did begin what some regard as a disturbing intervention by the Royals into areas which, in the end, directly involve party politics. The nation would soon learn, for example, of Prince Charles's private discussions with Mrs Thatcher on urban decay. The continuing debate into which he had projected himself would attract bitter criticism, and eventually he would be backed by the Queen, when she saw him being forced into a corner.

Unperturbed by the prospect of any comeback – or could it be that that's exactly what she wanted? – Princess Anne agreed to an interview for the *Sunday Mirror*, where the author was then deputy editor. As with all interviews that Anne gives now, and they usually number two or three a year, the point of the discussion is made known in advance and a list of questions submitted and strictly adhered to. She does not like to deviate from that outline, nor talk about any personal matters unless previously agreed through the Palace press office. In this case, she wanted to talk about her work with the SCF, and she specifically agreed to discuss the gypsies controversy. She gave a down-to-earth, most professionally handled interview. Bearing in mind the bitter exchanges she had had recently with members of the press, one is perhaps left wondering who is manipulating whom.

She is to be found on these occasions at her suite in Buckingham Palace, which contains her office and personal apartment. The door is opened by Princess Anne herself. A brief but engaging smile, firm handshake, her blue-grey eyes reflecting a steely, determined look. She smiles and signals towards a chair. She discusses the subjects that are closest to the heart of our most outspoken Royal. For the best part of an hour, she relaxes in her chintz armchair and pinpoints what she considers, in her role as President of the SCF, the vital issues of the day. It doesn't take her long to get on to a better understanding of the most unwanted group of people in Britain, the gypsies. Princess Anne forms her opinions from first-hand experience – and remains unmoved by the controversy. The point is, she said, that these people have children: "Those children are growing up in quite the worst conditions anywhere in Britain. Now you might say it is the fault of the parents. But in my work with the SCF, that's neither here nor there. What we're trying to do is to improve conditions for those children, for their health and development. The Fund has a mobile classroom and a playschool to generally improve the life around these youngsters ... but it is a particularly difficult area because they're not the sort of communities that inspire a great deal of support from outside. I want to make it clear that I went to those sites as a fact-finding tour ... I don't know enough about the subject to be drawn on what steps need to be taken regarding the gypsies themselves. I won't be drawn on the questions of whether gypsy sites have any right to be there, or how dirty they are. That's irrelevant, and not helpful to the Fund or the children we are trying to help. These people could be any community of any shape or size in the UK. But they are gypsies and people don't like to think about them. It's a problem they rather wish wasn't here so everybody gets frightfully uptight when I go along and take a look. Well, I'm sorry, but you know they exist and their children exist and quite a lot of their children don't grow up very healthy because of the conditions they live under." Princess Anne added with ferocity: "Anyway, all the hue and cry about these travellers making such a mess ... I don't think the British public have got a great deal to be proud of with the litter they leave all over the country. The picnic sites and places they go to are covered with litter. The cast-offs of modern society. But no one seems to want to change that."

So could we expect to see a gypsy site at the bottom of Princess Anne's garden? She shook her head wearily: "That's a wonderful over-simplification, isn't it?" She responds to serious questions with an enthusiasm that displays her desire to show her knowledge. "There are plenty of people who see no reason to support charities that work overseas because they think we've got enough problems at home. As for putting its own house in order, SCF has precisely done that for many years. It has always been conscious of the problems in Britain." She highlighted the Fund's playgroups in decaying inner city areas, community health care clinics, playschools, care service in hospitals, drop-in centres where hard-pressed mothers can call at any time for a chat or advice. She is proud that Fund centres seem to avoid the plague of vandalism in even the toughest areas of Britain. In Belfast the Eliza Street Family Day Centre was opened on a day of great tension after the death of a hunger striker; fighting devastated the neighbourhood but the centre was untouched, and local mothers of both religions placed trust in the SCF counsellors.

The fund's extension into other areas of British life is also encouraging, said Anne. The Milestone Project in Sunderland is not the place for the genteel or faint-hearted: it's filled with tearaways and teenage law-breakers. It displays the Fund's lateral thinking and modern outlook. Anne is impressed: "It is an intermediate treatment centre for the more habitual young offenders in the region. An alternative, with the agreement of the courts, to custodial sentence. There is very intensive counselling. Questioning them about their backgrounds leading up to whatever it was they have done wrong. It's too early to tell just how successful it will be but I think it has a slightly higher degree of success than plain custodial sentencing. It is our hope that through counselling, they will realize they have done wrong and decide there are other ways of living their lives."

It was while on a visit to the Midlands that Princess Anne had come into contact with what she called the "no hope" generation, unemployed youngsters with no prospect of jobs. She then goes into what she describes as her favourite story, one which sums up her attitude towards youngsters in the dole queue, which on reflection perhaps sounded rather insensitive: "I was on a walkabout and I met three youngsters on the Youth Training Scheme who were smartly dressed enjoying the opportunities they had to improve their job skills and possibility of work at the end of the day. On the other side of the same square were three untidy, scruffy youngsters who weren't doing anything. They said they had a band and I asked if they had ever contemplated the YTS and one of them said 'Well that's slave labour innit?' (she said in an accent mocking of the lower-class kids). That was as far as he was prepared to go. If he and his pals feel happier playing in a band then that's up to them. I don't know if there was anything available but he said he wasn't going to look and find out." Some might have thought Mrs Thatcher could not have put it better herself!

Anne talked constantly of "self-help in the community" and said: "If by setting an example you can encourage people to enjoy their lives more or become better citizens then you're achieving something ... It's all about increasing the level of awareness, a level much closer to home. For mothers to be alerted to avoiding serious illness and long-term problems with their children. To remember things like vaccination, particularly polio. Some people tend to think that because you don't read about it anymore it doesn't exist; but polio will always exist."

She introduced another emotive issue in discussing whooping cough jabs for babies. "Whooping cough is still a great killer. There has been a lot of dangerous and irresponsible panicking over statistics for brain-damaged children. It is a great shame that the figures for children who have died from a whooping cough epidemic are not put alongside the numbers who have died from the brain-damage through the vaccine."

These are her favourite topics and she could talk for hours with a knowledge that bears no contradiction. Anne the Worker is seen on these occasions at her professional best.

ELEVEN

Into Africa, Again

The title of Princess Royal was always on the cards for Princess Anne but it was never to be given lightly. The Queen had originally planned to reward her only daughter with this recognition of status and endeavour when she had turned forty and thus had completed more than twenty-one years in the service of her nation and the Commonwealth. It would be a title which would take her into the second half of her life and one which would be suited to a more matronly figure.

It was not always a certainty that the title would be reserved for Princess Anne. Her aunt, Princess Margaret, might well have claimed it some years ago had her personal life not developed into so much turmoil. That alone put her out of the running, leaving Anne the clear candidate to carry this honoured position into the next century. Two things happened which encouraged the Queen to make the announcement. First, by the middle of 1987, Anne's untiring efforts for charity had earned her world-wide acclaim; even her most ardent critics could not begin to undermine her work and there was by now no question that she had earned this fitting tribute. Secondly, the Queen was apparently anxious that her daughter's seniority and status in the Royal family would not be overwhelmed in the public eye by the Princess of Wales and the Duchess of York, as theirs became the world's two most famous faces, appearing regularly on the covers of major magazines in every country. As the press recorded every move of her two sisters-in-law, Anne's position in the limelight became more confined. Her publicity is now restricted to three areas: her charity work, which the popular press grudgingly record with scant references; her sporting achievements; and areas of controversy.

Controversy came to the fore again when the *News of the World* delivered her a Christmas present of huge banner headlines on the front page, in December 1987, declaring: "Anne

169

and Anthony's Three Nights In Paris". It was an entirely factual headline, but the story beneath the facts left the paper's readers to put two and two together and come up with five. It aroused in Anne a state of rage, not to mention disquiet in Anthony Andrews with whom she was once again supposed to be having an affair. The story claimed that the princess and the actor were "fuming last night after their hotel-hopping antics in Paris were revealed". Two days earlier, Chris Hutchins, the gossip diarist on *Today* newspaper, had reported that Andrews had arrived in Paris to meet Princess Anne. The *News of the World* then sent two reporters to the French capital to find out more. Andrews had checked out of his hotel at Roissy, fifteen miles from Paris, where he was filming with Jane Seymour for the television production of *The Woman He Loved*, a rather wet account of the romance between the Duke and Duchess of Windsor. Andrews booked into another hotel, the Plaza Athena, just around the corner from where Princess Anne was staying. She was in Paris for an international equestrian conference, accompanied, incidentally, by her father, Prince Philip, who was staying at the same hotel. Anne was sharing a suite with her lady-in-waiting. When the reporters contacted Andrews, they wrote that he was " ... angry and refused to deny he had been calling and meeting the princess in secret during their time in the city of lovers"; a statement couched in such terms as to leave readers with little to imagine.

Furthermore, the report went on: "The dashing star raged, 'People are always trying to make something out of something' (his exact words)." The 'something' Andrews was referring to was that he and his wife had been friends with the Phillipses for years and he was fed up with having to deny he was having an affair with Princess Anne.

It was, of course, good gossip for the *News of the World* and that day's issue achieved excellent sales, as is always the case with Royal "scandal" stories. But for Princess Anne it was a further incentive to regard the press with mistrust and contempt to the point that she now adamantly refuses to give interviews on matters relating to her personal life. "The trouble is," she said with some feeling, "I am constantly in the public eye ... always travelling and meeting people ... but the media coverage, particularly on the Continent, mainly consists of pure gossip. It's only social events they bother about, but I can understand it to a degree, and if I can bring the public's attention to the SCF then the rest is immaterial."

She manages to turn most of her interviews into a plug for her beloved Fund and it is now difficult to imagine what course her life would have taken without it. Anne admits that the SCF gave her a chance of a working life, and that's exactly how she has approached the challenge, interspersed as it is with countless other engagements. She appreciates that her work for the Fund is an important and prestigious part of her life and one which raises her above the level of a flimsy princess doing the Royal bit. In that respect, she has also had more success than her brother Prince Charles, in his involvement with the state of British architecture and inner cities, and she even overshadows his charitable Prince's Trust, which was started to aid unemployed youngsters in depressed areas.

No doubt she would have found some other cause but, without the SCF as her public anchor, there would have been obvious temptations for her to drift rather aimlessly through her Royal life – a plight which has befallen other members of her family. Her youngest brother, Edward, has yet to show himself in the Royal traditions of public duties. It was interesting to note, also, that, as the Royals came out of their Christmas hibernation and into 1988, advisers to Princess Diana began moulding her image to give her more "weight". She had been the Royal glamour girl for too long, and it was the Queen Mother who said that perhaps it was time for her to take on a more serious tone. The Duchess of York was now available to share some of the popularity, and Diana's engagements would in future be carefully scrutinized to cut away those now considered too whimsical for our future Queen.

Princess Anne had looked forward to the Christmas holiday; during 1987 she had carried out two hundred and forty-three official engagements, in addition to seventy-nine receptions and banquets, forty-five investitures, audiences, Palace functions, plus her overseas work. She was abroad for a total of sixty-seven days during which she carried out a further three hundred and thirty-seven engagements. Her re-emergence from the holiday was heralded by controversy. In January, she was hurled back on to the front pages – rather fortuitously, considering that she was less than a month away from another major SCF tour – with an outspoken view on AIDS. In a speech she wrote herself, the Princess Royal declared at a conference of health ministers and doctors from one hundred and fifty countries: "AIDS is a

171

classic own-goal scored by the human race on itself." She said the self-inflicted wound on society served to remind man of his fallibility. She spoke of innocent victims, young babies born to carriers of the disease, those who had caught it through blood transfusions and the few infected knowingly by sufferers seeking revenge.

Naturally, her remarks at the World AIDS summit were immediately condemned by homosexuals and gay rights activists. America's surgeon general, Dr Everett Koop, said: "We try not to use words like 'innocent victims' because it implies others are guilty." Peter Tatchell, of the UK AIDS Vigil organization was less polite in his responses, and insisted the princess had been badly advised. "We reject as divisive and discriminatory the Princess Royal's categorization which implies some people are guilty and deserving of their illnesses." Whatever the protesters said, however, she had once again hit the mark because a large percentage of the public agreed with her, tinged though these views were by the attitudes of blue-rinse women in the shires. Soon she would be in the thick of the disease, seeing for herself the ravages in its wake. Kampala, which has more cases of AIDS per head of population than any other city in the world, was the first stop on her 1988 SCF tour, another gruelling excursion lasting fourteen days, covering fifteen thousand miles and visiting Uganda, Mozambique and Somalia.

In preparation for the trip, she had once again undergone debilitating courses of injections and inoculations, including an anti-rabies jab. This time, a doctor would be in permanent attendance, carrying an AIDS kit, containing syringes and plasma matching Anne's blood group. She was also given a personal fly-swatter, an aide whose sole job was to prevent insects and mosquitoes settling upon her.

The difficulties of Uganda, a country once described as the garden of Africa, where trees and crops sustain luscious growth, are, of course, man-made. It has suffered at the hands of mad tyrants like Idi Amin and the genocide of Milton Obote. As she entered Kampala, Princess Anne drove past mounds of skulls and bones, which are heaped for all to see as memorials to the half million or more people systematically slaughtered in the years under Obote. At the British-built Mulago hospital in Kampala, part of which had been given a coat of white paint for her visit, she saw patients, many of them dying from AIDS, lying on dirty floors or on beds that had no mattresses. Running water had only just been restored. Doctors battle against ever-mounting disease, for the equivalent of £7 a month in wages. In the Luwero Triangle, the following day, she saw what remained of an area caught in the most bitter fighting between Obote's soldiers and the resistance army of Yoweri Museveni for most of the first half of the 1980s. The mechanics of civilization had been wiped out: whole villages burnt to the ground, clinics, hospitals and schools razed, farms deserted and run wild. Here Museveni had ordered that human skulls should be hung from the banana trees as a permanent reminder of the mass killings and, whenever visitors arrive at Luwero, it is an instruction that they are shown the mounds of human remains.

For years, relief organizations such as the SCF could not operate here. On every day of that conflict, children were being violated, mothers and fathers were being indiscriminately put to death. The place was awash with orphans. When Princess Anne arrived, community life was showing signs of revival. The SCF had re-established its positions and had set up nutritional centres and clinics. Some of those who survived were able to tell her, in descriptive and galling words, of the horrific suffering. In the village of Kapeka, she visited a home where three children aged between eight and fourteen were living on their own, with the help of Fund people. Both parents had been massacred, and the children fled into the bush, living for months on berries and whatever food they could scavenge. They were found by SCF workers soon after the coup that toppled Obote. Anne was shown the devastation by Fund official Dr Doreen Gihang who told her: "The Obote army looted and raped, and left this place totally naked of any kind of organizational help to the communities. This country has suffered the most appalling crimes since Hitler." The SCF had quickly set to work after the coup, and the Red Cross re-established a health centre in 1985 which was almost immediately looted by fleeing soldiers. Only in 1988, when Anne arrived there, was it being re-equipped and it was then the only health centre to serve an area within a twenty-mile radius. The SCF earmarked one million pounds to be spent in Uganda during 1988, and more is planned for the coming years. At Masuulita, another village Anne visited, the people themselves have built a new school with the aid of the Fund, and, as she entered, the children stood by the dusty roadside singing the songs that relived the war; the verse told the story: "It was a life of terror, murder and robbing."

By the end of that first week, Anne had seen sights which would have sent less experienced travellers into convulsions of tears. What happened next, even she was not expecting. At a reception for the Princess Royal, the conquering President, Museveni, suddenly turned on her in his speech and berated her, as the Queen's daughter and representative of Great Britain, over Britain's past neglect of his country. There, in the magnificence of the State House in Entebbe, a splendid relic of colonial rule set in tranquil lawned grounds overlooking Lake Victoria, he insisted that Britain had done nothing to stop the rape of Uganda by its former rulers Amin and Obote; that it suppressed the truth about the atrocities; and had continued to assist the Obote army even when it was fighting Museveni's guerrilla resistance. Princess Anne took the brunt of his attack without losing her dignity, and, afterwards, it was made quite clear to Museveni that her visit, under the auspices of the Fund, was also a gesture of friendship by Britain towards the new regime.

Ahead were more sights of ghastly poverty, offset by the new and rewarding centres being set up by her Fund in Mozambique and Somalia, where she would spend the next eleven days, before her return to England at the beginning of March. Press coverage of the trip was sparse. Papers like *The Times*, *Telegraph* and *Guardian* carried regular reports; other journalists were less enthusiastic this time about following Anne on another of her jaunts, partly because of the logistics of travel and accommodation, and partly because in some areas, northern Uganda for example, lawlessness was still rife and visitors entered at their peril.

She returned home having lost almost a stone. Mark Phillips brought the children from school to welcome her back; and, now reunited with her family again after days in aircraft, hours in jeeps on dusty dirt tracks, endless visits to sights of despair, hundreds of handshakes and well-meaning official receptions, it could well be expected she might want to get her feet up and take a long rest. But she returned to work straight away.

As she surveyed her diary for the coming week, she had engagements for the SCF on four out of the five days on duty, many of them to report back on her latest journey and to receive the applause of her British organizers. Nor was there any let-up for the rest of March, while the month of April was going to be a particularly busy one. The Palace had given her thirty-four public engagements, over a period of thirty days, compared with fourteen for Prince Charles, thirteen for Princess Diana and four for Prince Edward. Her commitments included unveiling a statue to the Grand National Horse, Red Rum, and attending a St John Ambulance Jamboree. She opened a fertilizer factory and a new British Rail link line. She attended an equestrian conference in Switzerland, and a Country Fair for the Missions to Seamen. She travelled more than five thousand miles, by car, helicopter and plane.

A typical day was April 21. It began with an early morning call at Buckingham Palace, where she had stayed overnight after a late evening engagement. She was up and about by 6.30 am; showered, took a light breakfast and scanned the morning papers. She dressed in sensible, fairly plain clothes and selected her shoes. She had to choose an outfit that would suit all the day's engagements because there would be no time to change during the busy schedule. She picked out a cream skirt with a green, blue and yellow patterned top, that looked elegant, yet relaxed. Her shoes were navy blue, with matching handbag. She had her hair swept up and pinned at the back, and her face attended to, before a meeting with her staff and duty lady-in-waiting, to discuss the previous day's duties and to discover her arrangements for the current day's events. The first was scheduled for 9.15 am, when she was to meet the Marquesa Neneta de Valera who had secured an interview with the princess which was to be published in the first issue of a new Spanish-owned magazine to be launched in Britain, called *Hello*.

By 10.30 am, she was travelling in a Rolls Royce with police motor-cycle outriders down the busy Strand, in the heart of London, to attend a book launch for the Save the Children Fund. She was greeted by Mr Nicholas Hinton, Director General of the SCF, who guided her inside for private discussions with Fund workers and a meeting with the Fund's African review committee; then into a press conference, where she spoke for fifteen minutes. There followed an informal "open house" in which she agreed to answer questions from the floor. By mid-day her lady-in-waiting was looking at her watch. It was the signal to move on, and the princess brought the conference swiftly to a close, ready to attend the buffet luncheon that had been laid on for her. She took a light meal which she just picked at, and sipped a glass of Coca-Cola.

At 12.52, she swept from the luncheon into the Rolls, which was waiting outside with its engine running and police outriders revving their machines to escort her on a speedy journey to Heathrow Airport. There an aircraft of the Queen's Flight was ready to take her to Norfolk. She touched down at RAF Honington at 3.02 pm; transferred to another Rolls Royce; and, at 3.30 pm precisely, was moving slowly up the gravel drive to Overa House Farm in Larling, for her appointment at the Equine Rehabilitation Centre. More handshakes from the waiting reception committee, and she was led by Captain Chris Bennington, Director of the International League for the Protection of Horses, on a tour of the stable blocks and then to meetings with the staff.

At 4 pm, she was moving again, a mile's journey to Hall Farm where she formally declared open another stable block for the ILPH, and informally walked among the waiting crowds who were there to cheer her arrival. Her lady-in-waiting took charge of the armsful of flowers she was given, which were later dispatched to a local old folks' home.

She joked and laughed, and shook more hands, and at 5 pm the engine was running again. Forty minutes later, she was driving up to Bixley Manor, the estate of the Lord Lieutenant of Norfolk. Time for ablutions: a freshen-up and a quick cup of tea. Then back to the Rolls for the remainder of the journey to Norwich where she was due at 6.30 pm, this time for a fund-raising reception for the British Olympics team at Norwich Castle. Guests had paid £50 each for the privilege of being in Princess Anne's company, and her very presence had raised more than £6,000. She was supposed to stay only half an hour, but carried on talking to them for more than an hour.

At 8.15 pm she reached Norwich airport where a Wessex helicopter of the Queen's Flight was ready with rotor-blades whirring to fly her off to Gatcombe Park. It would be 9.45 pm before she would be able to kick off her shoes and relax. A typical, fairly unspecial day which passed like most, without any major press coverage apart from the formalities of official work, and, as far as the rest of the world was concerned, she might as well have been enjoying herself back on the farm with her husband.

The prospect of finding Captain Phillips at Gatcombe might,

however, have been remote. During the first half of 1988, he had been flying back and forth to Gleneagles to supervise the finishing touches to the equestrian centre bearing his name. He travelled to Canada three times, too, in connection with his equestrian work, spending a total of six weeks in that country; and to Spain to look over a new leisure complex, the Sotoclub at Jardines de Sotogrande, in which he has an interest.

Excluding the Christmas holiday period, Mark and Anne were together at home for full days on only twenty-nine occasions during a full six months in 1988.

After the opening of the Gleneagles centre by the Princess Royal on June 2, Mark flew off to Canada for a two-week working tour for which he would receive substantial fees and sponsorship. The tour was almost as busy as one of his wife's overseas trips and, apart from his equestrian clinics, tutorship and other work such as commentating on Canadian television for a major international event, he attended charity banquets and helped raise money for disabled riders. It was during this tour of Canada that the *Sunday Mirror* began to tail him and to monitor his movements. As he was about to return to England, he discovered that the newspaper was preparing to run an investigation into his association with "stunning blonde divorcée, Kathy Birks, aged 44". It would be claimed that he went to extraordinary lengths to conceal his secret liaisons with her.

Miss Birks runs a public relations business which handles many of Mark's interests in Canada and was the subject of newspaper speculation a year earlier when she and Mark were seen out to dinner. Now, the *Sunday Mirror* was able to reveal exclusively, under bold front page headlines, details of a "dossier [compiled by reporters] on the couple's mysterious behaviour in Canada". The report went on to claim that they had been seen enjoying private, candle-lit dinners, had stayed in the same hotel (when her apartment was only a few minutes away), had appeared at breakfast together at the isolated Mill Croft Inn, fifty miles from Toronto, which is a well-known rendezvous for lovers and hideaway for famous stars. He was also seen being driven away from a dinner in her jeep when an official car was waiting to drive him. Reporters interviewed staff at the Mill Croft, and one was quoted as saying that Mark Phillips knew of the inquiries into his association with Miss Birks and "was frightened what might come out".

Once again, Mark found himself confronted by reporters.

He said: "I have a thoroughly professional relationship with Katherine Birks. She organized my tour of Canada; she organized the whole trip. That is the basis of my relationship with her." Miss Birks, when tackled, slammed the door in a reporter's face.

Mark flew back to Britain and went straight to Gleneagles, not home to Gatcombe. That weekend he had promised to captain a shooting team with Jackie Stewart, and now he refused to let his friends down. So another sixteen days passed during which Mark and the Princess Royal did not set eyes on each other. There were, of course, telephone conversations when he was away; though not many. During that period, Anne was busy enough herself, completing twenty-four engagements.

Throughout this time, the Phillipses were experiencing personal worry which neither showed publicly, nor was it taken into account by the press. Mark's mother, Anne, had been ill for some time with a pancreas condition and, soon after he arrived back from Canada, was taken into hospital and, a week later, was on a life-support machine. She died on July 25. Her death was a great blow to them, not just from the standpoint of losing a loved one. Mrs Phillips had become an integral part of Anne's and Mark's life; she was a great supporter of them both, a confidante and a best friend to Anne, and a loving grandmother to Peter and Zara. She, above all, had been ever-present to lend a hand and care for the children when their parents were away. With their maternal grandparents away so often, and as busy as their mother herself, the Phillips children were often with their paternal grandparents, whom they loved, and by whom they were perhaps indulged.

Like his wife, Mark is something of a workaholic. Neither Anne nor Mark could let the personal tragedy affect their lives. As well as his commitments in Scotland, Mark had to throw himself into the organization of the 1988 British Open Horse Trials at Gatcombe Park, which were staged at the beginning of August. Barbour were the sponsors of this event, and throughout this important time, Mark had to make himself available for interviews and personal appearances, as well as team performances, also for Range Rover who sponsor his own competitive activities. He sometimes works a sixteen-hour day. He was aware as he approached forty, that his days in competitive horse-riding were numbered and was planning retirement from serious sport to concentrate on his farming and tutoring, which in themselves will continue to take him all over the world. Like Princess Anne, he is constantly on the move and is well aware that he spends far less time at home with his wife and children than he should. On average, he travels about four months of the year and is sometimes away from home more often than Princess Anne, who hardly ever goes with him on working trips. He said: "When I am away, my work takes up practically all of my time, over ten hours a day minimum. I appreciate it is rather trying for my wife and family but at the moment it is a necessity. Also, when I am not away, our farm keeps me very busy." Because of this, certain family events which would, in most households, be a time of celebration, tend to get overlooked. The couple's past seven wedding anniversaries, for example, have been spent apart. In 1982 and 1983, Anne was in Australia on both occasions; in 1984 Mark was in Dubai and in 1985 he was in New Zealand. He was in Australia in 1986, she was in the Far East in 1987, and he was abroad in 1988.

Anne and Mark probably qualify as the world's most travelled couple, after the Queen and Prince Philip. It must be said that they usually go their separate ways. Until Anne's workload is cut back, the situation is unlikely to alter; for Mark continues to insist that he has to earn a living and he's doing it the only way he knows how, which is with horses and equestrian activities, and there are not enough openings in Britain to keep him sufficiently well employed.

Through all this hard work, there are the children, Peter and Zara. What of them? Anne and Mark, as we have seen, go to great lengths to keep them out of the limelight, which is understandable enough; things will undoubtedly alter as they get older and the press begin to focus their lenses on the growing grandchildren of the Queen. Psychiatrists and child experts might say that the prolonged absences of one or other parent from the home, and sometimes both at the same time, could be a recipe for trouble in later life. The aloofness and lack of parental love of George V and Queen Mary, for instance, has often been cited as the cause of the problems which showed up in some of their children, notably the waywardness of Prince Edward (Duke of Windsor) and his brother George (Duke of Kent) and the extreme shyness and speech impediment of Prince Albert (King George VI). There was, of course, uproar when the Duke and Duchess of York left their newborn Princess Beatrice for a ten-week visit to Australia in September 1988 and few recalled that when the last Duke and Duchess of York (later King George VI and Queen Elizabeth) visited there in 1927, they were away for six months. On that occasion, they were applauded by the press for putting duty before parenthood. But Anne's and Mark's situation is somewhat different because he is a working father, and she is a working princess, and they go out of their way to make up for their absences. Their love and devotion to their children is apparent to all. The children are well to the fore in all family matters and appear not to suffer from their parents' busy schedules.

Peter, aged eleven in 1988, is at boarding school and will remain away from home during term-time until he eventually leaves university. Anne told the Marquesa de Valera: "My boy is one of the most gregarious people I have ever met and he is infinitely happier at school than he would be stuck at home. I think that children are quite capable of enjoying themselves without their parents and they have to learn to cope on their own." Zara, at eight, is still attending a local school. When her parents are away, she remains in the care of Nanny, Sarah Minty. The Queen also keeps in touch on an almost daily basis when she is at home, especially while Anne is away, and so did Mrs Phillips before her death.

Both parents spend a great deal of time with their children during the holidays and it is these areas of family life that are sacred to Anne: she allows nothing to interfere with her plans then. Life at Gatcombe is far less formal for the children than in many other Royal households. Laughter and games ring out, muddy shoes never matter, toys and untidiness illustrate the family atmosphere. Peter spends hours with his father out on the farm. Both children are always keen to join their parents at horsey days out. Zara, of the two of them, shows more promise of following her parents into equestrian activity, though neither as yet has the same aptitude that Anne had at their age.

The children themselves are bright and athletic and seem to have adopted their mother's traits of being strong-willed and occasionally outspoken. Zara, in particular, has to be pulled up sharp now and again and Peter, whose boarding school discipline has quietened him down, still has occasional lapses. There was a huge row at one horse show when he allegedly shouted at photographers: "Get lost, you spastics," the admonishment being not for shouting at the photographers but for insulting the sufferers from that illness.

Both Peter and Zara have no Royal title. They will not be expected to perform Royal duties, nor will they qualify for allowances from the Civil List. This situation could change if Mark decided to accept a title. However, they will always be the Queen's grandchildren, direct descendants of the Monarchy, and can expect that the rest of their lives will not be as shielded from public glare as Princess Anne has so far managed to achieve for them. For example, as Zara and Peter advance in years, they will inevitably become increasingly aware of continual press references to the state of their parents' marriage. Already, it will not have escaped the attention of their school friends that their mother and father have figured in front page headlines about "secret liaisons" and Peter particularly will not have been spared the cruelty of child wit. Nor is there at the moment any reason to suggest that this type of reporting will subside. Gossip is something they will learn to live with, and disregard. Otherwise, if they pay any attention to it at all, as their mother once said: "It'll drive you nuts."

Their parents will always be there to guide them and little can arise for the children in terms of publicity that Anne and Mark haven't already experienced. Pressure from the press is likely to continue, because there is no sign that they plan to amend their life-style to spend more time together. As one of those the author spoke to put it: "I think, at best, theirs is now a marriage of convenience; no overpowering displays of love and affection, yet no animosity either ... They love their children, they love their home and they like being together, as long as it's not for too long. It is an arrangement that works, though it could never have been easy to reach that point where they had virtually eliminated the rows and disregarded the outside influences and comment on their lives and marriage. They worked at it; it has taken time to get it right and now they are well organized, with supportive friends. Perhaps they do have their flirtations but they are not hurting anyone, and especially they don't want to hurt their children."

However, her separations from Mark are occasionally a cause of displays of short-temper and intolerance, as was noticed by a television crew who met her by appointment while preparing a film on her work for the Save the Children Fund. As is normal on such occasions, the head of the television unit lined up his crew for presentation to her. "Is this really necessary?" she asked with weary disdain and then, throughout the subsequent interview, she was diffident and uncooperative. So much so, that when it was over John Haslam, from the Palace press office, apologized and explained that she had just had words with Mark which had upset her. However, the television people were moved to write a letter of complaint over their treatment.

The year of 1988 was something of a turning point in Mark's career. He reached forty in September. His primary business of farming is now well established, under the management of his staff. He now attends chiefly to the business side, though he occasionally likes to indulge in the physical side, too, such as helping with the harvest which he enjoys.

Just as important, now, are his equestrian interests which will undoubtedly make him a millionaire in his own right. As this side of his activities takes more of his energies, we can expect to see him develop into a more popular and public figure. That is not to say that Mark is going out looking for the same kind of media attention that his wife receives. But he is now recognized the world over as an inspired and brilliant tutor. At Gleneagles, where more than three million pounds has been invested by the owners, Guinness, in the centre bearing his name, he will attract residents from home and abroad for the riding courses which start at £250 per person for a weekend. Membership of the centre costs £300 a year and private lessons are priced at £34 for forty-five minutes. He has been hosting riding weekends at the 750-acre hotel complex since 1985, but the new venture will, by its very nature, mean he will have to spend much more time in Scotland. Mark himself has said the centre is the best he has seen anywhere in the world. He was involved in the design, the building and the staffing, and will supervise the overall management of the establishment. It is no small undertaking. Focused around a grand arena which is larger in size than Olympia, there is seating for almost a thousand people. Next to it, is an 800-square metre practice arena, plus a maze of hacking and riding trails. There is private stabling for members, a lecture hall, club rooms, tack shop and leisure facilities. The whole complex is also geared to television so that major international events can be staged there. He has also moved part of his Range Rover-sponsored team of horses and riders to Gleneagles as a permanent base.

In December, Mark's business ventures moved further into the realms of total commercialism when a new fashion catalogue was released under the logo of "Mark Phillips at Gleneagles". It was a glossy, up-market mail order production, complete with male look-alike model with attractive female companions, displaying everything for the fashionable and wealthy, and not restricted to the horsey set. The collection featured items he had personally selected, and ranged from his hall-marked cashmere sweaters to a gentleman's gold watch engraved with the Phillips' logo, a snip at £6,650. There was even a blanket, in his own tartan, at £59.60.

Mark has always gone out of his way to remain just below the surface of the Royal aura, and has often been viewed as a rather nervous outsider in the nation's foremost family. As a Royal escort, he remains, still, a background character and admits to a continued shyness in these situations. But his confidence and ability shine through in the equestrian world which has long been aware of his talent and energy. In the not-too-distant future, he could well be elevated to celebrity status in his chosen field.

The time he is able to share with his busy wife and his family will become even more limited.

When he was selected for the Seoul Olympics, everyone was hoping he would become the golden hero once more, and return victorious with a medal from what could be his last opportunity of representing his country. When he failed in that aim after his horse, Cartier, was pulled up lame in the three-day event, the spotlight of the world's press was once again turned on the couple's private and very separate lives – perhaps not without cause. There were headlines about The Princess and The Pauper when their sleeping arrangements became known. The Princess Royal, as the newest member of the International Olympics Committee, stayed in a pleasant hotel suite at £60 a night, while Mark joined the rest of his team in the spartan apartments of the competitors. There was further scrutiny when Mark failed to arrive at the glittering ceremony when his wife was sworn in as an IOC member and it later emerged he had spent the time practising at an equestrian centre ten miles away. But perhaps a more telling example of how their lives are becoming more distant, through the very weight of their personal schedules, occurred after the Games.

Mark, who didn't see a lot of his wife during the month-long Olympics, remained in the Far East for a lecture tour which would earn him £80,000 – and keep him away from home until December 6, 1988. For almost three months, they hardly had time to say Hello.

Anne also had major commitments to attend both before and after the Olympics. Just before she went to Seoul, for example, she resumed what is becoming another important facet of her work, her prison visits as Patron of the Butler Trust which, it would seem, she is treating with a growing seriousness. Prison reform has clearly become a cause to which she is planning to devote more of her time. She went to Scotland's infamous Barlinnie Prison, which was the scene of violent riots not long before, and she talked and joked with criminals. One encounter with prisoner William Ellis, who presented her with a brooch, was recorded with alarm – that the princess should be put in the position of having to exchange words with a convicted murderer and bank robber! In October, she spent two hours inside the top-security Parkhurst Prison on the Isle of Wight, where she chatted to prisoners serving life and ignored words of caution that her involvement in the controversial cause of prison reform can only lead to embarrassment of herself and the Government.

The following month, November, Anne came under close observation in Canada. The press were speculating that Mark's business acquaintance, Kathy Birks, had been told to keep a very low profile during the visit. What was obvious to everyone, however, was that their joint workload has placed an incredible strain upon the marriage of Anne and Mark, and the fact that it survives must be seen as a credit to them both.

By the end of the year, the Princess Royal had completed a record six hundred and thirty four official duties for 1988, which was one hundred and ten more than the Queen herself. She had also visited fourteen countries. Prince Charles logged four hundred and sixty nine engagements and the Duke and Duchess of York's combined total was two hundred and fifty three.

The Future

The role of the Princess Royal, in years not-too-far distant, can only become even more demanding as she moves closer to assuming the mantle of a kind of matriarchal figure which she will be forced to adopt by the simple course of nature. She will be at the centre of significant events, heralded for the next decade and beyond, which will change the face of British Monarchy. Influences for change will come from the outside, but also from within the Royal family itself, and not the least is the contribution we can expect from its leading lights, especially the Queen, the Queen Mother and the Princess Royal.

Time will tell. For example, the Queen Mother, though she has shown no signs of giving up her public work, must soon come to the day when she can no longer go flitting about the country in her helicopter. The Queen herself, as she edges closer towards her three score years and ten, will eventually have to face the fact that she cannot keep up her world-wide activities with the same vigour she has displayed for the past thirty-five years. Consequently, more work will fall to the Princess Royal.

Will the Queen retire, and abdicate to give her son a more positive role? The author thinks this is unlikely, but that Prince Charles can be expected to assume some of her workload as the years go by. The Duke and Duchess of York will also be brought more into the public arena and will take over some of the tasks previously done by the Prince and Princess of Wales. (The Yorks' Australian tour in the autumn of 1988 is an example of this.) The Princess of Wales, as our future Queen, will eventually rank senior to Anne, but the Princess Royal is the more experienced, and, at the moment, the harder working in public life.

If there is a staff shortage among the Royal family in the coming years, this will bring only pleasure to those who would like to see a cut in the Civil List allocation. Only those who perform public duties get money from the Civil List. The children of Princess Margaret, the Duke and Duchess of Kent, Princess Alexandra and the Princess Royal, for example, show few signs of following their parents into public life. Indeed, most are doing their best to avoid it, as they develop the pursuits of more ordinary working young men and women, such as carpentry and secretarial work. Unless they show an abrupt about-turn in later life, there will certainly not be as many working Royals as the Queen has had to support her during her reign so far.

As these changes begin to occur, the fear in many quarters is that the Royal family will diminish in its importance and relevance to modern society. For those of a republican view, this will be seen as a welcome and natural progression for which there will be supporting elements outside the Queen's control.

In 1992, Britain will be tied irrevocably, both politically and economically, to the European Community. Unless there is a radical change in public opinion, Prime Minister Margaret Thatcher will continue to strengthen her grip on the political scene, which is already at the point where some of her more devoted followers see in their leader something of the mystique that the Court of Windsor has for so long tried to maintain. Although Mrs Thatcher herself has been somewhat apprehensive about the creation of a United States of Europe, on the lines advocated by more ardent supporters of that philosophy, such as Mr Edward Heath, the move towards the Community is bound to affect the British Monarchy. If a single European currency is created, it would presumably have the effect of removing the Queen's portrait from the coin of the realm.

Was it also significant that, when the Queen made the first visit by a British Monarch to Spain in October 1988, she was preceded in that excursion by Mrs Thatcher? It is an interesting phenomenon of the late 1980s that, while the Royal family has faced the increasing trivialization of its deeds through the popular press, Mrs Thatcher has established herself as a sort of mother-figure to the nation. Barring crisis, scandal or death, she will probably sustain her own matriarchal role, and become a Churchillian figure, revered in a strange love-hate way by millions, regardless of political persuasion. Hitherto, the British Monarch has often been seen as a symbol of unity, above faction; but now Mrs Thatcher, hated though she is by many, has inspired an aura of confidence and security that cuts right across British society, not only among the well-off but even among those in the lower reaches of the great divide she has so often been accused of creating. At the end of the last Labour Party conference, a national opinion poll put her leagues ahead of Neil Kinnock as the person the majority would like to run the country.

As the nation becomes more tied to Europe, it will be Mrs Thatcher – or one of her successors – who will perhaps be seen as the leader of Britain. Our Monarch will make unimportant courtesy visits. The prospect of sharing the British Royal family with, say, the French or the Germans in any significant or powerful way is as unlikely as seeing the Spanish Royal family in the same role in Europe.

On occasions of great importance Mrs Thatcher will be in the limelight. Even if the financial crisis, in which some pundits believe, sinks the Conservative Government and sends Mrs Thatcher into the wilderness, the Monarchy can hardly seek comfort in the election of a Labour Government. Labour's election pledges may contain an additional hazard. Some still wish to disband the House of Lords and, if that happens, some of the pomp, pageantry and ancestry that links the Crown and Her Majesty's Government will be stripped away for ever. Many earnestly desire this, others will regret its passing.

There are other changes, also. There is no longer an Empire for the Monarch to rule over. An increasingly republican opinion in Australia, New Zealand and Canada has stimulated efforts in Britain to attempt to retain the popularity of the Royal family and to sustain some sort of public devotion, lest these major English-speaking countries go the same way as India (once the jewel in the Monarch's crown) or Africa (where the Queen now has little loyalty or following). A majority of government leaders in the Commonwealth have, in reality, long since divorced themselves from Britain which they see as a supporter of their arch enemy, South Africa. Most, anyway, are anxious to sever all the threads of colonial history, content perhaps only to accept Third-World aid from their former rulers.

This decline in the Monarchy's international influence will undoubtedly continue, as more senior members of the family begin to take a back seat, and as the great bonds between Britain and countries that once were part of her Empire fade into distant memory, and as the special relationships forged during crises and war die with the last remnants of that generation.

I have canvassed many opinions about the future role of the Royal family in the course of interviews for this book, and the consensus is beyond doubt that the Monarchy will survive. The question that carries more doubt is: In what form? Jeffrey Archer, for instance, is of the view that the strength of present members of the family, and the work of the Princess Royal in particular, will see it in good stead. He told me: "Say what you like, the British are a sentimental race and I think the Monarchy is as popular now as it's ever been and it will survive the trivialization of its work. The only problem that might occur – and it will not, I think, with Prince Charles – is that on occasions we get a bad Monarch; every fourth or fifth seems to go wrong and if we get a bad Monarch in the twenty-first century, the Monarchy as we know it today might well begin to crumble. It will survive if the standards of public duty set by the Queen, Prince Charles and the Princess Royal are maintained."

My former colleague, Victor Knight, a respected political journalist who has spent much of his working life during the last forty years in the House of Commons, agreed. "The Princess Royal is an integral part of the system and operation of Monarchy which exists today, and which the Queen herself has moulded to twentieth-century requirements. Her importance is beyond measure and can only increase in the next couple of decades because she has set an example of the way in which members of the Royal family can extend its respect and following. Far from the Monarchy facing the prospect of demise, I would say that it is now more popular than it has ever been, but it goes deeper than that. The Princess Royal, in her career role, has travelled hundreds of thousands of miles, she has met dozens of politicians and world leaders, she has met more people in more countries than many of our senior politicians and that experience cannot be taken lightly. In reality republicans are thin on the ground and I cannot believe that the Monarchy faces extinction. What would we put in its place? A superannuated politician as president, as they have in other European countries? With due respect to the personalities it is laughable to suggest we should replace the Queen with some retired statesperson like Jim Callaghan, Ted Heath, or even Mrs Thatcher. Britain's great pride and heritage is its Royal family and, if there were a referendum tomorrow, I am sure eighty per cent of the British electorate would vote to keep it. But their influence is not just in popular pageantry. The Queen, and latterly the Princess Royal, all have immense experience of world affairs. They are actually able to say to ministers when discussing problems overseas: 'I've been there' or 'I've talked to him' and warn of possible problems. The Queen is the most experienced person in British life; she has been reading the Cabinet papers for almost forty years and, while there is never any question of a more politically active role for any of them without a change in the constitution, their very presence is of great benefit to any government which may be in power. She is also very sensitive and protective about her role, and when Mrs Thatcher once referred to Her Government, the Queen promptly pointed out that it was Her Majesty's Government."

Victor Knight's assessment of the nation's support for the Monarchy was proved to be remarkably accurate by a Gallup Poll conducted for the *Daily Telegraph* at the end of 1988. It showed eighty-two per cent of those interviewed were in favour of retaining the Monarchy in its present form, although forty per cent also thought that the annual Civil List awards to the Royal family, which amounted to £5,250,000 in 1988, were too high. Almost half those questioned were also of the view that the Monarch had little influence on affairs of State and the Walter Bagehot adage that the Monarch has the right to be consulted, the right to encourage and the right to warn now seems a little dated.

The Princess Royal came top in the category of "caring" but also collected some brickbats for her displays of arrogance and snobbishness. Apart from Anne's acclaim, the public seem now to view the Royal family's function principally in the role of super-public relations at home and overseas and, doubtless, if the Civil List cost was laid against their benefit to tourism there would be few complaints. However, it is clear that the public does notice when Royalty goes astray, and perhaps it is time for a more concerted effort by the Palace to correct certain unfortunate images.

Perhaps it is a pity that attractive young stars like the Princess of Wales and the Duchess of York have brought a following which is more in line with Hollywood than with the House of Windsor, in which they have been eagerly assisted by the media and have little control over. But other aspects of Royal life can be re-examined so that their activities do not add to the downgrading effect. Perhaps it is a pity that the Prince and Princess of Wales were used, blatantly, to sell British products in

America. (Or is that to be one of their prime roles in the future?) Perhaps it is a pity that Prince Michael and Captain Mark Phillips go cap in hand to sponsors to finance their sporting activities and, by association, allow the Crown to be tainted by the lust of commercialism.

The Royal family must be able to be taken seriously. It must remain aloof, regain some of its mystery, take itself out of the Soap Opera category and restore some of the lost glow that has evaporated through familiarity. Buckingham Palace has its own responsibility for the trivialization of the family. The Queen's advisers are not always on the mark; Lord Mountbatten was largely instrumental in edging the family towards a more open life, and, as the popular press dived in, the Monarchy suffered the consequences.

Certain Royal personalities who damaged the aura of the Crown, such as Princess Michael, have been quieter of late; but some viewers questioned the televised performance of the Duchess of York in Australia, when she kept insisting when speaking to distant children over a two-way radio: "This is The Duchess here," as if were some joke title. She was matched by a child's answer: "Yes, your Royalty." Andrew was also going too heavily on trying to be "just one of the boys" when everyone knows that he is not, never has been and never will be. During his tour of Lockerbie after the PanAm air disaster in December 1988, he was heavily criticized for his abruptness and ill-considered remarks. And, if Prince Charles was unhappy with the ITV programme on his own private life, he probably has his advisers to blame. Didn't anyone consider telling him that he was laying himself open to the possibility of over-exposure? Prince Charles's excellent documentary for BBC TV on British architecture was rightly acclaimed. Opinion polls showed massive support for his views, and applauded his courage. But do we want our future King to adopt the role, however creative and polemical, of television presenter?

The Princess Royal has deftly sidestepped many pitfalls, and has tried to keep her private life within the confines of Gatcombe. She is touchy even over the annual intrusion of visitors for her husband's equestrian event.

Have the press been unfair to her over the years? Have they belittled her good deeds, in the shadow of stories of bad temper, rude behaviour and salacious stories? I sought some answers from within the newspaper industry itself, and went first to an agony aunt, my old friend and former colleague, Marje Proops who was granted one of the first open interviews with Princess Anne and Mark Phillips in the 1970s. Marje said: "I think the hostility with which Princess Anne was treated in the tabloids was largely due to her own hostile attitudes towards them. She has made no attempt to hide her impatience and irritation and it is not surprising they reacted in the way they did. They changed, though, when her devotion to Save the Children became obvious and she now appears to be among the top of the royal polls with the mass media. Certainly when I met her at her home, I liked her enormously; she was funny, cordial, relaxed and consequently I was too. Often since then, I've found myself defending her when other journalists have made snarling remarks about her. I am also inclined to believe that the unconfirmed 'news', or gossip, about the Royals has been stretched by some of the tabloids beyond an acceptable level and Muggeridge is right; it is a Royal Soap Opera which HM's subjects find utterly enthralling, and since it is very difficult indeed, if not impossible, to get accurate information out of the Buck House press office, it is hardly surprising that the gossip is all too often reported as hard news. I doubt if it bothers the Royal stars very much though, I expect they are both amused and inured."

Meanwhile, David Montgomery, editor of *Today* and formerly editor of the *News of the World*, agrees that the Princess Royal suffered a tremendously bad press in the early part of her working life, but this was brought on largely by her own attitudes and actions. "However, I feel this has been replaced by a true respect," says Montgomery, "which newspapers reflect in their coverage of her. She has become a public figure, who happens to be a member of the Royal family, much admired for her qualities of leadership. Like the Queen, she is a leader of her people, a tireless worker and the esteem in which she is now held was earned the hard way, by showing and proving to everyone just what she could do. In the main, the media have accepted her importance and regard her with much greater understanding; there will always be the other side of the the coin, and sensational stories surrounding her, but they are balanced by the good things. During the coverage of the claims by her detective Peter Cross, for example [published at a time when Montgomery was editor of the *News of the World*] Princess Anne was herself not criticized and she was seen as the victim, a person under pressure who was also lonely and in need of support. But she has grown out of all that. She is quite unlike any other member of her family, particularly some of the lesser Royals whose public display of wealth and extravagance is turning the public against them. Princess Anne has never relished wealth and material things; she started out as someone who would have happily made her way in life successfully from more humble beginnings. She has always sought a life, privately, which was as close as possible to normal, and people I know who have met her at horse shows tell me she is pleasant and casual and doesn't show any of the arrogance seen in some other members of her family. In public life, like the Queen, she retains the mystique. Andrew and Fergie, I think, are succeeding in doing the opposite; the extravagance they have shown at the start of their married life has brought critical reaction. Many people see Andrew as a bit of a buffoon who seems intent on extracting what he can from his position. They are swanning around, looking overfed and fairly useless, and the public is becoming contemptuous of them. Prince Charles is a different kettle of fish; unlike Anne he has never had, nor been given, a definite aim or purpose other than to be the King-in-Waiting. He is a highly sensitive and very shy man who is facing the dilemma of knowing what to do with his life until he is crowned King. Perhaps it is the system that is wrong."

Montgomery agrees with me that a lot of the blame rests with Palace advisers who, he thought, were of pretty poor quality, bearing in mind the importance of the people they were working for. "Charles especially," said Montgomery, "is a victim of stunts and things that his advisers haven't properly thought through or guarded against; consequently he dips into things, here and there, without a real role. Anne wouldn't have stood for it if she was in his position, as heir apparent; she has always forced her own pace and has never let anyone get in her way. That is why she is what she is, a woman in tune with reality and the modern world and not restrained by the old-fashioned ties of the system of Monarchy."

As for the future, Montgomery is among those who believe that with a more sophisticated populace, the Royal family will have difficulty in surviving in its present form in the next century. "People will be less and less willing to accept the view that they are above ordinary mortals," he said, "and more and more anxious to see them earning an honest living. The more senior Royals who work hard and define a role for themselves will continue to command respect. The junior members of the family will not be tolerated if they indulge themselves hunting, shooting and holidaying and generally having a good time with vulgar and frivolous displays of their wealth and status. The press will continue to pursue them. Quality papers will be questioning their political influence and views more intensely. The popular newspapers will still look for the juicy scandals and no doubt find them. In retaliation, I think the Royals will be more likely to use the law to curb the media's attentions. But as one senior Royal said to me: 'When you lot stop pestering us, no one else in the country will care about us either. Then we will be out of business.'"

Buckingham Palace press people are always on hand, because the Royal family seek and enjoy the *right* kind of publicity. But the gushing coverage of the Duchess of York's pregnancy and the eventual arrival of Princess Beatrice reached new heights. The *Sun*, the *Star* and the *Daily Mirror* rejoiced with the two-inch headline: "It's a girl", a fact of which few could have been unaware, since the news had been broadcast repeatedly on radio and television and since Fergie had her baby at 8.18 on August 8 1988 – all the "eights" which allowed *Today* newspaper to insist that the young princess was "Born Lucky". *Today* devoted ten of its thirty-two pages to the Royal birth, compared with eight in the *Sun*, six in the *Mail* and *Mirror*, and a more manageable three in the *Daily Express*. The *Guardian*, *Telegraph* and *The Times* recorded the event with front-page news coverage, while Mr Andreas Whittam Smith, editor of the *Independent*, carried only a small paragraph. He said: "All this intense coverage makes them a running TV serial. A charming couple have a baby. That is all the story there is. The rest is complete synthetic hysteria."

Twenty-four hours later, the whole scenario was repeated when the Duchess stepped out of the hospital with her new arrival. She was greeted by over two hundred photographers, and, since most of them use motorized cameras, something over five hundred pictures of her would have been taken in that first second of her appearance. Jean Rook, of the *Daily Express*, led a chorus of those who felt it was all getting too much. "Since the first coming, no infant's birth has been so prophesied, heralded and all but starred in the East. But it is not over yet;

split seconds after the happy hospital snaps the bitchier fashion critics will be focused on Fergie's shape." The *Sun* did, of course, and under the headline "Return to Slender" advised the Duchess of York to lose fifty-six pounds!

The Princess Royal was brought into the press ravings, first with the "exclusive" that the Queen had asked the Duke and Duchess of York to make her a godmother because of her disappointment at not being asked by Charles and Diana; and then with the news that she would not be asked, after all, which rather cancelled out the first exclusive.

What is it that makes the popular newspaper continually go for overkill and saturation about anything to do with Royalty? What is it that inspires editors and publishers to part with large sums of cash to bribe servants, hairdressers, fashion people or plain snoopers to tell all about Diana's wardrobe, or Fergie's labour, or Mark's dinner with a blonde, or Anne's liaison with an actor? The answer is simple. Circulation. Every sensational Royal story will guarantee lots of extra newspaper sales, tens of thousands. A good royal souvenir issue will not only sell lots of extra copies, it will also attract top-money advertising content. The interest is purely commercial, in the end, and it is also self-perpetuating. Because, seemingly, the more the masses get in terms of Royal coverage, the more they apparently want. It can be compared to the early days of Hollywood, when movie producers discovered their actors becoming known and followed avidly by filmgoers, and the word filmstar was born. These icons of the screen became so famous that fan magazines just could not get enough material to publish about them. The same has been happening these past few years with British Royalty. Magazines around the world, in every language, have built them up into glittering, glitzy stars.

So where is all this synthetic hysteria leading? My view is that it is leading in a direction which will make the Royal family so accessible to the public, and so stripped of their dignity, that in the end they will just become media figures, like Joan Collins and Elizabeth Taylor.

Years ago, when Joe Haines, the *Mirror* Group's political editor, was press secretary to Prime Minister Harold Wilson, he was asked to draft a definition of privacy to protect people in public life from the intrusive camera and notebook. Joe told me: "My answer was simple. It read: 'That every citizen should be accorded the same right to privacy as is accorded to the families of newspaper proprietors.' That would be a revolution as far as the Royal family is concerned, indeed, as far as anyone is concerned, but there has to be a middle way between total privacy and relentless exposure. It is time, for the Royal family's sake, the newspapers' sake and the country's sake, for the media to start backing off. To put it crudely: to stop speculating about the size of Fergie's backside, to stop peering at Diana to see if her nipples show she isn't wearing a bra, and to stop mocking Charles as he struggles to find some meaning to an often meaningless life."

It is not only Royalty who suffer either, as a recent example clearly showed. In September 1988, television personality Mike Smith and his girlfriend Sarah Greene were taken to hospital after a helicopter crash. Some time after his admission, Smith noticed the presence of an unfamiliar "doctor". The man was wearing a white smock and carried a rather large, old-fashioned doctor's bag. When challenged, it was discovered he was not a doctor at all; he was a Fleet Street photographer and one end of his bag had been cut away to allow his camera lens to focus on Mike Smith lying in his hospital bed. It didn't end there. Soon afterwards, Smith heard noises outside his room window; two journalists, a reporter and photographer, were posing as workmen and were actually in the process of climbing a scaffold tower to get to Smith's bedroom window and take his picture. It is this kind of intrusive and scurrilous behaviour that is giving journalism a foul name.

This view is shared by Magnus Linklater, editor of the *Scotsman*, who analysed the situation for me thus: "There is something distinctly manic about the way the popular press today sets about the Royal family. The mania has its peaks and troughs. An early symptom may be a simple front-page picture of a pensive Princess of Wales. Within days, this can swell into an outburst of competitive hysteria, with each paper claiming its share of foaming exclusives about the collapse of the Royal marriage or the nervous breakdown of the heir to the Throne. This is followed, in the nature of the disease, by a period of depression as the Royal couple in question continue to live perfectly normal lives and fail signally to conform to the lurid picture presented of them. There is a distinct sense of resentment that they have somehow fallen short of the fictional drama in which they were meant to star. If on the other hand, Royalty occasionally slips from some arbitrary standard of public morality set for it by the same newspapers there is outrage. What, they demand, has our Royal family come to? How can the British public maintain its respect for a Monarchy that is so flawed? Any psychiatrist analysing this pattern of behaviour would immediately reach for the lithium or prescribe a rapid course of intensive psycho-therapy, but so long as the fierce competition at the bottom end of the newspaper market continues, the popular press will continue its mad habit of adulation and denigration."

Linklater posed an interesting question: How much does all this matter? For Royalty itself, the attentions of the press are doubtless irritating, occasionally maddening; and for the rest of us, they are shocking or amusing, according to taste. The danger, if such there is, lies in the increasing irrelevance of this mass coverage and consequently to the Monarchy itself. Linklater said: "Shorn of its more serious contribution to British life, it becomes merely entertainment, and gradually, the entertainment loses its appeal. Sooner or later, someone may ask the dreaded question: Do we need it? If you are a republican all of this will be excellent news. As Royalty floats away on an ebb-tide of massive inconsequence, you look forward to a new and healthier constitutional era. If, on the other hand, you believe the British Monarchy to be important, you may be more concerned. For those who fall into the latter category, Princess Anne is a saving grace. She has been through the denigration period when she was derided for being arrogant and toffee-nosed. She has survived the adulation period when her work in Africa with Save the Children elevated her to near-sainthood. She has had her share of soap opera stardom, though there may be future roles in reserve. What she has become is herself, a remarkable collected, sensible and down-to-earth lady who has chosen some important and interesting public work to do and who does it extremely well. Her prison role is perhaps the most innovative and effective one that any members of the Royal family have yet chosen. Because it is an area where reform is both necessary and unpopular, her patronage of the Butler Trust which highlights the work that is going on inside prisons, contributes to breaking down the clichés about life inside prison walls. Because she has the ability to talk without condescension to prison officers and prisoners alike, she helps bridge the gap between them. And because she maintains a certain brisk objectivity, she can deliver the odd home truth where it will be most effective. Prison work was a risky choice for her to make; but it has been a great success."

If any future member of the Royal family were seeking a model, the Princess Royal might well be the one to choose. As Linklater says: "In short, she makes the best case for the Royal family today because she uses the natural attention she receives for wholly practical ends. What she does is not spectacularly glamorous but, at the same time, it is not so routine that it ceases to be interesting. At the forefront of social reform on the prison front, drawing attention to starvation and neglect with her Save the Children work, she has used her royalness to singular effect, without in any way cheapening or undermining it. What she has also managed – so far – is to hang on to her own personality rather than one created for her by the popular press. She has done so by maintaining friendly if distant relations with the media and yet without incurring their resentment. Altogether in this day and age, that is quite an achievement."

So where does the future of the Royal family lie? One thing is fairly certain: readers demand Royal stories and editors, until they note a change in that climate, will not alter their approach. As satellite and "tabloid" television channels join the ever-increasingly competitive media, saturation coverage will get worse before it gets better.

Secondly, the Royal family will have to discover ways of adapting to avoid an evaporation of their effectiveness. The Princess Royal, who could already lay claim to a Nobel prize for her work, will be a prominent and influential voice in maintaining dignity and achieving this effectiveness. Her stature, I am sure, will be unscathed by any feelings of worthlessness or diminished by trivialization. At the outset of this chapter, I offered the view that she will be forced to adopt the role of mother figure to the Royal family. Eventually, probably long before she becomes the matriarch, she will be the ardent protector of her family's status.

As a last word on the subject, I put forward an assessment made for me by Mr Edward Heath, whose experience in Royal circles is a sound basis for his comment: "In Salisbury Cathedral recently, the Princess Royal had a packed audience spellbound with a lecture that was so obviously her own work and answered questions spontaneously with such a mastery of her subject that everyone was full of admiration for her grasp of the issue and

197

her detailed knowledge of the situation in so many countries. As a member of the Brandt Commission which has produced two reports on relations between developed and developing countries, I fully appreciate the immense contribution the Princess Royal is making to increasing public understanding of these world-wide problems and mustering support for the underprivileged. In her sporting activities, in her work for children, she maintains a personal elegance combined with quiet dignity worthy of her mother and grandmother and acknowledged by those who meet her the world over."

The Princess Royal has earned this honest respect through sheer endeavour in which she is matched by few other members of her family. She still has an irritable impatience, which will mellow; she still has a tart haughtiness, which will subside. Her abrasive goodness will, eventually, convert itself into a loving regard from her nation.

The Princess Royal Fact File

Born:

August 15, 1950, at Clarence House, second child of Queen Elizabeth II (when she was Princess Elizabeth) and the Duke of Edinburgh. She was baptized at Buckingham Palace on October 21, 1950, by the late Dr Cyril Garbett, Archbishop of York and was given the names Anne, Elizabeth, Alice, Louise. She received the title of Princess Royal in June 1987. She was educated first by private class at Buckingham Palace and, in 1963, became a pupil at Benenden School, Kent.

Work:

At the age of eighteen, Her Royal Highness began to undertake public engagements alone for the first time and notably the following year when she opened an education training centre in Shropshire. She also began to accompany the Queen and the Duke of Edinburgh officially on State Visits, the first being in Austria in May 1969. Since then she has travelled extensively on her own account, especially in her capacity of president of the Save The Children Fund.

Sport:

In 1971, she won the Raleigh Trophy in the Individual European three-day-event at Burghley and was nominated Sportswoman of the Year by the Sports Writers Association, the *Daily Express*, *World Sport* and the journal of the British Olympics Association. She was also voted the BBC's Sports Personality of the Year in 1971. She competed in the European three-day-event at Kiev in 1973, as a British Team Member in the Federal Republic in Germany in 1975 and won silver medals in both individual and team competitions. In 1976 she was a member of the British Three-day-event Team in the Olympics at Montreal and has been a consistent competitor in major three-day-events throughout Britain and Europe. She has competed in the Horse of the Year Show at Wembley and latterly has achieved success as a jockey in horseracing.

Offices:

She became President of the Save the Children Fund in 1970. Her many other appointments include: Commandant in Chief of the St John Ambulance Brigade, Chancellor of London University, President of the Riding for the Disabled Association, President of the Missions to Seamen, President of the British Academy of Film and Television Arts, Patron of the Jersey Wild Life Fund, President of the British Olympics Association, member of the International Olympics Committee, Patron of the British School of Osteopathy, Patron of the Spinal Injuries Association, Honorary President of the Chartered Institute of Transport, Honorary President of the British Knitwear and Clothing Export Council, President of the International Equestrian Federation (succeeding her father), Patron of the Intensive Care Society, Patron of the National Union of Townswomen's Guilds, and Patron of the Butler Trust.

Services (main appointments):

Colonel in Chief of the 14th/20th King's Hussars, of the Worcester and Sherwood Foresters Regiment, of the Royal Corps of Signals, of the Royal Scots and of the 8th Canadian Hussars; Commandant in Chief of the Women's Royal Naval Services, Commandant in Chief of the Women's Transport Services, Patron of the Association of WRNS, President of the Women's Royal Naval Services Benevolent Trust, Patron of the Army and Royal Artillery Hunter Trials,

Family:

She became engaged to Lieutenant (later Captain) Mark Phillips of the Queen's Dragoon Guards on May 29, 1973; they were married in Westminster Abbey on November 14, 1973. Their first home was Oak Grove House, Royal Military Academy, Sandhurst, where Captain Phillips was an instructor. Moved to Gatcombe Park, Gloucestershire, a house and farm bought by the Queen in 1976. Their first child, Peter, Mark, Andrew, was born at St Mary's Hospital, Paddington on November 15, 1977 and he was christened at a service in the Music Room of Buckingham Palace by the Archbishop of

Canterbury on December 22, 1977. Their second was born on May 15, 1981, also at Paddington, and was christened Zara, Anne, Elizabeth at a service at the Chapel at Windsor Castle by the Dean of Windsor on July 21, 1981.

Principal Overseas Visits

(The Princess Royal has also made unofficial visits overseas with members of her family, has taken part in skiing holidays, and has been on cruises in the Royal Yacht. All private visits and holidays are excluded.)

1954 **LIBYA, MALTA and GIBRALTAR** In April and May, went to Tobruk with Prince Charles to meet their parents who were returning from a Commonwealth tour; also visited Malta and Gibraltar.

1962 **FRANCE** Made a private educational visit in the summer as guest of the Marquis and Marquise de Saint-Genys at their château at Chapelle-sur-Ondon, Anjou.

1964 **GREECE** Visited Athens in September with Prince Philip and the Prince of Wales for the wedding of King Constantine and Princess Anne-Marie of Denmark, where she was one of six princesses who were train-bearers to the bride.

1966 **JAMAICA** Visited Jamaica in August with the Duke of Edinburgh and the Prince of Wales to attend the Commonwealth Games.

1969 **AUSTRIA** In May, joined the Queen and the Duke of Edinburgh on their State Visit.
NORWAY Made a five-day semi-official visit in HMY *Britannia* in August with the rest of her family.
FEDERAL REPUBLIC OF GERMANY In October and November, paid a three-day visit to Paderborn, to the 14th/20th King's Hussars, of which she is Colonel-in-Chief.

1970 **FIJI, TONGA, NEW ZEALAND and AUSTRALIA** Accompanied the Queen and the Duke of Edinburgh on their spring tour of Fiji, Tonga, New Zealand and Australia (the Prince of Wales joining the party for the latter two countries).
FEDERAL REPUBLIC OF GERMANY In June, laid foundation stone of the Florence Nightingale Hospital at Düsseldorf-Kaiserwerth and visited army units at Paderborn.

CANADA and UNITED STATES   Made a ten-day visit in July to Canada with the Queen, the Duke of Edinburgh and the Prince of Wales, marking the centenaries of the North-West Territories and the Province of Manitoba. Following this, she and her brother paid a three-day visit to Washington as guests of President Nixon's daughters and son-in-law.

FEDERAL REPUBLIC OF GERMANY   Visited the RAF in Bruggen in September and presented the Queen's Colours to the Royal Air Force, Germany, on behalf of the Queen.

1971   **KENYA**   With Prince Charles, made a two-week visit to Kenya in February, mainly to see the work of the Save the Children Fund.

CANADA   Accompanied the Queen and the Duke of Edinburgh to British Columbia (3–12 May) for the centennial celebrations of the Province.

IRAN and TURKEY   Visited Tehran in October with the Duke of Edinburgh to attend the 2,500th anniversary celebrations of the Iranian Monarchy, after which they joined the Queen for the State Visit to Turkey.

HONG KONG   Stayed in Hong Kong for five days in October and November, where she visited the 14th/20th King's Hussars, of which she is Colonel-in-Chief, and toured hospitals, schools and nurseries which are assisted by the Save the Children Fund.

1972   **THE FAR EAST**   Accompanied the Queen and the Duke of Edinburgh on the first part of their Far Eastern tour in February and March, visiting Thailand, Singapore, Malaysia and Brunei.

FEDERAL REPUBLIC OF GERMANY   Went to Munich with the Duke of Edinburgh for the Olympic Games in August and September.

YUGOSLAVIA   Accompanied her parents on their State Visit to Yugoslavia in October.

1973   **ETHIOPIA**   During February carried out official engagements in Addis Ababa and other places and also did a mule trek in the Simien Mountains.

SUDAN   In February visited Khartoum for official engagements.

FEDERAL REPUBLIC OF GERMANY   Went to Berlin in June to visit the Worcestershire and Sherwood Foresters Regiment (29th/45th Foot), of which she is Colonel-in-Chief.

SOVIET UNION   Visited Kiev to take part in the European Three-Day-Event Championships.

ECUADOR, COLOMBIA, JAMAICA, MONTSERRAT and ANTIGUA   Paid official visits during December with Captain Mark Phillips following their honeymoon cruise on HMY *Britannia*, which took them from Barbados to the Galapagos.

1974   **CANADA**   Paid an official visit to Ottawa with Captain Phillips.

NEW ZEALAND, NORFOLK ISLAND, NEW HEBRIDES, BRITISH SOLOMON ISLANDS, PAPUA NEW GUINEA and AUSTRALIA   With Captain Phillips, accompanied her parents on their visit.

FEDERAL REPUBLIC OF GERMANY   In March visited the 14th/20th King's Hussars at Herford.

CANADA   Visited Toronto in November with Captain Phillips, to go to the Royal Agricultural Winter Fair.

1975   **AUSTRALIA**   Visited Australia in April and May for a fortnight's tour.

FEDERAL REPUBLIC OF GERMANY   In June visited the 14th/20th King's Hussars.

FEDERAL REPUBLIC OF GERMANY   In August and September took part in the European Three-Day-Event.

1976   **CANADA**   In July competed in the Olympic Games at Montreal as a member of the British Three-Day-Event Team.

FEDERAL REPUBLIC OF GERMANY   In May visited the Royal Air Force station at Gütersloh.

1977   **UNITED STATES**   In June, accompanied by Captain Phillips, visited Washington and Maryland, where she unveiled a statue of Queen Anne in Centerville, Queen Anne's County.

1978   **FEDERAL REPUBLIC OF GERMANY**   In July visited the 14th/20th King's Hussars at Hohne.

FEDERAL REPUBLIC OF GERMANY   In October visited the Canadian Forces, Communications and Electronics Branch, at Lahr.

NORWAY   In November visited Norway in connection with Redd Barna and the Save the Children fund.

1979   **PORTUGAL**   In May visited Portugal for three days with Captain Phillips.

FEDERAL REPUBLIC OF GERMANY   In June visited the Royal Corps of Signals and also the 14th/20th King's Hussars.

THAILAND   In July, accompanied by Captain Phillips, visited Thailand.

GILBERT ISLANDS   Accompanied by Captain Phillips,

represented the Queen at the independence celebrations in July.

NEW ZEALAND   Visited New Zealand briefly in July.

AUSTRALIA   Visited Australia at the end of July.

BAHAMAS   Accompanied by Captain Phillips, attended the celebrations in honour of the 250th anniversary of the Bahamas Parliament at the end of September.

CANADA   In November visited Ottawa and Ontario in connection with the Save the Children Fund.

1980   **CYPRUS**   Visited the Royal Corps of Signals in February.

FRANCE   Visited Paris to attend the dinner of the Académie des Sports in June.

BELGIUM   In June visited Brussels to attend the Ball at the British Embassy in celebration of the 150th anniversary of Belgian independence.

FIJI   Accompanied by Captain Phillips, in October attended the tenth anniversary of Fiji's independence celebrations.

1981   **FEDERAL REPUBLIC OF GERMANY**   In October visited the Royal Corps of Signals in Berlin.

NEPAL   In November visited Nepal in connection with the Save the Children Fund.

FEDERAL REPUBLIC OF GERMANY   In December visited the 14th/20th King's Hussars and the Worcestershire and Sherwood Foresters Regiment (29th/45th Foot).

1982   **FEDERAL REPUBLIC OF GERMANY**   In June visited the 14th/20th King's Hussars and the Royal Corps of Signals.

UNITED STATES   In June visited Colorado, New Mexico and Texas.

CANADA   In July visited Yukon, Saskatchewan, Manitoba and Ottawa.

SWAZILAND, ZIMBABWE, MALAWI, KENYA, SOMALIA, DJIBOUTI, NORTH YEMEN   Tour in October and November in connection with the Save the Children Fund.

LEBANON   In November visited Beirut in connection with the Save the Children Fund.

1983   **NETHERLANDS**   In March visited the Netherlands in connection with the Save the Children Fund.

FRANCE   Accompanied by Captain Phillips, in March attended a gala performance at the Moulin Rouge in Paris in aid of international children's charities.

JAPAN   Accompanied by Captain Phillips, in April visited Tokyo to attend a gala performance by the Royal Ballet and carry out other official engagements.

HONG KONG In April visited The Queen's Gurkha Signals.

PAKISTAN In May visited Save the Children Fund projects near the Afghan border.

FEDERAL REPUBLIC OF GERMANY In July visited the Royal Air Force station at Wildenrath.

SINGAPORE In October visited Singapore to open the Missions to Seamen Centre.

1984 **UNITED STATES** In January visited Houston and New Orleans as President of the British Olympic Association.

YUGOSLAVIA In February attended the Winter Olympic Games at Sarajevo as President of the British Olympic Association.

MOROCCO, THE GAMBIA and UPPER VOLTA In February, attended the Independence Day anniversary celebrations in The Gambia and also made visits in connection with the Save the Children Fund.

UNITED STATES In early July visited Los Angeles in her capacities as President of the British Olympic Association and of the British Academy of Film and Television Arts, and also Atlanta as President of the British Olympic Association. She then visited North Carolina to attend the 400th anniversary of the first English attempt to settle in the New World at Roanoke. Later in the month she returned to Los Angeles to attend the Olympic Games.

BANGLADESH and INDIA In October made a visit to Bangladesh in her capacity as President of the Save the Children Fund, followed by a similar visit to India. After only a few days in India the visit was terminated by the assassination of Mrs Indira Gandhi on October 31. Princess Anne stayed on in Delhi and represented the Queen at Mrs Gandhi's funeral.

UNITED ARAB EMIRATES In December, accompanied by Captain Phillips, attended the Dubai International Horse Show and visited Abu Dhabi and Sharjah.

1985 **FEDERAL REPUBLIC OF GERMANY** In February attended the British National/Army Cross-Country Ski Championship at Zwiesel, Bavaria. She then visited the 14th/20th King's Hussars at Hohne.

INDIA In February continued the visit to India cut short in November 1984.

FEDERAL REPUBLIC OF GERMANY In June visited the Royal Corps of Signals at Verden.

TANZANIA, MOZAMBIQUE, ZAMBIA and SUDAN In November and December made a three-week visit to Africa in her capacity as President of the Save the Children Fund.

1986   **BRAZIL**   In March visited Rio de Janeiro for Royal Gala Performance by The Sadler's Wells Royal Ballet.

FEDERAL REPUBLIC OF GERMANY   In May visited 1st Battalion, Royal Scots at Sennelager.

FEDERAL REPUBLIC OF GERMANY   In May visited 21st and 16th Signal Regiment, Royal Corps of Signals at Wildenrath.

FRANCE   In June attended the Prix de Diane at Chantilly.

BELGIUM   In June visited 11 Signal Brigade (Volunteers), Royal Corps of Signals.

CANADA   In June visited Alberta, Ontario and New Brunswick.

FEDERAL REPUBLIC OF GERMANY   In July attended World Jumping Championships at Aachen.

SWITZERLAND   With Captain Phillips attended a garden party in Berne given by the British Residents' Association.

1987   **AUSTRALIA**   In February visited Western Australia for the closing stages of the America's Cup.

UNITED ARAB EMIRATES, QATAR, KUWAIT and JORDAN   In February visited the United Arab Emirates, Qatar and Kuwait and was joined by Captain Phillips for a visit to Jordan.

FEDERAL REPUBLIC OF GERMANY   At the beginning of March visited Isny, Bavaria, for the International Lowland Cross-Country Ski Championships and later in the month attended the Essen Trade Fair with Captain Phillips.

FRANCE   As President of the International Equestrian Federation (FEI) attended the Volvo World Cup Final for Jumping Riders in Paris.

SWITZERLAND   In April attended an International Equestrian Federation meeting in Lausanne.

NETHERLANDS   In May as President of the Missions to Seamen, opened a new Missions to Seamen Club in Flushing.

CYPRUS   In September visited the 1st Battalion, Worcestershire and Sherwood Foresters Regiment, and the Royal Corps of Signals.

REPUBLIC OF KOREA   In November attended a meeting in Seoul of the International Equestrian Federation to discuss planning for equestrian events at the 1988 Olympic Games.

FRANCE   In December attended the General Assembly of the International Equestrian Federation in Paris.

1988 **CANADA** Visited the Winter Olympic Games in Calgary, Alberta, in February.

UGANDA, MOZAMBIQUE and SOMALIA From February 22 to March 5 visited Africa in her capacity as President of the Save the Children Fund.

AUSTRALIA At the end of March opened and attended the Royal Easter Show in Sydney.

FEDERAL REPUBLIC OF GERMANY Took the salute at the Queen's Birthday Parade in Berlin in May.

HONG KONG In September, engagements in the colony en route to the Olympic Games.

REPUBLIC OF KOREA At the Olympic Games, where she was sworn in as an IOC member.

CANADA In November, various engagements in connection with SCF and equestrian activities.

Sources and Reference Points

Short Bibliography

CAMPBELL, Judith; *Anne: Portrait of a Princess*, Cassell, 1970.

CATHCART, Helen; *Anne and the Princesses Royal*, W H Allen, London, 1988.

COURTNEY, Nicholas; *Princess Anne: A Biography*, Weidenfeld and Nicolson, London, 1986.

DAILY MIRROR; *Princess Anne Grows Up*, Daily Mirror Newspapers, 1963.

EVERINGHAM, Barry; *Marie-Christine: The Adventures of a Maverick Princess*, Bantam Press, London, 1985.

HOEY, Brian; *HRH the Princess Anne: A Biography*, Country Life, 1984.

HALL, Unity; *Philip*, Michael O'Mara, London, 1987.

HOWARTH, Patrick; *George VI*, Hutchinson, London, 1987.

JAMES, Paul; *The Royal Almanac*, Ravette Ltd, London, 1986, and *Anne, The Working Princess*, Piatkus, 1987.

KING, Cecil; *The Cecil King Diary* (1965–1970), Jonathan Cape, London, 1972.

LACEY, Robert; *Majesty*, Hutchinson, London, 1977.

MATHESON, Anne; *Princess Anne: A Girl of our Time*, Muller, 1973.

MORROW, Anne; *The Queen*, Granada, London, 1982.

PARKER, John; *King of Fools*, Macdonald/Futura, London, 1988.

PEARSON, John; *The Ultimate Family*, Michael Joseph, London 1986.

PHILLIPS, Pearson; *Mark and Anne: The Story of a Royal Romance*, Battersea Books, 1973.

RIPPON, Angela; *Mark Phillips: The Man and his Horses*, David and Charles, London, 1982.

VICKERS, Hugo; *Cecil Beaton, The Authorised Biography*, Weidenfeld and Nicolson, London, 1985.

WHEELER-BENNETT, Sir John; *King George VI*, Macmillan, London, 1981.

Other Sources

Published interviews with Princess Anne, consulted by the author, and quoted:
With Princess Anne and Captain Mark Phillips, jointly for the Press Association on behalf of all newspapers, November 1973; with Alastair Burnett and Andrew Gardner, for television, November, 1973.
Princess Anne, with Marjory Proops, of the *Daily Mirror* and for *Woman's Own*, February, 1976; with Kenneth Harris for the *Observer*, August 1980; with Georgina Howell, for the *Sunday Times Magazine*, August 1985; with Tony Frost, the *Sunday Mirror*, October, 1986; with the Marquesa de Valera, for *Hello Magazine*, June 1988.
Articles and news reports have also been researched from the files of the following: *The Times*, the *Daily Telegraph*, the *Guardian*, the *Daily Express*, the *Daily Mail*, the *Daily Mirror*, the *Sun*, *Today*, the *Star*, the *Daily Sketch*, the *Sunday Times*, the *Sunday Telegraph*, the *Mail on Sunday*, the *Sunday Mirror*, the *Sunday People*, *News of the World*, the *Sunday Express*, the *Observer*, the *New York Times*, *Washington Post*, *Look Magazine*, *You Magazine*, the *Sunday Times Magazine*, the *Sunday Telegraph Colour Supplement*, *Woman's Own*, *Woman*, *Picture Post*, *Illustrated*, *Majesty*, *Time*, *Life*, and *Royalty Monthly* magazine. In the scanning of this material, the author extends his thanks to the staff of the British Museum Library, the British Museum Newspaper Library, Colindale, and particularly the Hans Tasiemka Archive, London.
Also consulted: reference material and research data from the Foreign and Commonwealth Office, the Central Office of Information and Buckingham Palace Press Office.

Index

211